The Biblical Doctrine of Original Sin

The
Biblical Doctrine
of Original Sin

A. M. Dubarle

Translated by E. M. Stewart

HERDER AND HERDER
NEW YORK

1964

1964
HERDER AND HERDER NEW YORK
232 Madison Avenue, New York, NY 10016

THIS BOOK WAS FIRST PUBLISHED BY LES EDITIONS DU CERF, PARIS, UNDER THE
TITLE *Le Péché originel dans l'Écriture, Lectio Divina* NO. 20, IN 1958.

© TRANSLATION, 1964, GEOFFREY CHAPMAN LTD.

QUOTATIONS FROM SCRIPTURE ARE IN THE *Revised Standard Version*.
OCCASIONALLY, A DIRECT TRANSLATION HAS BEEN MADE FROM THE FRENCH TEXT
OF SCRIPTURE, IN ORDER TO FIT THE AUTHOR'S SENSE. WHERE THIS HAS BEEN
DONE, IT IS INDICATED IN A FOOTNOTE.

LIBRARY OF CONGRESS CATALOG CARD NO.:- 64-19731

NIHIL OBSTAT: JOANNES M. T. BARTON, S.T.D., L.S.S., CENSOR DEPUTATUS.
IMPRIMATUR: GEORGIUS L. CRAVEN, EPUS. SEBASTOPOLIS, VIC. GENERALIS.
WESTMONASTERII, DIE 20a APRILIS 1964.
THE *Nihil obstat* AND *Imprimatur* ARE A DECLARATION THAT A BOOK OR
PAMPHLET IS CONSIDERED TO BE FREE FROM DOCTRINAL OR MORAL ERROR.
IT IS NOT IMPLIED THAT THOSE WHO HAVE GRANTED THE *Nihil obstat* AND
Imprimatur AGREE WITH THE CONTENTS, OPINIONS OR STATEMENTS EXPRESSED.

MADE AND PRINTED IN GREAT BRITAIN.

Contents

Contents

Foreword

The object of these chapters, which are meant to form an organic whole, is to conduct a progressive enquiry.

Chapter 1, on the human condition in the Old Testament, consists of general considerations and prepares the way for the story of the Garden of Eden, the subject of chapter 2. The few pages on the Gospels (chapter 4) have a similar role to play with regard to the pauline texts (chapter 5). Chapter 3 concerns the Wisdom literature and may seem rather negative. If it has not a very substantial contribution to make to the doctrine of original sin, for all that it is not useless. The sages did not have the same way of looking at things as Genesis : for this very reason their evidence should balance that of the ancient authors. In the same way chapter 6, on God's justice, draws attention to some views that would have to be taken into account in any systematic construction. The original French edition of the book ended here. But this present edition includes a final chapter which outlines some of the main issues in a modern and biblical approach to the subject, with the emphasis on points that our contemporaries find of especial interest or difficulty.

The words 'original sin' are the result of doctrinal elaboration, the work of Christian centuries. The present enquiry wants to ascertain the mind of the inspired authors on this subject in the first place. But this is meant to be a starting-point, not the end of the discussion.

The negative reality of sin cannot indeed be the last word of a Christian theology, any more than it is the last word of

Scripture. It must be set in its place in the whole divine plan
of salvation. If God has allowed sin, has allowed it even to
abound, it is only to make his mercy and grace superabound.

This translation has been prepared with the author's collaboration. Some errors of reference in the original have been
corrected, and a few slight bibliographical additions made to
the footnotes.

A.M.D.

I

The Human Condition in the Old Testament

Pascal's attempt at an apology of the doctrine of original sin is well known : 'Nothing, to be sure, is more of a shock to us than such a doctrine, and yet without this mystery, which is the most incomprehensible of all, we should be incomprehensible to ourselves. The tangled knot of our condition acquired its twists and turns in that abyss; so that man is more inconceivable without the mystery than the mystery is to man.

'Whence it seems that God, desiring to make the mystery of our nature intelligible to us, hid the knot so high up, or better, so low down, that we are quite incapable of reaching it.'[1]

In spite of such an authority we may be permitted to think that the idea of original sin is not a starting point but a point of issue, the outcome of a laborious process of observation and reflection on the part of the people of God. Inspired and directed by the Spirit of God, and carried on through long generations of the people of Israel, a spiritual and intellectual process of great complexity slowly worked out the facts of a more general problem, the problem of evil. The different

[1]Pascal, *Pensées*, (Brunschvicg n. 434). Translation, *Pascal's Pensées*, Martin Turnell, (London, 1962), p. 170.

9

1*

answers given by the inspired authors to this question which springs so naturally to the human mind are recorded for us in the Scriptures. It is in this far wider context that the doctrine of original sin must be seen in order to be understood properly. The best preparation for an understanding of the account of the Fall in Genesis and for a fair interpretation of the idea of original sin that it contains is to set them back in a wider context. That is why, before approaching these problems in the next chapter, it will be a good idea to gather together a certain number of texts in which we find an expression of the mind of the men of the Old Testament on the human condition.

The biblical authors did not develop a picture of man and his situation before God in any systematic fashion. They expressed the idea as the occasion arose, and the modern reader has to group together the scattered clues and descriptions in order to grasp an idea which, although expressed rather sporadically throughout the Old Testament, is nonetheless of great importance; and in order, also, to experience for himself the feeling of fear and oppression in the face of an irremediable wretchedness and uncleanness which weighed so often on Israel. In this way chapter 3 of Genesis will be seen not as an isolated monolith but rather as the meeting point of a great number of threads which can to some extent be followed throughout the Bible.[1]

[1] On the rather vague subject of this chapter, the following may be consulted, F. R. Tennant, *The Sources of the Doctrines of the Fall and Original Sin*, (London, 1903), chapter 4; W. Eichrodt, *Theologie des Alten Testaments*, (1935), Vol. III, pp. 81-118; A. Feuillet, 'Le verset 7 du Miserere et le péché originel', in *RSR.*, XXXII, (1944), pp. 5-26; O. Procksch, *Theologie des Alten Testaments*, (1950), pp. 640-53; J. Guillet, *Thèmes bibliques*, (1951), chapter 4, pp. 100-16.

I. THE WRETCHED CONDITION OF MAN

Death and the wretchedness of man

Is man's condition a sign of something abnormal, does it betray some fundamental disorder, which could only be caused by sin, granted that everything is the work of a good God? The mind of Israel did not envisage such problems all at once. It was with the asking of these questions that reflection on death and all the wretchedness that death epitomizes and symbolizes turned gradually under the guidance of the Spirit towards the doctrine of original sin, according to which the present state of man is the wages of sin.

For a long time death appeared as a normal thing, when it came at the end of a long life. There is no scandal to be seen, the fact is simply recognized, when a biblical author concludes the life of his hero by mentioning that he died 'in a good old age, an old man and full of years': this was the case with Abraham (Gen. 15:15; 25:8), Isaac (Gen. 35:29), Gideon (Judges 8:32), David (1 Chron. 23:1; 29:28), Job (Job 42:17) and Tobias (Tob. 14:1). The friends of Job themselves, in spite of their strict view connecting suffering with sin, describe such a death in the happy image of a harvest:

> You shall come to your grave in ripe old age,
> as a shock of grain comes up to the threshing floor in
> its season (Job 5:26).

And an idea of this nature still inspires the picture painted by a prophet of the happiness of paradise (Isaias 65:19-23).

Even when death is seen in a more sombre light, it is still frequently resignation in the face of the inevitable that accompanies it. 'We must all die, we are like water spilt on the ground, which cannot be gathered up again' (2 Sam. 14:14), says a simple woman to David. And the king himself said of his own son who died at an early age: 'I shall go to him, but he will not return to me' (2 Sam. 12:23). Death is 'the way of all the earth' (1 Kings 2:2), that is to say a universal condition. There is no reason to demand for man, any more than for the grass of the field, an existence without end which is proper to God alone (Isaias 40:6-8; Psalm 103:15-16).

Gradually, however, a more pessimistic view of life appears, finding expression alongside an optimistic appreciation. The patriarch Jacob feels that his years have been short and bad, and the account of his death has none of the serenity of the brief mention given to his fathers (Gen. 47:9; 50:1). Moses is weary of living and dies without having satisfied his wish to enter the Promised Land (Num. 11:11-15; Deut. 4:23-28). Naomi recalls sadly a life full of bitterness, contrasting it with the omen of happiness contained in her name (Ruth 1:20-21).

Two psalmists lament the fact that life is so short. And to their lamentations they join the idea that God punishes man for his iniquities. The one foreshadows the remarks of Ecclesiastes on the vanity of efforts which are never sure of achieving the desired ends (Psalm 39). The other contrasts the eternity of God and the fragility of a creature like the grass of the field; he seems to be alluding to Gen. 3:19, by mentioning the divine command which makes the sons of men return to dust; he feels himself pursued by a mysterious and powerful anger (Psalm 90). To attribute to them the doctrine that death itself is a punishment for sin would probably be making too much of something that is only a very hazy feeling on the part of the two psalmists; but their thoughts are certainly turning in that direction.

It is the same with the great poet who, under the guise of Job, complains bitterly of his unbearable sufferings. Sometimes, in fact, he extends the scope of the debate and passes from his own case to the consideration of the wretched fate that awaits the son of woman. His life is short and full of sorrow (Job 7 : 1; 14 : 1-2). And worse, his fate is more deplorable than that of a tree : once dead, he cannot, like a stump left in the ground, send out new shoots (Job 14 : 7-12). These sad remarks on the human condition have all the more importance since for Job the wretchedness is bound up with a divine displeasure and since he feels the weight of this without knowing the reason. Suffering is not an entirely profane matter : it involves separation from God. And so the problem arises as to the origin of this universal wretchedness.

The facts that lie at the root of such a question are stated by Ecclesiastes even more clearly than by Job. He also considers the human condition to be miserable, taken as a whole, and complains of the inevitability of death (Eccles. 2 : 15-17; 8 : 8; 3 : 19-20; 11 : 7-12 : 7). This fact is all the more distressing since God has put duration in the heart of man, that is, he has given him the faculty of raising himself above the present moment in order to grasp with his intelligence the sequence of time, and has consequently inspired in him the desire to act for the future (3 : 11). For this distressing contradiction Ecclesiastes can find no explanation; and he says this quite openly (3 : 11; 7 : 23; 11 : 5). All the same a short sentence which he offers as the result of much research turns our thoughts in the same direction as the texts of Job or the psalms already quoted :

Behold, this alone I found, that God made man upright, but they have sought out many devices (7 : 29).

It is suggested, then, that man is responsible, at least collectively, for his deplorable condition : he has spoiled the work of God, which was good.

And so, in a fleeting and unemphatic way, in Ecclesiastes the realization of the essential wretchedness of man, apart from individual accidents, draws its importance from a fundamental idea, expressed much more clearly and frequently in the Old Testament. Suffering is a punishment for sin.[1] A good God, powerful and wise, such as the God recognized by Israel was, could not be the direct author of evil, even if certain phrases seem to put the responsibility for evil on him without stressing the fault of the creature.

It is quite a common occurrence, then, that misfortune makes men look for the sin which must be at its root. So it is with Pharaoh, who has taken Sara (Gen. 12 : 17-18). So it is with Joseph's brothers, arrested as spies in Egypt (Gen. 42 : 21). So it is with Joshua after the people have been defeated in battle (Joshua 7 : 6-13). Naomi thinks that Jahweh has shown his displeasure by afflicting her (Ruth 1 : 21). Saul concludes from the silence of the divine oracle that some fault has been committed in the army under his command (1 Sam. 14 : 38). David looks for the causes of a famine that has lasted three years (2 Sam. 21 : 1). The widow of Sarephtha who receives Elias into her house, seeing her son seriously ill asks the prophet if he has come to bring back the memory of her sins (1 Kings 17 : 18).

On the other hand it is not often that the Bible clearly distinguishes the temporal punishment of a fault and the loss of

---

[1]This view underwent, after a fairly long time, a certain loss of emphasis or at least some clarification, mainly to distinguish collective and individual responsibility, or to show the educative value of suffering, for example Deut. 8: 2-18; Prov. 3: 11-12.

divine favour.[1] For such a distinction to be commonplace, it would be necessary for the existence of close and affectionate ties with God to be considered as a thing of value independently of blessings in the material order. And that is something that happens only rarely, and it is not formulated in an abstract way till late in the Old Testament. Most frequently, then, Israel closely associates a misfortune affecting some sphere of human life with sin, which troubles good relations with God.

A sign of this is the fact that the same words serve indifferently to designate the actual sin, the guilt which results or the punishment which follows. And every suffering takes on a religious aspect; there is no purely profane suffering. The physical suffering of sickness or the mental suffering of men's hostility go hand in hand with the anguish of being the object of divine anger and the fear of being rejected by him (Psalm 6; 88; 102). Death is a final separation from God. In *sheol* nobody praises God (Psalm 6 : 6; 30 : 10; 88 : 6-13; 115 : 117; Isaias 38 : 18; Baruch 2 : 17).

Naturally we must avoid attributing to the biblical authors conclusions which they did not explicitly draw, or according the same positive value to all their expressions, when it would be necessary to take into consideration ready-made formulas and references which do not involve personal commitment. In any case what remains is the refusal to make the various parts of the human being into watertight compartments, and the religious significance seen in suffering and death. The thought which is reflected throughout the Old Testament formed the atmosphere in which the story of the Garden of Eden and its interpretation of human fate in the light of sin could arise.

[1]The clearest case is the pardon granted to David simultaneously with the announcement of the punishment (2 Sam. 12: 13).

The tendency to evil

Several times the Old Testament denounces the inborn perversity of the human heart, which is inclined to evil from the earliest age.

In texts without a doubt very old, where the wording is anthropomorphic, Genesis attributes to Yahweh himself the statement 'that the wickedness of man was great in the earth, and that every imagination of the thoughts of his heart was only evil continually' (Gen. 6 : 5).

The word translated as 'imagination' *'yeser'* is the word which the Rabbis will later use to denote the inclination to good or to evil. Here it seems to express a state of fact, an actual sin, rather than a tendency which as such would not be blameworthy, although inclining to sin. Evil has spread over all the earth.

This does not imply that the author is thinking of a strict and absolutely universal incapacity to do good : an exception to the general corruption is mentioned at once, that of Noah, who found favour in the eyes of God. In spite of temptation man retains the power to do good, if he wishes. That is the lesson to be drawn from the words addressed by God to Cain, who was already irritated at the preference shown to his brother. Sin, represented as a wild beast lying in wait for its prey, or perhaps even as one of those evil spirits accepted by popular beliefs, can be overcome by the one whom it threatens (Gen. 4 :6).

After the Flood, the story shows Yahweh declaring that he will not curse the earth any more on man's account, 'for the imagination of man's heart is evil from his youth' (Gen. 8 :21). This text can be understood, either as expressing through the mouth of Yahweh himself an excuse for sin or a mitigating circumstance, by recognizing an inborn propensity to evil, or

16

better still as simply representing the precocious culpability of man as something which has been the cause of past punishment, but which should not in future cause such a universal cataclysm. In order not to have to exterminate again, with one blow, a humanity corrupt save for one just man, God now makes a law about the vengeance of blood, which will prevent the spread of violence. He states a fact and acts accordingly. Penal sanctions, established or approved by God, limit the growth of evil. The book of Proverbs will express a similar thought in more abstract terms :

Folly is bound up in the heart of a child,
But the rod of discipline drives it far from him (22 : 15).

Although the Genesis texts speak of a universal malice and not expressly of an inborn, perverse disposition, it is fairly obvious that one can conclude from the first to the second : the suggestion of Genesis is so strong that the word used, *yeser*, 'imagination', becomes the technical term to denote the inclination to good or bad.

The prophets begin by proclaiming the radical perversion of the heart as the origin of that constant malice revealed by experience. Jeremias, the messenger tormented by the mission which he has received, perhaps finds in the resistance to the divine will which he feels in his heart of hearts a revelation of the deepest dispositions of all men :

The heart is deceitful above all things,
And desperately corrupt;
Who can understand it? (17 : 9).

The sins of Jerusalem bring to his mind the irrepressible necessities of nature :

17

As a fountain casteth out her waters,
so she casteth out her wickedness (6:7 Authorized Version).

Elsewhere the image is different but the idea remains the same, with an allusion to habit, that second nature, contracted as a result of social influences:

Can the Ethiopian change his skin
or the leopard his spots?
Then also you can do good
who are accustomed to evil (13:23).

This state of affairs is not limited to the people of Israel who have been unfaithful to their calling (cf. Baruch 1:22; 2:8). All the pagan nations, too, follow 'their own evil heart' (Jer. 3:17). All peoples, Israel as well as her neighbours, are uncircumcized of heart (Jer. 9:25; cf. Ezech. 44:9): even if they bear circumcision in the flesh, their moral and religious dispositions are not altered for all that; they are not really devoted to Yahweh. Even in Israel, where circumcision was the sign of the divine alliance, a radical transformation must take place, the circumcision of the heart: this is the exhortation of Jeremias to his contemporaries (Jer. 4:4; cf. Lev. 26:41; Deut. 10:16), while Deuteronomy seems to think that only God is capable of bringing such a work to a successful conclusion in the days of the final salvation (Deut. 30:6). A parallel image is the image of uncircumcized ears, incapable of listening to the word of God with attention and joy (Jer. 6:10).

These metaphors, drawn from a ritual custom, express the conviction that the native state of man is a profane one, implying a separation from God, that spontaneous psychological dispositions offer an obstacle to the normal growth of religious and moral life, that this state of affairs must be remedied and that finally only God can succeed in doing this.

Ezechiel has recourse to a still stronger image: a heart of stone. This expression was perhaps originally meant to describe the paralysis and insensibility caused by apoplexy (cf. 1 Sam. 25 :37). Leviathan, the monster described in the Book of Job, has a heart as hard as stone, that is to say incapable of fear (Job 41 : 16). In the same way Israel, deaf to all warnings, rebels against any fear. But on the day of salvation Yahweh will gather together his exiled people, purify them and give them a new heart and a new spirit: he will take the heart of stone from their flesh and give them a heart of flesh, so that they can observe the commandments. The relationship of alliance will thus be re-established (Ezech. 36 :26; cf. 11 : 19). This renewal presupposes as its starting point a condition which is not only inferior but abnormal: the heart of stone. The prophet assumes this as the state of affairs without questioning its origin: whether an immemorial sin or a sin committed since the historical epoch of the exodus from Egypt.

The Wisdom books re-echo the prophetic voice, but in a different key. The sentence, quoted above,

Folly is bound up in the heart of a child,
but the rod of discipline drives it far from him (Prov. 22 : 15),

anticipates the good effects, not from a law supported by sanctions, nor from an impassioned appeal to the good will of the individual, nor from Jahweh's direct action on the heart, but from a firm education. The counsels of severity, which the Wisdom writers give so freely (Prov. 13 :24; 15 : 10; 19 : 18; 23 : 13-14; 20 : 17; Ecclus. 7 :23-24; 30 : 1 and 7-13; 42 :5 and

11), presume that there is an inclination to evil, which is not, however, irresistible.

Ecclesiasticus once or twice speaks of the 'evil imagination', borrowing from Genesis the words which were eventually to become an expression used by the rabbis to denote the 'evil inclination', known to Christian theology as concupiscence.

> O evil imagination, why were you formed
> to cover the land with deceit? (Ecclus. 37 : 3).

It is not certain that there is question here of any tendency to evil : perhaps the writer is thinking simply of the actual decision taken by the will. This writer, who stresses the reality of human freedom so much, used the same word, *yeser*, 'imagination', when speaking of freedom :

> It was he who created man in the beginning,
> and he left him in the power of his own inclination (15 : 14).

Perhaps he wishes only to state the fact of liability to sin without trying to attach it to any evil tendency. The fragility of a creature goes without saying :

> What is brighter than the sun ? Yet its light fails,
> So flesh and blood devise evil (17 : 31).

We should have to take the thought of Ecclesiasticus beyond the direct and certain sense of the texts if we wished to attribute to him the idea of a tendency to evil existing in every man and yet proceeding from an original fault. This would not be a contradiction of the passage attributing the origin of mortality to the first sin of a woman (Ecclus. 25 : 24), but it would go beyond the explicit testimony of the book.

In conclusion, then, the clearest statement of a congenital perversion of the human heart is to be found in the prophets and the book of Proverbs, in spite of the fact that the classical terms for the further development of this doctrine come from Genesis and Ecclesiasticus.

The universality of sin

It is not easy to distinguish those texts of the Old Testament which refer to an inborn evil tendency and those which refer to a sin actually committed. The actual words, hard heart or heart of stone, can sometimes mean a deliberate sin. 'They made their hearts like adamant lest they should hear the law and the words which the Lord of hosts had sent ... through the former prophets' (Zac. 7 : 12). We must not expect at the very beginning those distinctions which were to emerge in the course of a long tradition but rather a general description of an abnormal situation, in which the various factors brought to light by further analysis are not carefully distinguished.

The whole people without exception is guilty (Isaias 64 : 5-6). What is more, sin or the tendency to evil is universal among men. The biblical authors frequently return to this thought.

For there is no man who does not sin (1 Kings 8 : 46; 2 Chron. 6 : 36).

Surely there is not a righteous man on earth
who does good and never sins (Eccles. 7 : 20).

One sentence from Proverbs goes further and adds that it is never certain that expiation has cancelled the fault :

Who can say, 'I have made my heart clean'? (Prov. 20 : 9).

One of the psalms is very radical in its judgement:

> The Lord looks down from heaven upon the children of men,
> to see if there are any that act wisely,
> that seek after God.
> They have all gone astray, they are all alike corrupt;
> there is not one that does good, no, not one (Psalm 14 : 2-3).

There may be some exaggeration in such a condemnation which could be compared with many prophetic accusations. Some verses later the psalmist himself seems to suppose that some exceptions to this general statement, beginning with the oppressed people. But even the most just have some infidelity with which to reproach themselves, so that it is only a question of degrees of guilt. So it happens that some psalmists invoke their devotion to Yahweh to obtain protection against wicked enemies and at the same time to implore pardon for their own faults (Psalm 25; 38; 39; 40; 69). All men, then, need to appeal to the mercy of God:

> If thou, O Lord, shouldst mark iniquities,
> Lord, who could stand? (Psalm 130 : 3).

> Enter not into judgement with thy servant:
> for no living man is righteous before thee (Psalm 143 : 2).

This feeling of universal guilt appears again in the importance attached to rites of expiation, regulated at such length by the ceremonial law: sacrifices for sin and the great day of expiation every year (Lev. 4; 5; 16; Num. 15 : 22-29; 28 : 11; 29 : 38).

Ecclesiasticus echoes those who have gone before him, when

he warns against the attempt to appear just in God's eyes
(Ecclus. 7 : 5), and remembers that we all deserve punishment
(8 : 5), for all have committed some faults, even if it is only a
matter of thoughtless speech (19 : 16). Thus the writer himself,
in his morning prayer, asks pardon for his sins (39 : 5). Just
as it has spread universally to all men, sin goes back, beyond
youth even, to the first beginnings of individual existence. This
is the conviction expressed in the Psalm *Miserere*, the most
profound cry of repentance to be found in the Scriptures.[1]
The penitent confesses that he has been a sinner since his first
moments :

> Behold, I was brought forth in iniquity,
> and in sin did my mother conceive me (Psalm 51 : 5).

Perhaps the psalmist implicitly considers that his condition
is also the condition of every man. This is not a question of the
special case of illegitimate conception, since he mentions the
birth itself and even gives it the first place. It would be contrary to all biblical thought to attach any strict moral guilt to
the conjugal act. But, like the confinement, it was affected by
a ritual uncleanness. And it was assumed that, by physical
contact, the child conceived was affected by it. It is probably
by an extension of the effects of such contact rather than by
reason of any moral solidarity between the parents and their
offspring that the psalmist maintains that he shares his mother's
state of sin. While many of the biblical authors see the cause of
uncleanness before God merely in man's corporal nature and
fragility,[2] this verse of the psalm *Miserere* clarifies and
accentuates their idea by drawing attention to the unclean

---

[1] For the theological content of this psalm, see A. Feuillet in the article
already mentioned, p. 10, n. 2; H. Gunkel, *Die Psalmen*, (1926), p. 223.
[2] Cf. p. 27.

origin of the body. The crudest of terms are used : the word translated as 'conceive' is elsewhere used only of animal heat.

Before he has committed any personal act, then, the initial condition of every man is sin, which at the very least means a certain separation from God, which propagates itself from generation to generation. Although, strictly speaking, the words 'in iniquity . . . in sin' could characterize the state of the child alone or the state of the mother alone, the fact that the two parallel lines have one after the other, as subject, 'child' and 'mother' suggests that in the eyes of the psalmist both share in the one sin which affects the whole race. There is nothing else to indicate the existence of an evil tendency. It is not expressly stated that this state of sin goes back to a deliberate transgression on the part of an ancestor, although the idea would be quite acceptable to an Israelite mind, steeped in the feeling of racial solidarity. But the expressions chosen suggest in the first place the uncleanness inevitably attached to procreation : and there is nothing to prove that the author was looking for any further causes. He expresses a first global apprehension, in which distress at the feeling of being far from God is far more predominant than the abstract analysis of the situation.

A comparison between this Psalm 51 and a verse of Job might come to mind : 'Who can cleanse what is born of tainted stock?' (Job 14 :4). But this is only the Vulgate translation, which has probably undergone the influence of the Christian doctrine of original sin. The original Hebrew text simply said : 'Who can bring a clean thing out of an unclean? There is not one.' The context speaks of the wretchedness and fragility of 'man that is born of a woman' (14 : 1). The connection between the uncleanness of man and his origin by procreation is much more tenuous.

24

More satisfactory parallels with Psalm 51:7 could perhaps be found in Isaias 48:8 : 'from birth you were called a rebel', or Psalm 58:4 : 'The wicked go astray from the womb, they err from their birth, speaking lies.' And yet such texts are not at all clear : one could understand 'from birth' just as well as 'from conception'; that is what is suggested by the words of Psalm 22:10 : 'since my mother bore me thou hast been my God,' or of Psalm 71:6 : 'upon thee I have leaned from my birth.' In these two quotations the parallel makes it clear that the relevant point of departure is the birth and not the period before birth.

It is this verse of the Psalm *Miserere* that remains the closest approximation to the doctrine of original sin outside Genesis : and still it does not expressly relate the native state of sin to a deliberate sin of an ancestor, as St Paul was to do. It is rather a foreshadowing of the Gospel words : 'that which is born of the flesh is flesh' (John 3:6), implying that this flesh has need of the purification of water and the Spirit.

The incompatibility of God and man

In short the Bible betrays the feeling that relations between God and man are not normal, instead of being full of the confidence which alone would seem to correspond to the divine goodness. Religion is steeped in fear : the word here means not only the respect a weak creature has for his infinitely perfect Creator, but also the vague consciousness of sin bringing down God's anger.

When God appears, the story often insists on the reaction of fear experienced by those who receive this favour. This fact deserves to be stressed, since it is likewise one of the first impressions experienced by the sinful couple of Eden after their act of disobedience. The Israelites at Sinai are terrified by the extraordinary phenomena accompanying the promulgation of the law (Exod. 19:6, 20:18; Deut. 5:20-24). Even favoured individuals are oppressed by fear. At Horeb, Moses dare not look at God even though God is about to send him to deliver his brethren (Exod. 3:6). In the Temple, at the sight of Yahweh surrounded by the Seraphim, Isaias realizes the risk he is running because of his own uncleanness and his solidarity with a people whose lips are sullied (Isaias 6:5). Simply at the sight of the divine glory, Ezechiel falls on his face (Ezech. 1:28; 3:23), just as he falls again when he sees punishment overtaking sinners (9:8; 11:13). In the book of Daniel the visions and apparitions, even when they only involve angels, fill the prophet as well as the pagans with terror (Dan. 2:1; 4:2; 5:6; 7:15 and 28; 8:18 and 27; 10:8-9; 10:16-17). Even in retrospect the witnesses of a theophany, who at the time thought it only a divine messenger, are seized with fear, when they later realize whom they have met; thus it is with Jacob (Gen. 32:31), and Gideon (Judges 6:22) and Manuel (Judges 13:22).

The fact is that it is a mortal danger for man to see God (Exod. 19:21; 33:20-23; Deut. 4:33; 5:23; 18:16). And the only possible escape is to fall on one's face as Moses did (Exod. 34:8), or to cover one's face as Elias did (1 Kings 19:13). More generally speaking, man cannot stay in the presence of God and his worship should express and reinforce this spontaneous conviction. The priests must leave the Temple when the glory of Yahweh comes down on it (Exod. 40:33; 1 Kings 8:11; 2 Chron. 7:2). The High Priest himself, if he does not want to die, must not enter the innermost sanctuary where Yahweh appears (Lev. 16:2); he goes in only once a year, protected by the smoke of the incense (Lev. 16:13).

This state of affairs, which amounts to incompatibility

between God and man, is due to sin.[1] Yahweh refuses to go in the midst of Israel because they are stiff-necked people, who would be consumed at once (Exod. 33 : 3-5). And in fact when God shines the light of his presence on the hidden faults of men, sinners are consumed in his anger (Psalm 90 : 7-8). Where this is not the effect, it is because the unswerving fidelity of God tempers his justice (Mal. 3 : 6).

Other passages in Job, which appear more theoretical, describe man as an unclean being. And in this word, so meaningful for an Israelite accustomed to ceremonial washings, is expressed the lowliness of man's origin and at the same time the stain of sin. Probably no importance is to be attached to the fact that the accent is laid on the weakness of the earthly creature (Job 14 : 17-19; 25 : 4-6), now on the moral transgressions (15 : 15-16), for some Psalms (39; 78 : 38-39; 90 : 3-9; 102 : 11-12; 103 : 9-16), and later Ecclesiasticus (17 : 26-27), associate the shortness of human life and the sins of these miserable creatures in the development of one idea.

For all things cannot be in men,
since a son of man is not immortal.
What is brighter than the sun? Yet its light fails.
So flesh and blood devise evil.
He marshals the host of the height of heaven;
but all men are dust and ashes (Ecclus. 17 : 30-32).

This conviction of the fundamental uncleanness which is a part of man—the idea upon which the friends and adversaries of Job dwell with such complacency—is not the point of the

---

[1] A text such as Jer. 30 : 21 seems isolated. Without sin being mentioned at all, it seems that man is still incapable of approaching God.

discussion. The unfortunate patriarch himself is also convinced of this uncleanness which cannot be remedied by man (14 : 14). He does not deny that he has committed some sin (7 :20-21; 10 :14-15; 13 :27; 14 :16-17). He only claims to be as innocent as a weak creature can be, incapable as he is of avoiding the sins of youth (13 :26). If he feels that he has not deserved the sufferings which have come upon him, he cannot help seeing in them the expression of a divine anger which is all the more painful to him for being unjustified (9 :15-31; 10 :16-17; 13 :24-27). For he too does not clearly distinguish the misfortunes of the human condition and the consciousness of a lack of harmony with God.

And so the Old Testament bears witness to the wretchedness of man and proclaims that it is of a universal and religious nature. But in this state of wretchedness the individual is not in isolation : sin and evil propagate themselves from one man to the next. And this second idea forms an essential element of the doctrine of original sin, and one which was also equally familiar to the Israelite mind.

II. THE CONTAGION OF SIN

The people of Israel were profoundly convinced of the solidarity binding each person to his family and nation, not to mention his physical environment. This is an immediate truth for them, a self-evident fact which does not need preliminary proof. This solidarity enters in on the religious level as on other levels, and was often felt as a solidarity in sin.

The solidarity between successive generations[1]

Frequently the admission of sins embraces at one and the same time the faults of the believer or of the people and those of previous generations, whether it is a question of recognizing oneself guilty along with one's fathers or of imploring God not to punish one for the sins of one's fathers (Jer. 3 : 25; 14 : 20; Dan. 9 : 16).

> Do not remember against us the iniquities of our forefathers;
> ... deliver us, and forgive us our sins, for thy name's sake
> (Psalm 79 : 8-9).

> Both we and our fathers have sinned;
> we have committed iniquity, we have done wickedly (Psalm 106 : 6).

> Do not punish me for my sins ... and those which my fathers committed before me (Tob. 3 : 3).

The calamities of the Babylonian exile are explained by the faults which piled up over several generations (Lev. 26 : 39-40; Jer. 9 : 13; 16 : 11). Even the 'first father' of the people, which probably means Jacob, sinned (Isaias 43 : 27). These texts show how spontaneously the Israelites looked upon themselves as bound in solidarity with the family or national past, without

---

[1]On this subject, see J. de Fraine, 'Individu et société dans la religion de l'Ancien Testament' in *Biblica*, XXXIII (1952), pp. 324-55, 445-75. The reaction of the author against the excesses of a purely collective view of Israel's religion leads to some excesses in its turn. For example it is not easy to see what reason he has to suppose complicity (p. 459) on the occasion of the collective punishment inflicted on the family of Core or Achan (Num. 16: 27; Joshua 7: 25). In spite of this the article contains a good explanation of the facts. See also F. Spadafora, *Collettivismo e individualismo nel Vecchio Testamento*, (1953), especially chapters 2 and 3.

trying to assume an individual responsibility. Only a late development was to teach them to distinguish between sin and punishment, and clearly to assert individual retribution, which seems so normal to us. But the old way of looking at things which is to be found in the Scriptures must have some lesson for us : if not a definitive theological explanation then at least some indication of fact.

What really appears in these texts is the conviction that children not only feel the consequences of their parents' faults and are often led astray by the bad example given them, but that they do in a certain way share in their sins. A race should not be considered as a succession of morally independent individuals, but also as a living unit. That is why Yahweh is the 'jealous God, visiting the iniquity of the fathers upon the children to the third and the fourth generation of those who hate me, but showing steadfast love to thousands of those who love me' (Exod. 20 :5; 34 :7; Num. 14 :18; Deut. 5 :9; Jer. 32 :18). The state of mind behind this old formula lost nothing of its vitality until the approach of the Christian era. The last of the Wisdom books echo it :

Children will blame an ungodly father,
because they suffer reproach because of him (Ecclus. 41 :7;
cf. 3 :11; 23 :24-25).

But the prolific brood of the ungodly will be of no use,
and none of their illegitimate seedlings will strike a deep root
(Wisdom 4 :3-6; cf. 3 :11; 12 :10-11).

The historical books offer numerous examples illustrating this law. Cham, who had insulted his father, was to be punished in his descendants, who where reduced to miserable servitude

(Gen. 9:25-27). The tribes of Ruben, Simeon and Levi were condemned to lose their importance because of the faults of the ancestors who gave them their names (Gen. 49:3-7). Core, Dathan and Abiron, who rebelled against Moses's authority, were swallowed up by the ground together with all their family, even the little children (Num. 16:24-25). Achan, guilty of a sacrilegious theft, was stoned together with his sons and daughters (Joshua 7:25-25). The descendants of Heli, the priest at Silo, who showed an unworthy weakness with regard to his sons, were reduced to the humiliation of begging (1 Sam. 2:31-36). The violation of an oath of truce by Saul was avenged after his death by the execution of seven of his descendants (2 Sam. 21:5-6; cf. Joshua 9:15). The child born of the adulterous union between David and Bethsabee died because of his father's sin (2 Sam. 12:14). Joab, David's general and the murderer of his rivals, was always to have ailing or unfortunate men in his family (2 Sam. 3:29). On account of Giezi's cupidity and lie, leprosy was to cling to him and his descendants (2 Kings 5:27).

The royal dynasty of David was humiliated because of the unfaithfulness of Solomon : ten tribes were taken away (1 Kings 11:39). The royal house of Israel which led the people into sin was regularly the victim of a complete massacre : this was not merely a precaution taken by the usurpers against any possible revenge by the survivors. The prophets approved this merciless procedure, or at least saw in it a certain providential justice. Such was the case with Jeroboam (1 Kings 14:10-11; 15:29), with Baasa (1 Kings 16:7 and 12) and with Achab (1 Kings 21:21-22; 2 Kings 9:7-10, 26 and 36; 10:10-17 and 30). It must be added that this extermination of a whole family is the last related in the book of Kings. About forty years later Amasias, king of Juda, punished the assassins of his father,

31

Joas, but not their whole families (2 Kings 14:6). The prophet Osee, almost a century after Jehu, implicitly condemns the cruelty of a man who had been regarded in his own time as an instrument of Yahweh (Osee 1:4). He does declare, however, that this blood will be revenged on the house of the one who shed it, still recognizing the fact of racial solidarity, while at the same time no longer considering it the expression of a perfect justice.

That does not prevent Isaias from foretelling to Ezechias the enslavement of his sons as a punishment for his foreign policy, which was too profane (Isaias 39:7). In the same way Jeremias announced to Joachim, the oppressor of the people, that his son Jechonias would be delivered into the hands of his enemies and that none of his family would possess the royal throne again (Jer. 22:18-30). This law of solidarity holds true even outside the Chosen People: a massacre of the members of the reigning house of Babylon is prepared by God because of their fathers' crimes (Isaias 14:21).

Such are the points of fact and of law recognized by popular tradition and which still reveal themselves to careful scrutiny. And yet, in spite of this long habit of Israelite thought, a shift of attitude, which would correct what was incomplete in this view, was to appear. As the reorganization of the judiciary advanced, the law came to forbid the execution of sons for the sin of their fathers or vice versa (Deut. 24:16; cf. 2 Kings 14:6). The idea of individual responsibility became current and was confirmed both by the priests, custodians of the law, and by the prophets, bearers of the word of God, who were to apply the new idea to the sphere of relations with God. Jeremias and Ezechiel, contemporaries of the Babylonian exile, had the opportunity of hearing in their presence the words: 'The fathers have eaten sour grapes, and the children's teeth are set on edge' (Jer. 31 :29-30; Ezech. 18 :2). These words could be interpreted as an irreverent jest against a Providence that was supposed to be just, or as a sign of discouraged fatalism, abandoning the effort to shake off the weight of a crushing heritage : 'Our fathers sinned and are no more; and we bear their iniquities' (Lam. 5 : 7). But there could be little doubt, it seemed, about the truth of the fact contained in this popular saying, the summing up of an already long experience.

The prophets, however, do not hesitate to attribute to their God the perfect justice that takes only individual merits into account. Leaving aside the past, they proclaim a future era in which none will die save for his own personal sins (Jer. 31 : 30; Ezech. 18 :4). In this declaration, so categorical in face of all the facts, is the clearest expression of a truth which is borne out more or less obscurely in every book of the Bible : God renders to each according to his works.

Solidarity with the race and independence of the person in his immediate relationship with God : both these aspects of the human condition are asserted alternately by Scripture, but without any effort to present an elaborate synthesis. Consequently the exact nature of this solidarity with one's fathers is left to some extent unclear : does it mean that sons suffer or benefit from the repercussions of acts in which they had no part, or again that they are incited more to evil or to good by examples which affect them more closely, or finally that they share in the sin or merit of their ancestors? It would probably not be in accordance with the mind of the inspired authors to exclude this last meaning completely, for the earlier parts of the Bible, in particular, do not distinguish clearly between subjection to punishment and guilt, both ideas being included in the same word, sin.

Solidarity with contemporaries

Just as there is a bond between successive generations, there is also a bond between the members of one and the same national community. The inspired authors are profoundly convinced of this and delight in stories illustrating it. They describe a calamity striking the whole people as a consequence of the fault of one single person or of a minority. And the words they use do not make any clear distinction between the fault itself, which according to our modern way of thinking should bring down God's anger only on those responsible, and the punishment which follows and can fall on the innocent as well.

The whole house of Pharaoh and that of Abimelech, the king of Gerarar, are stricken with sterility as a penalty for the abduction of Abraham's wife, Sarah (Gen. 12 : 17; 20 : 18). And if the High Priest broke any of the ceremonial laws, he would run the risk of angering Yahweh against the whole assembly (Lev. 10 : 6). Moses intercedes with God so that the revolt of one faction may not call down the ruin of the whole assembly (Num. 16 : 22). The sacrilegious theft of Achan is the cause of a military defeat until the guilty man has been duly punished (Joshua 7). The idolatry of Baal-Phogor brings on a plague which decimates the people before their entry into the land of Canaan; and several years later, when the conquest is over, the memory of this infidelity still weighs on the survivors, who do not feel that they are yet purified (Joshua 22 : 17). The involuntary failure of Jonathan, Saul's son, to fulfil a vow made by his father prevents the divine oracle from giving a reply in the course of the battle (1 Sam. 14 : 36-46). The perjury of Saul with regard to the Gaabonites leads to a famine from which the country suffers under the reign of David (2 Sam. 21 : 1). The sin committed by David in the census of the people brings on a fatal plague (2 Sam. 24 : 1-7). The story begins with the mention of God's anger against Israel, when God incited the king to a sinful deed which was destined to be punished in due course. Antiquity was not shocked at this simple and yet profound way of representing divine justice precipitating the wicked into a series of crimes to be followed by punishment and downfall. A similar story in Herodotus (*Hist.* I, 159) concerning an apparently deceptive reply of the oracle of the Branchides could provide a good parallel to the book of Samuel, which expresses in its naïve way the very vivid realization of the bonds created between men by sin, especially between a people and their leader. In Israel, however, a finer appreciation of the divine transcendence and of individual retribution leads gradually to a modification of the religious interpretation of this episode. The book of Chronicles (1 Chron. 21) traces the king's fault to the temptation of Satan, hostile to Israel. The reference to the anger of Yahweh against the people, of his use of David as his instrument and finally of his feeling of repentance with regard to the land disappears from this new version of the events.

On many occasions the Babylonian captivity is connected with the crimes of Manasses (2 Kings 21:10-15; 23:26; 24:3-4; Jer. 15:4). And here solidarity between successive generations and solidarity between king and people are united in one and the same case. The murder of Jeremias would mean that his blood would be upon the whole town of Jerusalem as well as on the guilty party (Jer. 26:15).

Collective sins

The Bible is not concerned only with individuals or with society directly in terms of the individual. It also takes into consideration social facts, where it is impossible to discover those responsible so that they go unmentioned and where the individual is absolutely without any means of acting against the current of the realities into which he is plunged. He comes under the malign influence of his environment without being able to resist or even think of resisting. Two examples of this are particularly stressed: the dispersal of the peoples and idolatry.

In the story of the Tower of Babel, as we read it in Genesis (11 : 1-9), little importance, from the point of view of religious instruction, is to be attached to the circumstantial detail and the extreme oversimplification of the account, as a result of which the division of tongues is represented as instantaneous; even some of the Fathers of the Church did not take this literally. The narrator takes it for granted that his readers are acquainted with *ziggurat* or pyramids built in stages. These were designed by the Babylonians to offer an earthly abode to the gods, and their unusual height gave simple folk the idea that they were trying to reach the sky. But according to the belief of the Israelites God and not man can alone take the initiative in relations between heaven and earth: even when Solomon builds a magnificent temple, they continue to feel the impossibility of a work of human hands providing an abode for an infinite God (1 Kings 8 : 27; Isaias 66 : 1). So the biblical author overlooks whatever genuine religion there may have been in the intention which led to the building of the *ziggurat*, and concentrates only on the proud pretensions which could attempt to reach the divine dwelling-place by man's own unaided power, or on the greed for power dominating the gatherings of men in great empires: 'Let us make a name for ourselves, lest we be scattered abroad upon the face of the whole earth' (Gen. 11 : 4). Mankind wants to assert its strength by keeping itself grouped together, contrary to the divine command to fill the earth. God will achieve his ends in spite of man's efforts. He causes confusion in the language of the men building Babel and so makes them abandon the enterprise. An unfinished tower in Babylon could provide the believer in Yahweh with a symbol of the inevitable failure to which great enterprises inspired by pride are doomed. By a play on words and a distortion of etymology, the capital of the greatest empire which the ancestors of Israel had ever known was associated with this example of human pride—for this is what the tower was—and with its punishment : Babel, the gate of the gods, was finally only *Balal*, confusion. In this old story details of geography and folklore merge with profound realization of a basic human condition and with the pessimistic view of mankind adopted by the biblical authors.

As soon as a child is integrated into a community by virtue of the language he has learned, he inevitably becomes fatally cut off from other people. [1]The impossibility of mutual understanding determines differences of mind, character and culture, and makes men aware of them. When a man imbibes a language, instrument of men's collaboration and intercourse, he imbibes at the same time the latent opposition between groups which is the result of a multiplicity of languages. Subjugation by a conqueror is all the more hateful because his speech remains unintelligible.[2] And thus the great empires instead of welding men together in a stable union, which was their intention, often ended by hopelessly dividing them. Conversely the conversion of the pagan nations to Yahweh entails their adoption of the language of Canaan (Isaias 19 : 18).

The story of the Tower of Babel is a forceful resumé of all those facts against which individual strength is powerless and which spring more or less directly from sin. By making

[1]There is an example in Neh. 13 : 24.
[2]Cf. Deut. 28: 49; Isaias 28:11; 33: 18-19; Jer. 5: 15.

the sovereign judge, who directs the course of history, intervene directly to cause confusion of tongues, it points to a fateful solidarity between those responsible and those not responsible, cut off as all are by a wall of incomprehension from other peoples. This is only one typical example from among many of those collective and anonymous faults which eventually create a corrupt atmosphere, in which religious and moral life is exposed to inevitable deviations.

Idolatry was another case that held the attention of another, much earlier book, the book of Wisdom. The author is combating the immemorial and almost universal mistake of identifying the godhead either with the stars or the elements of the world (Wisdom 13 : 1-9), or with images representing men or animals (13 : 10, 15-19). This is not the place to repeat the arguments which he uses to show how ridiculous and foolish idolatry is. But we must point out the texts which echo some of the invective passages from the prophets (cf. Jer. 9 : 13), in which he insists on the corrupting effects of these practices.

Therefore there will be a visitation also upon the heathen
idols,
because, though part of what God created, they became
an abomination,
and became traps for the souls of men
and a snare to the feet of the foolish (14 : 11).

Not only are they a sign of the sin of those who indulge in them, but also a danger to those who see them.

Sometimes it was not directly a religious aberration that led to the making of an idol. A father, in his inordinate affection for his dead son, wants to preserve his likeness. A king wishes to have his authority respected in his absence. The crowd is

attracted by the beauty of the work, falls victim to this excess
of esteem accorded to a man and ends by seeing in him a god :

> And this became a hidden trap for mankind,
> because men, in bondage to misfortune or to royal authority,
> bestowed on objects of stone or wood the name that ought
> not to be shared (14:21).

But Israel had the good fortune to know the true God and
to find in this knowledge the strength to resist this temptation.

> For neither has the evil intent of human art misled us,
> nor the fruitless toil of painters,
> a figure stained with varied colours,
> whose appearance arouses yearning in fools,
> so that they desire the lifeless form of a dead image (15:4-5).

The past is somewhat idealized in this hymn of gratitude.
The prophet Ezechiel had occasion to reproach Jerusalem for
venerating painted figures (Ezech. 8:10) and for the adulterous
passion to which the mere sight of these pictures gave rise
(23:14-15). Historical detail is of no great importance here.
The author is either speaking only of the recent period of his
people's past, since the exile, or he wants to consider only the
faithful nucleus who had not allowed themselves to be led
astray like the majority under the kingdom, and at this point
he shows the power of attraction exercised by the idols. These
have an almost irresistible influence, for

> Folly is bound up in the heart of a child,
> but the rod of discipline drives it far from him (Prov. 22:15),

as the Wisdom writers said of old. Their successor, in a pagan
land, has to admit that this discipline has not been present
among the pagans, who are 'most foolish, and more miserable

than an infant' (Wisdom 15 : 14). Thus they were deceived by
the most outrageous frauds, the trickery of the maker of
idolatrous statues, for example, exploiting public credulity out
of covetousness (15 : 12-13). Thus they descended to the worship of the most repulsive animals (15 : 18).

St Paul was to repeat this condemnation of idolatry. Like
the book of Wisdom (14 : 22-31) he showed religious error
leading to moral corruption (Rom. 1 : 18-32). But he ap-
proached it from a different angle and was more concerned
to show the culpability of paganism, at least in its origins and
even though it was impossible to pinpoint one particular individual responsible for it, while *Wisdom* is more interested in
revealing the corrupting and almost irresistible pressure exercised on a great number by the first aberration. From this point
of view the lesson it offers completes the lesson of Genesis in its
story of the Tower of Babel and focuses attention on the solidarity in sin which is one of the characteristics of the human
condition.

The contagion of uncleanness

According to the Bible, evil religious influence does not
occur merely between one man and another. Physical contact
with certain things can also contaminate him, thus affecting
his relations with God. No doubt the laws concerning uncleanness, promulgated particularly by Leviticus, seem to a modern
mind simply a relic of primitive ideas tainted with magic. But
a Christian cannot so lightly dismiss the whole of this legislation which holds so large a place in the codes and actual ways
of life described by the Bible.[1] If we recall Christ's words :

[1]Judges 13: 4, 7, 14; I Sam. 14: 33-34; 20: 26; 21:6; 2 Sam. 11: 4;
2 Kings 7: 3; 15: 5; 23: 16; 2 Chron. 30: 3, 18; Isaias 52: 11; Ezech
4: 14; Aggaeus 2: 13; Tob. 2: 5, 9; Ecclus. 34: 25; Acts 10: 14.

. 'Think not that I have come to abolish the law and the prophets; I have come not to abolish them but to fulfil them' (Matt. 4 : 17), we shall have to ask whether these practices, so disconcerting for us at first sight, do not nonetheless contain some still valid lesson.

There is no point in entering into detail here about forbidden foods and the classification by which an attempt was made to introduce some order into the law against eating certain species of animal, nor about the casuistry which regulated the duration of the uncleanness resulting from diseases such as leprosy, from contact with a corpse or from various sexual acts. It is enough to point out that in this sphere uncleanness did not result from moral factors. Nothing could be more in order than to bury the dead. And in the same way the various manifestations of sex, whether voluntary, as in marital relations, or involuntary, as in various normal or pathological discharges, and childbirth itself were all affected by a state of uncleanness which strictly speaking had nothing to do with any guilt.

The rules determining the conditions of contagion and purification from these various states of uncleanness do not merely constitute social taboos or duties; they do not simply codify what was or was not done 'in Israel'. In the eyes of the biblical writers they affect the sphere of religion, in order to protect its sanctity. Contracting uncleanness did not burden a person with sin in the modern sense of the word, but rendered him unsuitable, for a longer or shorter period, to participate in the liturgical worship of the community : he was forbidden, before the prescribed ablutions and delays, to enter the sanctuary (Exod. 19 : 10-15; 30 : 21; Lev. 12 : 14; 15 : 31; 22 : 3-4; Num. 19 : 13-20), to take part in a sacred meal (Lev. 7 : 20-21; 22 : 3-7; Num. 9 : 6-12; 1 Sam. 20 : 26; 21 : 5), or to remain

41

inside the camp during a military expedition (Num. 5:2-4; Deut. 23:10-12). It was a type of excommunication, more or less rigorous, which penalized the uncleanness, whether it was voluntary or not.

From this casuistry, whose details inevitably include something of an arbitrary nature, there does emerge something of real value which we Christians ought to try to see, formulate and integrate into our religious thought.

When one attempts, after the event, to find in this primitive legislation some reason which might have been even dimly perceived, the first possibility that arises is to connect it with the idea, expressed at the end of the story of the Garden of Eden, that the physical world and corporal life suffered the repercussions of sin. As a complement to the optimism shown by the account of the six days of creation, punctuated as it was with the affirmation that every one of God's works was good, some minds were struck by a lack of harmony in the natural world, which they explained by sin: the suffering that goes with work, death, the pains of childbirth, the subjection of woman to her husband and the rapid multiplication of harmful plants, to mention only what is contained in the sentence passed by Yahweh on the sinful couple (Gen. 3:16-19). While many make much of the blessings that God gives to his own in marriage, in the happiness of a table surrounded by a crowd of children, in a long life (Psalm 128), there are prohibitions of very ancient origin which recall not only that corporal life can cause men to suffer, but that even its most normal uses can bring about a separation from God.

There is no duality of principles here. In Genesis, which reveals profound reflection on these questions, the origin of all things is attributed to the beneficent will of the Creator and the introduction of evil to a deliberate sin on the part of man.

It is not that pessimism comes to contradict the optimism evident here as on many other pages of the Bible; but clear-sightedness gives depth to statements which were oversimplified. Certainly the world remains basically good after sin; for it is the world we actually experience now, and not a wonderful world gone for ever, that is described by the six day story of creation, which states that the divine work was very good. But that does not prevent the final author from adding to this bright picture another with sharply defined shadows. Man suffers and, as the ritual legislation adds, is defiled through his contact with the world.

But after this first interpretation of the facts of uncleanness, a second may spring to mind. In these prescriptions, which seem to us so arbitrary, there is a first clumsy and groping effort to raise man above the level of automatic impulses of feeling. Man is only man if he is capable of imposing discipline on his crude vital tendencies. The ritual taboos are a first attempt in this direction, often mixed with more or less mistaken ideas about the physical universe. A state of nature, morally and religiously neutral, must be left behind, if the faithful are to be worthy of approaching God. The crude realities of the organism or of the instincts cannot be accepted as such. A man must paint himself, or cut his hair, or forbid himself the immediate satisfaction of certain desires, and so on. A vague realization of this need led to a rather irrational proliferation of customs, which were handed on by tradition.

From this point of view one should speak of an initial deficiency and not of uncleanness, if by this word is meant a defilement coming after the event. But this was precisely the word that was used for those conditions which involved a certain religious incapacity. And the confusion that existed between two ideas which ought strictly to be distinguished is a sign of a conscience burdened by sin, which affected the neighbouring spheres of human life.

In conclusion, then, it is perhaps not absolutely necessary even were it possible to be sure what feeling, so difficult to express led to the appearance of the facts of uncleanness: a perversion of nature by sin[1] or an initial imperfection, or a combination of the two. The essential point is that the biblical authors recognized some influence independent of man's free will, yet having an effect on his religious condition. Here, without doubt, is one of the least intellectually elaborated elements in the biblical teaching on the solidarity of man with his environment, for good or ill. But it is nevertheless a contribution to the doctrine of original sin, insofar as it is presumed that religious defects can affect a person without any sinful action on his part or sometimes even any free decision.

Scripture does not give any theoretical explanation of the unworthiness caused by ceremonial uncleanness, and is content to define the practical consequences: the provisional prohibition against taking part in the liturgy. It is a limited effect, for liturgical worship is not the only way of entering into communication with God, and the prophets are at pains to teach other and better means: piety of heart and the observation of the moral laws. Thus the Old Testament as a whole distinguishes different levels on which relations with God can be established or broken. And it admits that, on the lower levels of ritual uncleanness, exterior causes, independent of any personal commitment of the heart, can cause a separation from God.

[1]Perversion either in itself or only in relation to a subject that has lost its innocence. It is still necessary to discuss the alternative here.—On these questions a good deal of information from the Old Testament, collected in view of St Paul's explanation, can be found in my article: 'Le gémissement des créatures dans l'ordre divin du cosmos' (Rom. 8: 19-22), *RSPT.*, XXXVIII, (1954), pp. 445-65.

2

Original Sin in Genesis

I. Preliminary Observations

Clearly the most important Scripture text concerning original sin is the story of the Fall in Genesis. This is the passage to which St Paul refers when he speaks of sin and death entering the world through one man, Adam (Rom. 5 : 12-19; 1 Cor. 15 : 22). To grasp the full meaning of this famous passage, we must read it with the general plan of the book in mind.

The first book of the Old Testament traces the origins of everything that might raise a problem in the Israelite mind : the whole world, the universal condition of man, all the various peoples of the earth, Israel itself, some of its major religious laws, its tribes and certain neighbouring and related tribes. This story of origins is also the story of sin and salvation. A general plan can be seen : the establishment of divine order, its perversion through the fault of man and its restoration by divine grace, or in other words : genesis, degeneration, regeneration. Even more than a plan, it could be called a constantly recurring theme. In fact, though the period from the creation to the call of Abraham (chaps. 3-11) is principally marked by the progress of sin and corruption, the mercy of Yahweh is already felt by the first couple and by Cain and Noah. Similarly, though the work of restoration is put in hand from the time of

45

Abraham onwards, many partial relapses are recorded, more or less seriously, compromising the future: for example, the relatively slight infidelities of Abraham, Isaac and Jacob and the more serious crimes of Jacob's sons. The original sin is the first of a whole series of faults which, in the course of time, disfigure the work of God.

One other important point must be made. Genesis was not composed all at one time by one historian who had fully weighed and digested his sources and then composed a story which was quite new from the literary point of view, retaining only those elements in the given information about which he was sure. The author did not work in the way a modern specialist would. After two centuries of analysis, it is today generally recognized that Genesis like a good many other books of Scripture was composed by a fairly arbitrary juxtaposition of pre-existing stories. Without rewriting what was contained in his sources to any great extent, the final editor added one to the other, sometimes using whole pages at a time, sometimes fitting them together in a more elaborate patchwork. Certain minor disagreements, certain difficulties in reconciling different passages, variations in style or point of view are all explained by this initial plurality and combination.[1]

[1]There is no need here to justify this literary theory in detail: it accounts simply for a great number of different difficulties. For chaps. 1-11, which form the early history and interest us specially here, two sources are recognized; the yahwist, an older and more psychological account, and the priestly code, a more simplified work, preoccupied with religious institutions. This theory is sufficiently probable for the theologian to be able to take it into account, at least insofar as it is a practical explanation of an undeniable fact: the composite character of Genesis. Attempts have been made to break down these two documents in their turn. The principle is plausible, but no hypothesis has won general support. The theologian may disregard these, since the final author, with whose intention he is concerned, worked with literary units that already formed a whole, not with a number of little fragments. Cf. O. Procksch, *Theologie des Alten Testaments*, (1950), p. 492, n. 2; p. 495, n. 1.

Consequently the intention of the inspired book is to be sought rather in the arrangement of the whole than in the detail of individual verses,[1] which were the work of more ancient authors who may perhaps have been outside scriptural inspiration. The final inspired editor, entirely concerned with profound religious lessons, respected the tenor of the traditional accounts without being very concerned about secondary details. Possibly, by their insertion into a wider framework, the older documents underwent a change of emphasis, and various intentions, which might be very obvious if such a passage were taken in isolation, may have faded into the background or disappeared altogether: the six days of creation, for example, or the age of the patriarchs. Exegesis must not be short-sighted when it is involved in seeking doctrinal statements in the canonical book; on the contrary, it must look at it from a distance sufficient to enable it to grasp the general outline.

II. THE STORY OF THE BEGINNINGS

Genesis opens with an account of the creation in six days, presenting and classifying the principal realities of the visible world, as the Israelite could see them, in a satisfactory order (Gen. 1 : 1-2, 4a). The comprehensive aim of this page, taken from the priestly code, is very clear. But the reason for its inclusion in the final work is the repeated statement that creation is good, very good, for it is the work of a power which knows no obstacle, of a wisdom which directs and discriminates and of a benevolence which provides solicitously for the needs of its creatures. Then comes another description of the beginning of things, borrowed from the yahwist. The outlook is

[1] J. Guillet, *Thèmes bibliques*, (Paris, 1951), p. 106.

much narrower and the order of creation is different here. Instead of the sequence : watery chaos, plants, animals and mankind, male and female, that we see in the priestly code, we find the dry earth watered by a spring, the male individual, the plants, the animals and the woman.

The two accounts may be difficult to reconcile from the point of view of cosmology, but they are complementary from the point of view of anthropology. Both result in the same essential lesson : man is superior to the animals, his destiny is the union of the sexes and he has duties towards God. The religious doctrine of the two accounts is equally complementary. With its insistence on the goodness of creation the first throws into relief the second, which begins with the formation of the first couple and ends, because of their disobedience, in a divine condemnation, which expresses the main characteristics of the human condition. All the ills that humanity is for ever experiencing are not the effect of the divine will or divine powerlessness; they come exclusively from a deliberate sin on the part of the creature.

We cannot linger here over all the problems raised by these passages. It will suffice to examine more closely the points concerning man's original state and his original sin. We can leave aside the exact psychological nature of the sin committed or of the knowledge of good and evil, forbidden under pain of death,[1] so long as we know that a sin was committed.

According to the priestly account, man was created in the image of God, a privilege that he alone enjoys : he was created male and female, a condition that he shares with the animals. He was called to multiply, to fill the earth and to have

[1] On this point see my position in *Les Sages d'Israël*, (Paris, 1947), pp. 16-19, and a history of the problem with a new solution in J. Coppens, *La connaissance du bien et du mal et le péché du Paradis*, (Louvain, 1948).

dominion over all other beings (1 : 26-28). However the exploitation of the resources of the material world is not his only object. God blesses and sanctifies the seventh day (2 : 3), by which it is suggested that he imposes certain duties of worship on his creatures. However nothing is said here of one of the most important laws for the people of Israel, the Sabbath rest. An obligation of this nature, intended to prevent any return of the bondage from which God had delivered his people in Egypt (Deut. 5 : 15), had no point in a creation that was very good. By his silence the author suggests a state of harmonious and painless work. Likewise there is mention only of an exclusively vegetarian diet : for man, cereals and fruit, for the beasts, green grass (1 : 29-30). The hierarchy is thus respected and no picture of death comes to disturb the initial peace. After the Flood, God will decree penalties for murder and, at the same time, permission to eat meat (9 : 1-7). The prophets expressly announce a state of peace and vegetarianism in the last days (Isaias 11 : 5-9; 65 : 25). The creation narrative suggests it, less clearly, and does not speak positively of immortality being granted to man.

The description of the creation of man in the Garden of Eden, the work of the yahwist, agrees in the main with the first account, although very different means are used to express the same ideas. Man and the animals are formed from the dust of the earth : but the gift of breath by Yahweh is mentioned expressly only in the case of man (2 : 7). No doubt this is with the intention of suggesting superiority, although in general the biblical authors regard the breath of animals also as coming from the breath of God. However that may be, man gives a name to the animals and does not find a helpmate fit for him among them. Only woman can fill this role. While the six days of creation narrative considers only the fruitfulness

49

of the union of the sexes, the yahwist account stresses the human characteristics of this union: a certain dependence on the woman's part, but with, in compensation, a special attachment on the husband's part (2 : 18-24). Perfect harmony, expressed by the state of nakedness, reigns in the little society formed by the first couple (2 : 25). At peace with God, man and woman are at peace with one another and have nothing to hide from one another.[1] Clothing is not necessary as a protection against an intemperate climate, for it has not yet rained (2 : 5), nor against thorns and brambles, which have not yet appeared (3 : 18).

Man is put in the Garden of Eden to cultivate it and take care of it (2 : 15). But this work of exploitation is not yet the hard labour, in the sweat of the brow, which will be imposed after the sin (3 : 17-19). To the Israelite mind the first man's condition, in a sort of oasis, would summon up that pleasant period before the gathering of the fruits and the vine harvest, when the mildness of the air made it possible to camp in the open to watch over the ripening harvest.

However, man, surrounded by this abundance, is commanded not to eat the fruit of a certain tree, the tree of the knowledge of good and evil (2 : 17). Just so, in the priestly account, he must submit to religious obligations, which here take the form of a prohibition, so frequent in primitive religions.

The serpent urges the woman, and through her the man, to disobey this divine command. The serpent is portrayed as a cunning being and its words are particularly subtle; but its punishment will be described in terms of an animal. It is not easy to attach a clear meaning to this rather symbolic language. At the very least the old storyteller means to show that man is subject to the influence of a malevolent power, and consequently that his sin is not entirely his own work.

[1] On this point see below, pp. 74-75.

The first couple, then, eat the forbidden fruit. And this disobedience is followed by a train of unhappy consequences. The two sinners see that they are naked and feel the need to make themselves some form of rudimentary clothing. After this embarrassment towards one another, they are too embarrassed to appear before Yahweh, as he walks in the Garden (3 : 7-10). Proceeding from culprit to culprit, the divine questioner arrives at the tempter, who is cursed without having the chance to defend himself. It is taken for granted that he has no excuse. The serpent is to crawl on its belly, as if it previously had a different posture; but this is not expressly stated. An enmity springs up between the seducer and his posterity on the one hand and the woman and hers on the other (3 : 15). So the consequences of the condemnation extend beyond the present actors to their descendants. There is no other mention of the hereditary nature of the punishments in the rest of the story; but it is clear that what is explicitly stated here about one of the consequences of sin holds good for all. It is the fate of all generations that is announced in the sentence passed on the woman and the man, and not simply the fate of the first sinful couple. Even earlier a passing remark stressed that the conduct of man towards the companion given to him by God was the prototype and cause of the conduct of all men when they marry (2 : 24).

Thus a perpetual struggle between the tempter and his victims is begun. The woman is condemned to the pains of childbirth and to subjection to her husband (3 : 16). The man is condemned to arduous work on the earth which will no longer be a lush paradise : he will have to struggle against thorns and thistles; and finally he will meet death, for he has been expelled from the Garden of Eden, far from the tree of life (3 : 17-24).

51

Such is the account which held a great place in Christian teaching, ever since the pauline parallel between Adam and Christ (Rom. 5:12-19; 1 Cor. 15:22). Long years of reflection have, justifiably, sought to develop all that is implicitly contained in the text. We must take this into account when we come to read it in our turn. This calls for a work of precision which, paradoxically, is at the same time a work of 'imprecision'. We are far from the naïvety of the first readers and today we must be conscious of the ambiguity or breadth of meaning of certain elements in the story, in order to guard against too hasty an acceptance of the highly definite notions which have since been arrived at.

It is necessary, then, to return to these first pages of Scripture, which have inspired so many theological doctrines through the centuries, in order to determine as accurately as possible just which categories subsequently made explicit literal exegesis can find in these passages. But there is one general question to be asked first, concerning literary genre.

III. ARE THERE MYTHS IN GENESIS?

These first stories of Genesis are commonly treated as myths, either with a view to denying or casting doubt on their value or with the intention of upholding it in spite of this fact. The latter case may involve refusing the account of any historical character at all, or of recognizing it in some restricted sense. We must, therefore, examine the way in which various authors have spoken of myth with regard to Genesis.[1]

[1] On this subject cf. I. Islop, 'The Christian Myth', in *The Life of the Spirit*, 7 (1952-53), pp. 185-88; J. Barr, 'The Meaning of "Mythology" in relation to the Old Testament', in *Vetus Testamentum*, 9 (1959), pp. 1-10.

Myth, said Gunkel, in a deliberately simplified definition, is 'a story relating to the gods'.[1] And he concludes that, since Israel had only one God, any traces of mythology in the Bible could only be faint. No battles and love stories of the gods are to be found there; instead the action takes place between God and man (with the angels as God's servants). And when God intervenes, the conclusion is very near.

Myth is also an attempt to explain (or simply to give expression to) natural facts in terms of concrete happenings, the development of which is attributed to the choice or freedom of the actors (gods, men, animals or plants). Myth is frequently aetiological, its aim being to account for the universe or certain of its details. From this point of view it is possible to see a difference between the Genesis stories and pagan myths. The God of Israel, being all powerful, needs only to will and to command a result. That is what we see in the six day creation account. In the story of the Garden of Eden there remain traces of the idea that God works in stages: he forms man, breathes life into him, then he removes a rib and makes a woman out of it. In any case, this is still far more sober than the pagan myths. The animist quality of the myths, attributing human feelings to animals, has disappeared. On this account some refuse to call the biblical stories myths and we can understand why.[2]

We can even go further. The first pages of Genesis are not simply a diluted version of pagan myths or an adaptation with the polytheism removed: rather, they are an adoption

---

[1]H. Gunkel, *Genesis übersetzt und erklärt*, 4, (1917) p. xiv.
[2]Thus F. R. Tennant, *The Sources of the Doctrine of the Fall and Original Sin*, (1903), pp. 83-84. This work contains a very complete and methodical discussion on this point, which has not lost its value, even if the comparative material has since become richer. W. Vischer, *Das Christzeugnis des A.T.*, 1 (1934) pp. 47-50, prefers the words story or legend.

of the opposite point of view. [Under the guidance of divine inspiration, they use the imaginative framework of the Babylonian cosmogonies in order to teach the opposite lesson.] And so the six days account also takes as its starting point an original state of watery chaos. But it shows God gradually producing order by his word, without any trace of that battle against a rebellious adversary of which certain more poetic pages of the Bible have preserved the picture.[1] To take only one example, the story of the Garden of Eden is preoccupied with the explanation of death, like the Babylonian stories. There is talk of a tree of life, as of a plant of youth or life potion in the pagan parallels. [But in Genesis death is not connected with some jealous decision or lie on the part of the gods but with a sin on the part of man.]

Myth can sometimes be an explanation of a particular fact of some outstanding landmark for example, and in the story of the Tower of Babel there is (together with other intentions) an answer to the problem posed by an unfinished or ruined building. But normally myths explain a recurrent fact : a state of affairs existing in many individual cases or in an entire race is accounted for by a contingent event, not by the nature or law of things. What is interesting about myths to a modern mind is not the explanation as such, but the material or spiritual fact that they observe and express and the religious meaning which they artificially attach to the fact. Or again, without claiming to give a real explanation, myths may simply give a representation of a general fact. What we do today in

[1] Psalm 89: 10-12; 104: 5-9; Job 38: 8-11; Prov. 8: 27-29 and passages that are less detailed or full of historical memories: Job 7: 12; 9: 13; 26: 11; Isaias 51: 9; Jer. 5: 22; Psalm 74: 13-16. P. Heinisch, *Problem der Urgeschichte,* Lucerne, (1947), has drawn attention to these cosmogonical fragments and given a brief account of the myths of the Babylonians and others about creation or paradise.

the form of a novel or a drama (intended to be fictitious) or in the form of abstract speculation, the primitive peoples liked to do through characters set in that past time when things began. When their story is told, the story of all men is told, even if the storyteller and his audience are not specifically conscious of this and have a naïve faith in the truth of the story. Today, thanks to the research that has been done on these products of pagan religions, we can make comparisons which allow us to pick out the laws of a certain literary genre and deny its historical character, in spite of the fact that the milieu from which it came was convinced that they were true, and so appreciate better where the real interest lies in these profound intuitions revealed by popular or learned traditions.

This is what leads many recent authors to consider that the primitive history or story of the Garden of Eden are myths : they think we must look there for an archetypal representation of man's state and not for details about individual facts at the dawn of our race. Very roughly the many individual opinions can be classed in two groups. For some the story of the Garden of Eden describes the arrival of mankind as a whole, or of the individual, at adult knowledge and the resulting realization of the limitations and sufferings of the human condition. Taking everything into account, then, this involves progress, not a fall.[1] For the others, more recent and at the moment, it seems,

[1] This interpretation goes back to Kant, *Muthmasslicher Anfang der Menschengeschichte*, (1786), modern Berlin edition, VIII, pp. 109-23, whose only object was to exploit a sacred text philosophically. For Kant the misfortune of the individual could be for the good of the species. The Germany of the Romantic period adapted this interpretation to hegelian philosophy; cf. J. Geiselmann, 'J. A. Möhler und das idealistische Verständnis des Sündenfalls', in *Scholastik*, XIX, (1944), pp. 19-37. An exegete such as Reuss begins to mention, among the consequences of the awakening of reason, the consciousness of sin. He opens the way to the second form of explanation: cf. *L'histoire sainte et la loi*, (1879), I, pp. 293-94.

more numerous, the story describes the religious experience of every man: [he discovers himself to be intelligent, eager for knowledge and at the same time radically separated from God, because he is voluntarily and freely a sinner; each individual, by virtue of a personal decision which is free and at the same time inevitable, is the object of divine anger.[1]

Is the exegesis of Genesis confronted with the alternative: an individual and historical fact or a general truth and myth? This opposition can be overcome and indeed some authors have already overcome it. They do not confine themselves simply to the statement of something that has always been recognized, namely that an individual fact can have the value of a prototype; instead [they describe a history of a special kind, which is expressed in traditional imagery, but in which the meaning of this imagery is profoundly transformed.

If history is understood as a detailed knowledge of certain facts in the past, based on testimony faithfully handed on by memory or in writing, then the historical character of the story of the Fall or of the whole of the early history can scarcely be maintained.[2] The findings of the natural sciences on man's

[1]This interpretation too is already present in Kant, though he treats sin as a violation of the moral law and not as an offence against God: *Die Religion innerhalb der Grenzen der blossen Vernunft*, (1793, I, iv), Berlin ed., VI, 41-43 (Trans.. *Religion within the Limits of Reason Alone*, Glasgow, 1934). Recently ¡G. Quell, art. 'αμαρταγω', *TWNT.*, I, p. 287; W. Zimmerli, *Die Urgeschichte*, (1943), I, pp. 251 and 242 (he may not deny the reality of the first sin, but he sees only its exemplary character and rejects any idea of transmission); A. Richardson, *A Preface to Bible Study*, (London, 1944), chap. 8; *Genesis I-XI*, (1953), p. 66; L. Ragaz, *Die Urgeschichte*, (1947), pp. 43-50; E. C. Rust, *The Christian Understanding of History*, (1947) pp. 213-15; G. Crespy, *Le Problème d'une anthropologie théologique*, (1950), pp. 42 and 118; F. J. Leenhardt, 'La situation de l'homme dans la Genèse', in the symposium *Das Menschenbild im Lichte des Evangeliums (Festschrift E. Brunner)*, (1950), pp. 1-29.

[2]The encyclical *Humani Generis* recognizes the fact and encourages us not to avoid the problem that it poses, when it follows up an earlier

origin, to keep only to the most modest estimates, do not allow us to think that an accurate tradition could have been preserved without alteration for a hundred thousand years. Besides, the Bible in no way supports this idea of a primitive revelation preserved intact in a privileged branch, since the ancestors of Abraham are represented as adoring other gods than Yahweh (Joshua 24 : 2).[1]

Apart from the remoteness of the origins of humanity, the resemblance (in form, not in content) with certain mythological stories of the ancient East, and the presence in the Bible itself of several variants of traditions about the beginning suggest that the stories of primitive history in Genesis were formed according to the same laws of psychology as the myths of other nations : [the observation of human nature or nature at large and the explanation of it from the point of view of religious beliefs.] And it is here that the difference becomes apparent.

The belief that the Bible contains revelation tells us nothing about how revelation worked in the mind of the inspired authors. Some prophetic oracles are the result of a chance association of images and ideas, or result from a play on words. In the story of the Fall revelation does not necessarily mean the instantaneous communication of a fact to the sacred author, with extraordinary, divine illumination taking the

letter of the Biblical Commission with the warning 'that the first eleven chapters of Genesis, although it is not right to judge them by modern standards of historical composition, such as would be applied to the great classical authors, or to the learned of our own day, do nevertheless come under the heading of history; in what exact sense, it is for the further labours of the exegete to determine', *Ench. Bibl.* n. 618 (CTS. trans. n. 38).

---

[1] M.- J. Lagrange, 'Héxameron', in *RB.*, V (1896) p. 406.

place of human testimony. It is more in accordance with the indications we have mentioned to assume that the facts were reconstructed by reason and imagination directed by the yahwist belief.

Israel, its religion based on the historical event of the exodus from Egypt, was more ready to think of the present as a result of a succession of past events than as the manifestation of a timeless nature or law. Accustomed to consider God's plan revealing itself over the generations, to discover a certain pattern followed over the course of long centuries, to see, for example, in the Exodus the realization of promises made to the patriarchs, the mind of Israel looked for objective facts at the root of the present, rather than rest content with ideal events set at the beginning as a simple prototype of present experience.

Convinced from other sources of the goodness, power and wisdom of God, who can do nothing that is not very good (Gen. 1:31) or perfect (Deut. 32:4), the faith of the Chosen People could not admit that man had originally been formed in the state of wretchedness and sin that he now experiences.[1] Here again we see the difference from pagan mythology, which does not hesitate to attribute to its gods powerlessness, arbitrary conduct and jealousy of man. This mental process, seeking the causes of universal facts of experience, was inspired and guided by God and consequently gained unique acute-

---

[1] This is a very brief summary of the essentials of the reasoning attributed to the faithful Israelites, which has been developed at length by A. Dillmann, *Die Genesis* 6, (Leipzig 1892), pp. 42-47, and recently by a Catholic, J. Guitton, *Le développement des idées dans l'Ancien Testament*, (Aix-en-Provence, 1947), pp. 124-26.

ness in its diagnosis of the human condition and complete truth in its explanation of it.[1]

But we must hasten to add that this reasoning, which we can reconstruct and express logically, was never present as an abstraction to the mind of Israel. Primitive peoples do not separate the need for explanation from concrete imagery: the ideological content in the image is not rendered consciously distinct. In the mental and narrative process which led to the story of the Garden of Eden, past events are rediscovered by faith and at the same time given literary forms which bear outward resemblances to the mythical stories of neighbouring peoples.[2] The state of mind of the storyteller here differs entirely from the case of parables, fables or allegories, where the imagery is deliberately introduced for pedagogical reasons. On the one hand there is inability to express thought in any way other than a picturesque account; on the other, there is the ability to render the image comprehensible by an explanation in clear language, when a question of fact is involved,

[1] P. Heinisch, *Probleme der Urgeschichte*, (Lucerne, 1947), pp. 102-03, rules out the possibility of the author being able to reconstruct the facts explaining our present sinful condition by reflexion; according to him there is too great a difference between the efforts of the various peoples and the result contained in Gen. 2-3. So it is necessary to assume a special illumination surpassing simple inspiration. The reason given is not conclusive, precisely because the other peoples had not the same knowledge of God as Israel and apart from that did not enjoy scriptural inspiration. The distinction between illumination and inspiration is artificial. It is quite true that, according to Catholic theology, inspiration does not necessarily include revelation of unknown facts, but it does not exclude it either. And there is no reason to deny that revelation could result from reflexion guided by inspiration.

[2] According to M. Noth, *Überlieferungsgeschichte des Pentateuch*, (1948), p. 257, the author of chaps. 2-3 did not follow any of the accounts of the creation in the ancient East but only used images of details to express what was his own creation.

or in abstract terms, when doctrinal teaching is involved.[1]

If a direct revelation has intervened to give instantaneous knowledge of the events of the origins, instead of inspiring a process of slow rediscovery, if the symbols that everyone concurs in recognizing in Gen. 2-3 were only a superficial literary clothing adapted after the event, it would be difficult to explain how the religious truths contained in this story had to wait so long to be formulated in a way which was not figurative: until the later Wisdom books (Ecclus. 25:24; Wisdom 2:24) and St Paul (Rom. 5:12-19). In fact it is difficult to give any solid proof of the storyteller's conscious symbolic intentions.[2]

These various considerations lead us to admit that the story of the Garden of Eden, and indeed the whole of the early

---

[1] Let us say at this point that the symbolic or figurative character of the literary genre in no way excludes a historical intention, which may be more or less clear according to the case. The majority of Gospel parables simply express general religious or moral truths: but the parable of the murderous vineyard workers (Matt. 21: 33-41) is a summary of Israel's history. To a lesser degree the parables of the weeds (Matt. 13: 24-30, 36-43), of the grain of wheat (Mark 4: 16-29), of the mustard seed (Matt. 13: 31-32), of the leaven (Matt. 13: 31) and of the net (Matt. 13: 47-50) have a historical meaning, because they describe the development of the kingdom of God from the beginning to the end. The allegory of the vine (John 15: 1-6) is timeless, but that of the shepherd contains some historical characteristics (John 10: 8, 15-18) and the allegory of the lioness in Ezech. (19: 10-14) is completely historical.

[2] That is what Y. Laurent says, 'Le caractère historique de Gen. II-III dans l'exégèse française au tournant du XIXe siècle', in *Eph. Theol. Lov.* XXIII, (1947) pp. 36-69, see p. 66.—G. Castellino, *La Storicità dei capi 2-3 del Genesi*, (1951) p. 22, admits that in the present case the hagiographer had no reflex idea of the distinction between matter and form, between the lesson and its clothing. The first Catholic exegetes, inclined to recognize some traces of a mythical origin in the story of the Garden of Eden, often supposed that there had been a conscious recourse to a procedure of literary expression for a doctrine already possessed by revelation (under what form?). Concerning these authors, see J. Feldmann, *Paradies und Sündenfall*, (Münster, 1913), pp. 574-84.

history, issues from Israel's faith by way of mental processes which, in religions less clearly founded on history and without the same knowledge of the true God, resulted in mythical accounts. This solution, which admits the close union of substance and form in the mind of the sacred author recognizes a very largely symbolic literary genre in these chapters, without having to distinguish the historical from the fictitious therein. There is no need for the exegete to involve himself in the difficult and arbitrary work of distinction to be able to say, for example, that the serpent is real but the tree of knowledge is not, that the site of paradise is unknown to us but its existence is certain, without showing on each occasion the positive reasons justifying this unequal treatment of the various elements of the text.[1]

The origin accounts, slowly elaborated by the tradition of Israel, acquired, if they did not already have it, a new historical significance with their incorporation into Genesis, i.e., into the early parts of that history of salvation which for an Israelite continues with the deliverance from Egypt, for a Christian with Jesus Christ, and for both with final judgment by God. This history, using the word in the sense of a view of time's unfolding, does not for eschatological events use human documents giving evidence of facts; nor is it an anticipated chronicle. The prophetic light does not reveal the details of events but simply the providential significance of the future.[2] And the same is true for the beginning: this biblical history does not derive its content and certainty from the historian's

[1] Cf. A. Bea, 'Neuere Probleme und Arbeiten zur biblischen Urgeschichte, in *Biblica*, XXV, (1944), pp. 70-87, see p. 76; G. Castellino, op. cit.' p. 23.
[2] About these peculiarities of the prophetic style and the imperfections of the picture of the future that it expresses, cf. E. Tobac-J. Coppens, *Les Prophètes d'Israel* 2, (1932), Vol. I, pp. 59-88.

ordinary procedure, which is the examination of witnesses.
It obtains the facts from sources which from the literary
point of view are related to myths but in which the content
and orientation of the mythical thought has already been profoundly modified by the historic faith of Israel.[1] It is not
arbitrary to call such a composition history, if it is agreed to
extend the scope of this word in rather an unusual way and
to understand by it a true knowledge of the past, however it
may have been obtained. One could quite justifiably speak of
a history of the solar system or of the earth, which would not
be based on contemporary observation of confirmed facts but
on calculation and reasoning from present facts. Nor is there
any reason why we should not give the name of history to an
account of mankind's past, in which reflection guided by religious faith has rediscovered real facts on account of their
resemblance to the present and their connection with the
present. The truth of this history is not to be judged from the
point of view of the literary genre in which it is expressed and
the mental processes which have given it birth. It is its adher-
ence to certain religious beliefs which will allow us to say
whether this special kind of history is true or false.

[Genesis intends to report real facts, not to teach timeless
religious truths in the manner of a parable. First of all it col-
lects, arranges and joins traditional accounts of the origins and
strictly historical memories, so that it is difficult to see where
one begins and the other ends. Amongst other peoples of

[1] W. Eichrodt, *Theologie des Alten Testaments* 2nd. ed. (Leipzig), Vol. II,
p. 86, n. 5; Vol. III, pp. 94-95; W. Vischer, *Das Christzeugnis des A.T.*,
(1934), Vol. I; 'Das Gesetz', pp. 47-50, (he prefers the word 'story' or
'legend' to 'myth'); O. Cullmann, *Christus und die Zeit*, (1947), chap. 7;
J. Guitton, op. cit., pp. 124-26 (he speaks of a 'popular account', which
would have been purified from all error); A. -M. Dubarle, 'L'histoire
primitive', in *RSPT.*, XXXIII, (1949), p. 202.

antiquity the myths were not subjected to any such treatment. Then again, what we know from the Bible itself of Israelite traditions, much closer to myth form than the early history of Genesis, allows us to see how Genesis 1-11 differs from the general structure and from the particular form its various constituent materials had received before being built into it.

The book of Job allows us to grasp the existence of a tradition very close to that of the Garden of Eden:

Are you the first man that was born?
... and have you stolen wisdom for yourself? (15:7-8).[1]

But in particular it is the prophet Ezechiel who develops, in a manner far more marvellous than Genesis, an account of a sin of pride committed by a being placed in the Garden of Eden, on the mountain of God, adorned with precious stones, walking amid the stones of fire, and then driven out; this text concerns a cherub, but one cannot be certain whether the culprit is the cherub himself or whether he is punished by the cherub (Ezech. 28:12-19). Such a parallel shows that the author of Genesis (or of the yahwist document) chose between several forms of his people's traditions or that he modified this tradition by eliminating its more extraordinary characteristics. Thus creations of imagination or the groping discoveries of the human mind underwent a complete literary assimilation, which gave them a sober, more historical form.[2]

[1] The second line of this quotation is a direct translation of the author's French text.—(Translator's note).
[2] A. van Hoonacker has quoted the parallel and the differences of detail between Genesis and Ezech. 28, to show how the two authors used popular traditions without confusing the essential teaching and the extraordinary elements that served as a means of expression. Perhaps he is giving the distinction a reflexly conscious character, which it did not have. If they do nothing else, the definite differences show that they

Thus, between history in the usual sense of the word and myth (with its implicit connotation of timelessness), the Bible presents us with a total view of the succession of time, the central part being properly historical and the peripheral parts drawn from sources of information other than witness : prophetic anticipation for the future and discriminating use of traditional symbolic stories for the origins. The knowledge of past or future obtained in this way cannot claim to report the concrete detail of the events as seen by those who lived through them, but only their significance in the drama of salvation.

Consequently the story of the Garden of Eden cannot be interpreted as if it were independent of the rest of Genesis, or we should be in danger of commenting on a figment of our own imagination. For it is possible and even probable that this account, in the form in which we read it in the first pages of the Old Testament, never existed independently and that its present form is the result of its insertion into a wider structure.

A symbolic theme, fable, legend, myth can be exploited in many different ways with more or less profound modifications. Even a text which fixes them in a definite form normally remains open to various interpretations. Any claim to discover the interpretation given by the author of Genesis to the Garden of Eden theme must take account of the evidence offered to us by the whole book. To isolate these chapters and, even more, to comment on what is claimed to be a more original form, obtained by literary dissection or rearrangement,

___

did not consider the details of the story as something of great importance and that there was progressive development. See 'The Literary Origin of the Narrative of the Fall.—Is the Narrative of the Fall a Myth?' in *Expositor*, (1914), VIII, pp. 481-98; (1918), XVI, pp. 373-400. I am familiar with these articles only through the Summary of J. Coppens, *Le Chanoine A. van Hoonacker*, (1935), pp. 15-20.

is too conjectural a task to be called exegesis. A written text is not to be interpreted as an actor interprets a dramatic role, or as a musician interprets a score, still less as a creative poet interprets an ancient theme.

IV. THE INSUFFICIENCY OF PURELY MYTHICAL INTERPRETATIONS

If Genesis is history of a special kind, using a traditional reconstruction and not witnesses in the strict sense of the word for its account of the origins, it remains to be asked what view of the unfolding of past events the author wishes to offer. The author means to convey that an inferior state, a mixture of good and bad, succeeded a state of excellence begun by creation. This is already clear in the story of the Garden of Eden taken by itself, contrasting the condition of man at his creation with the state that followed his act of disobedience. It is clearer still if this story is replaced in its context at the beginning of the yahwist document, which tells many other stories in which sin calls down divine anger.[1] Indeed the present order of Genesis, in which the book begins with the account of creation in six days, that hymn to the excellence of creation, shows clearly the final compiler's conviction that the world as we know it is not simply inferior to a divine ideal, but comes from an actual corruption of God's work. The story of the Garden of Eden cannot be just a myth describing a normal or inevitable process.

Thus exegesis which sees this passage as essentially a picture of human destiny, happy in the carefree days of childhood,

[1] Cf. W. Eichrodt, *Theologie des A.T.*, (1935), Vol. III, p. 95.

then more and more unhappy with the progress of psychological self-consciousness, and which considers the sin of disobedience a mere literary device without any real importance, cannot claim to be true to the thought of the book which we actually possess. Still less is it a question of the collective progress of humanity: that is the object of chapter 4:19-22, which tells of the origin of the arts and ways of life.

[Exegesis which sees in chapters 2-3 a representation of sin constantly recurring in mankind is already closer to the intentions of Genesis: this view makes the author, by a perfectly legitimate literary fiction, recount as an individual fact what is really only a synthetic picture of sin in all men, whether this involves free acts committed by each individual or the realization of the creature's state of inevitable separation from God.

All the same it may already be asked if this interpretation of the Eden drama as a schematic representation of a universal fact does not tend to treat personal sin as an inevitable necessity. This idea would be contrary to the general plan of Genesis and also to certain stories in the book. Not only are just men, like Enoch and Noah, mentioned, but brothers, whom one might suppose to have been placed in the most similar initial conditions, act quite differently: Cain and Abel in particular illustrate the freedom of divine preferences; one cannot say the same of Sem, Cham and Japhet. But we must not lay too much stress on something which is a possible consequence rather than a direct assertion of the kind of exegesis that we have envisaged.

What is more serious is the fact that this school of exegesis considers sin as a purely individual reality and dismisses the idea of any inheritance on this score. Modern ideas, alien to Genesis and ancient Israel, have come in here and disturbed the exegesis of the text.

In the story itself there are some points which show that the author certainly does mean to relate a drama with consequences extending to a whole race. The enmity Yahweh set between the serpent and the woman is also to exist between their respective posterities. A hereditary vendetta is begun. The expulsion from the garden of Eden concerns only the guilty couple themselves in the first place, as they are the only people in existence. But it is quite clear that access to the divine garden is forbidden from then on to all their descendants (cf. Gen. 4 : 16). The woman is called Eve, which means 'life', because she is the mother of all the living (3 : 20).

Furthermore Genesis as a whole, and the yahwist section in particular, is convinced that the ancestor's conduct and fate condition the destiny of his posterity, without it being necessary for the same free decision to be taken anew in each generation. Each population group is shown as the issue of a first father who gives it both its name and its ethnic and psychological characteristics. The vagabond fate of Cain, the murderer, is an image of the nomad life of the tribe of Quenites or Cainites (Gen. 4 : 14). Canaan is cursed at the same time as his father Cham, who lacked respect towards Noah (9 : 25). Ismael is a savage ass, at odds with everyone (16 : 12). Moab and Ben-Ammi, born of the incestuous union between the daughters of Lot and their father, are the founders of the hated peoples of Moab and Ammon (19 : 37-38). Of the sons of Jacob, Ruben loses the rights of the eldest son through an act of incest (35 : 22; 49 : 4). Simeon and Levi are condemned to dispersal, which affects the tribe bearing their name, as a consequence of their massacre of the Sichemites (34; 49 : 5-7). Judah separates himself from his brothers and allies himself to a Canaanite woman, and this foreshadows the future situation of his tribe (38 : 1). Joseph, who became the saviour of his family, enjoys precedence amongst his brothers, although not the first-born (cf. 1 Chron. 5 : 1-2). Two of his sons, Ephraim and Manasses, are adopted by Jacob, just as Joseph's house was to divide into two groups, which later became two of the tribes of Israel (Gen. 48 : 5-6). And above all the respective situations of the two brothers, Jacob who is Israel and Esau who is Edom, foreshadow the mutual relations of the two peoples bearing their name (27 : 28-29, 39-40).

These different stories may schematize and simplify to some extent. But the number of these examples leaves no doubt that, [for the yahwist and also for the final author of Genesis, a legacy is transmitted from one generation to another and that this is one of the most important laws of history] When they portray the sin of the first father at the beginning and do not give him a name, calling him simply Man,[1] it is quite clear that they do not mean in this case, and in this case alone, to suspend the operation of this general law of inheritance, both physical and moral, which is verified elsewhere. And this presumption is confirmed by positive evidence in the story itself, in the reference to the descendants (3 : 15 and 20).

The religious downfall of mankind is a real fact and not merely the remoteness of a divine ideal not yet realized. And in the same way it is a collective and hereditary downfall and not the sum of strictly individual faults. The sins of ancestors have repercussions on their posterity, without the latter even needing to make these sins their own by a new free act.

It would be wrong to allow modern ideas to blind us to the conviction of the biblical author. Still, a more detailed examination does certainly allow us to remove some of the

[1]Adam is a common collective noun, meaning man: the 'sons of Adam' are men.

68

difficulties felt by the modern mind. The author of Genesis affirms the reality of a legacy, both physical and moral, passing from one generation to another, but in no way has he clearly analysed the mechanism of this transmission, nor has he made any accurate division of the total effect between the two causes which he recognizes in general : physical heredity and social tradition. The idea of physical heredity was taken for granted : it is explicitly mentioned in a passage of the priestly code, where Adam is said to have begotten a son in his own likeness according to his image (5 : 3). The Israelites obviously did not have such a clear idea of the limits of this physical heredity as modern geneticists : this is not surprising. The yahwist experiences no difficulty in repeating the story of the procedure by which Jacob obtained striped lambs from white sheep (30 : 37-42). A chance psychological experiment produced an effect in the descendants by way of physical heredity. This points to a certain mentality but no excessive importance must be attached to this passing detail. The yahwist and, following him, the final editor recognized the part played by social tradition in the total legacy, alongside the corporal heredity. *social tradition* Quite a clear case is reported in Genesis 32 : 33. For the author of this story abstention from a particular sort of meat, mentioned there, became established because it was known, at least in the first generations, what had happened to Jacob. In many stories in which the conduct of one man is seen to predetermine the lot of his descendants the paternal blessing or curse—that is, a moral element—intervenes : Noah and his sons (9 : 25-27), Isaac and his sons (27 : 28-40) and Jacob and his sons (chap. 49).

[And so the author of Genesis emphatically states the existence of a physical and moral legacy passing from one generation to another] And he has distinguished physical and moral factors in this transmission. But it would be asking much more of him than he meant to give, if in his work we sought a theory of the relationship of these two factors and the exact part played by each. And to reduce the whole thing to physical heredity would be to simplify his thought unduly.

V. Original Sin in Genesis

If Genesis is permeated by the idea of a legacy, then, it remains to examine what the Garden of Eden story includes in the common heritage of all mankind and, correspondingly, how it represents the original state from which sin caused the downfall. The remarkably moderate tone of the description should be noted here. The author gives a straightforward description of the state following the sin, making us feel its abnormal and unhappy nature, but he only suggests what went before. The clearest contrast is between unembarrassed nakedness and shamed nakedness. For the rest, the account insinuates that there is a difference, without making clear what it is. In a similar fashion the cosmogony of the six days, which obviously means to describe the world as we experience it, suggests by its silences that there was no strife among the animals and that work was not drudgery, but does not say so explicitly. One detail gives us to understand that the 'very good' creation at the beginning was followed by a further cultural development: man receives the command to multiply, to fill the earth and to subdue it (1:28). Everything was not at once in a state of finished perfection. As a parallel, in the yahwist document, artistic and technical developments (4:19-22) occur in generations already remote from the first couple, whose state recalls in certain regards the state of childhood.

So it is in keeping with the spirit of Genesis to abstain from too much precision concerning the first perfection.

The story of the Garden of Eden gives us to understand that deterioration occurred on the religious level itself, that relations between the Creator and man were spoiled in a way that could be inherited. The first effect of the disobedience is that man and woman see their nakedness and hide from Yahweh. Their reaction is understandable, but it is remarkable that this is the reaction almost invariably pointed out in the Bible as the accompaniment of divine manifestations. Even when the one involved is a favoured one, who cannot be accused of any personal faults, for whom God's visit is a sign of a merciful intention, man is seized with fear, feels his uncleanness with sorrow and prevents himself from seeing God by falling on the ground or covering his face. And looking back he is filled with distress when he realizes that he has been in contact with God without knowing it.[1]

In the story of the Garden of Eden the actions and attitudes attributed to the first couple are those of all successive generations, as is obvious from the reflection on marriage (2:24); the punishment pronounced on the guilty ones is destined to strike all their descendants. The author, whose intentions to represent and explain are so clear, must have been thinking, when he described the flight from Yahweh, of the very similar reactions of any man who comes into God's presence: he certainly intended to account for one fact by the other. Mankind is now afraid to approach God, feels itself unclean and unworthy in his presence; but that is not a normal thing, resulting from the will of God; it happens because a heritage of sin deprives us of the confidence and familiarity which were the lot

[1]Gen. 32: 31; Exod. 3: 6; 19: 21; 33: 20-23; Deut. 4:33; 5: 23; 18: 16; Judges 6: 22; 13: 22; 1 Kings 19: 13; Isaias 6: 4; Ezech. 1: 28; 3: 23.

of original innocence. [Without necessarily bearing any personal responsibility for sin, all men find themselves, by virtue of their origin, in a state of embarrassment, difficulty and restraint with regard to him who in Israel's belief, is all-merciful.[1]]

The thought here is proposed with extreme delicacy : it emerges from parallel situations set side by side, not from explicit statements; there are some things at which it is better only to hint. But if we consider the general intention of the story, it is here that we find the first traces of the doctrine which St Paul formulated with absolute clarity when he blamed Adam for the introduction, not only of death, but of sin into the world. This revelation was not new, but expressed in abstract terms the real content of the old story : 'By one man's disobedience many were made sinners . . . Yet death reigned from Adam to Moses, even over those whose sins were not like the transgression of Adam' (Rom. 5 : 19 and 14).

A theological problem is raised by the question of the serpent. Later, Wisdom (2 : 24) and the Apocalypse (12 : 9;

[1]'If Adam is himself and at the same time his race (Kierkegaard), original sin concerns him and his race as well. It concerns them according to the law of causality, insofar as Adam is the first author of the sinful state in which his race finds itself, and not therefore according to the law of analogy, according to which his fall would be repeated in every individual, so that each individual would be created innocent but would fall into sin, once confronted by a similar temptation. In fact, through Adam, the whole human race is in a state of sin (Sünde), and therefore of guilt (Schuld).' O. Procksch, *Theologie des A. T.*, p. 639. 'This event has the character of an "original sin", that is to say of a lapse in the line of development desired by God, and acts in a decisive manner, as the sequel of the story shows, on the spiritual attitude of all men. It is with good cause that the teaching of the Church on hereditary sin should have come in here . . . ' W. Eichrodt, *Theologie des A. T.*, Vol. III, p. 97. He also notes that Genesis' teaching on this point is only comprehensible on account of the biblical idea of a bond between the generations.

20:2) identified the tempter with the devil and Satan. The same idea is implied by such expressions as Luke 10:19 and Rom. 16:20. No doubt the early author had not such a clear picture as the New Testament, or even as the books of Job and Chronicles (1 Chron. 21:1), of a tempter, enemy of God and men. But the final mention of the cherubim (3:24) shows that for him superhuman beings are able to intervene in the destiny of man. The ancient Orient's frequent association of the serpent with pagan deities[1] shows that the environment in which the story came into existence was quite ready to attach more than material significance to a character introduced in animal form.[2]

VI. THE STATE OF INNOCENCE AND THE FALL

The story of the Garden of Eden, then, shows us the guilty couple losing, both for themselves and for their descendants, their former state of peace and confidence with regard to God. But the few details that describe the primitive condition are

---

[1] Cf. the research of J. Coppens, *La connaissance du bien et du mal et le péché du Paradis*, (1948).
[2] W. Eichrodt claims that this identification of Satan and the serpent is right, *Theologie des A. T.*, Vol. III, (1935), p. 96. J. Guillet, *Thèmes bibliques*, pp. 130-40, has given a good review of the development of the biblical notion of the tempter.—To interpret the presence of the serpent as an expression of the inexplicable character of sin is to give the story a speculative and abstract tendency that is not very likely: this is done by W. Zimmerli, *Die Urgeschichte*, (1943), Vol. I, pp. 203-06; G. Crespy, 'Le problème d'une anthropologie religieuse', in *Études Th. et Rel.*, (1950), 1-2, pp. 107. n. 1. This view is already present in Kant, *Die Religion innerhalb der Grenzen der blossen Vernunft*, (1793), I, iv. (at the end); Berlin ed., VI, 43, who says explicitly that he is not concerned about the real thought of the biblical author. The latter does not write on this level of philosophical reflexion, but wants to show that the ills of mankind have superhuman dimensions.

very unsubstantial : Yahweh takes man, sets him in the garden
(2 : 15), where he seems himself to be in the habit of walking
to enjoy the cool air (3 : 8), brings the animals to man so that
he can get to know them as it were under his supervision, and
finally forms woman and presents her to her husband (2 : 19-
22). This is absolute benevolence on the part of the Creator,
to which there corresponds on the part of man a freedom of
approach without trouble or fear : this we may conclude from
the flight which is the immediate reaction to the sin.

There is no evidence in the story in favour of an exception-
ally developed knowledge. The text simply says that man gave
a name to the animals, which implies the exercise of his intelligence, and that he appreciated the value of the gift which
was made him in his wife. But the development of the arts
and crafts is left to later generations and there is no reason to
suppose that then they simply regained what had actually been
possessed before the sin. On the contrary, the attempt to
obtain higher knowledge through an act of disobedience supposes that this was not yet in man's power.[1]

To sum up the moral condition of the first couple before
the sin, Genesis uses these words : 'And the man and his wife
were both naked, and were not ashamed' (2 : 25). This detail
does not mean exactly what we might think. It describes a
state of confidence and mutual esteem, rather than the absence
of inordinate sexual impulses. In fact, the biblical authors
much more often saw in the state of nakedness the loss of
human and social dignity than the possibility of a dangerous

[1] Cf. M. -J. Lagrange, 'L'innocence et le péché', in RB., VI (1897), pp.
341-79. 'It is not that there are not many commentators with strange
and exaggerated ideas about Adam's knowledge', p. 362.—Let us note
here St Thomas Aquinas's reserve: unlike the angels, at his creation
man received a resemblance to God in knowledge, not in act, but only
in potency (S.T. IIa IIae, q. 163, a. 2).

excitement. Apart from the case of Bethsabee (2 Sam. 11:2), the question only arises with characters possessing some pre-eminence or authority which is compromised by the state of nakedness: Noah, the father of Cham (Gen. 9:21), the priests ascending to the altar (Exod. 20:26; 28:42-43; Ezech. 44:18; Ecclus. 45:8), King Saul caught in a prophetic trance (1 Sam. 19:24), King David dancing in front of the Ark (2 Sam. 6:20), the ambassadors sent to the King of Ammon (2 Sam. 10:4-5). The counsels of prudence about looking at women are general and do not concern nakedness in particular (Job 31:1; Ecclus. 9:3-9; 25:20; 41:20; 42:12). Putting adulterous women in the pillories naked seems to have been the usual punishment, though not sanctioned by the law (Osee 2:5; Nah. 3:5; Jer. 13:26; Ezech. 16:37; 23:10, 29 and 45). Nakedness was often the state of prisoners-of-war (Isaias 3:17; 20:4; 47:3; Mich. 1:11; Lam. 1:8) or of drunken persons (Hab. 2:15; Lam. 4:21). And so it is shameful. The state of a child at birth (Osee 2:5; Ezech. 16:4; Job 1:21) does not bring to the mind of biblical authors the idea of innocence but of destitution and weakness. It is shameful for an adult to be reduced to this state, in which all that the mind of man has been able to devise to protect himself from external dangers is lacking. Clothing is a sign of the richness and intelligence which make man suited to command (Isaias 3:6). Again, clothing is the epitome of all the dissimulations that make social life possible, and not merely the precautions taken to avoid sexual excitement.[1]

In such a mental context, the nakedness without shame of

---

[1] G. Quell, in the article 'ἁμαρτία', in *TWNT*., Vol. I, p. 286; W. Zimmerli, *Die Urgeschichte*, Vol. I, pp. 186-87; 202-03; H. Renckens, *Israel visie of her verleden . Over Genesis I-III*, (1956); see the German trans. *Urgeschichte und Heilsgeschichte*, (1959) pp. 244-46, and the account that appeared in *Eph. Theol. Lov.*, (1957), pp. 366-68.

the Garden of Eden presupposes the clemency of outside nature and the state of confidence, in which relations between people were not disturbed by fear or contempt. The later appearance of modesty, that complex feeling whose components go beyond the domain of sex, does not signify exclusively or even principally the disorder that has arisen in the senses, from now on rebellious to the rule of morality. It marks the beginning of an era in which man, separated from God, is also separated from his fellows and divided within himself: in sexual activity, both desire and shame; with regard to other people, the need both to communicate and to dissimulate; subjection to social conventions which gainsay our freedom of action. All this results quite naturally from sin. The very discreet tone of the story shows an ambiguity and a sense of constraint invading all the relationships of human life.

The moral condition of fallen mankind is expressed also in the image of a battle with the serpent. A curse is pronounced on it, condemning it to crawl on its belly. The author wants to suggest something else besides hostility between man and the animal world. The seducer has not won complete victory over his victims. Woman is mentioned to show that she is a morally responsible person. She and her descendants are to battle against the serpent and his descendants. The conflict is collective and permanent.[1]

[1] We are concerned here with the sense the author consciously gave this oracle (*sensus literalis*), not of the sense that it assumes when seen in the fulness of Christian revelation (*sensus plenior*). On this point it will be enough to reproduce some of the conclusions of a recent historical enquiry: 'Following him (St Irenaeus has just been mentioned) the Fathers, far from seeing any opposition between the collective sense and the christological sense, frequently unite them. As a rule they see Christ insofar as they see the victory. (Here the question of the *translation* adopted plays the important role that we have just analysed). This interpretation is made, at least among the promoters and leaders, in the light of the more explicit texts of the Old and New Testaments, particu-

There is no question of an immediate and complete victory
for either of the two adversaries. The efforts of the serpent
and those of the woman's lineage are described by the same
Hebrew word *šûf*, but its meaning is uncertain since it is so
rarely used. It probably means 'to trample underfoot' and so
'to crush'. Perhaps there is also a play with the similar word
ša'af, 'to spy on, to observe'. Hostility is constant, but its
results do not appear clearly at first sight. The two adversaries
watch out for one another and are able to harm one another.
So a continual vigilance is required on man's part, for the
serpent is dangerous, particularly as he hides and can attack
before being seen. Doubtless he cannot crush the heel but he
can inflict a mortal wound.

The terms of the curse point directly to a struggle. At first
sight that is a good symbol of the condition of mankind, in
which each generation in its turn has to combat evil. Here
there is a tacit statement of the freedom which remains after

larly Psalm 90: 13; Luke 10: 19; Rom. 16: 20. It seems, then, that the
christological sense and the *victory* belong to the profound sense that is
discovered, not from the analysis of the text alone, but by reference to
the whole of God's plan as the later Scriptures reveal it to us.' R.
Laurentin, 'L'interprétation de Genèse 3: 15, dans la tradition jusqu'au
début du XIIe siècle', an article appearing in *La Nouvelle Eve, Bull. Soc.
Fr. Et. Mariales*, XII, (1954) pp. 77-156. The passage quoted is on p. 110.
A note on this point adds 'that the inspired author believes in the
victory, that his text is provisionally open in this direction, *not that this
victory is clearly formulated*, in Gen. 3: 15, nor above all that this is the
first and principle idea.' The same note continues by suggesting that we
should consider 'not only Christ', but also the triumphant crushing of the
serpent, as belonging to the scope of the *sensus plenior*, (p. 110, n. 159).
It is from this verse of *Genesis* that the *Apocalypse* (chap. 12) describes the
battle between Christ and Satan. I have dealt with the marial sense of
this last text in a note, 'La femme couronnée d'étoiles', in *Mélanges
Bibliques (Mémorial A. Robert)*, (1947) pp. 512-18. On the marial sense of
Gen. 3: 15, J. Coppens, 'Le protoévangile. Un nouvel essai d'Exégèse',
in *Eph. Theol. Lov.*, XXVI, (1950), pp. 5-37.

the Fall. Man, fallen but not entirely subjugated by the power of evil, must still struggle against it. If he keeps on his guard he may gain the advantage : but the victory will not be easy. This gives a view of the moral state of mankind balanced between pessimism and optimism. The very next chapter gives a concrete illustration of all this in the story of Cain, tempted by envy and anger. Yahweh admonishes him and describes sin to him as a wild beast lying in wait for him, which he is capable of overcoming (4 : 7).

Probably the author wanted to suggest more than this. The position of the two adversaries seems rather to favour man. And in particular it is the serpent that is cursed, the man and the woman being spared this. The parallelism in the situations indicates that the serpent will be punished by its victims. Man has caused the ground to be cursed; and he is condemned to cultivate an ungrateful earth. Woman has tempted man : and she is put in subjection to him. In the same way the serpent will see its pride humbled by those whom it has urged to revolt for the first time.[1] In this way what the story contains is a promise of salvation. And this is all logical. The thought behind these first chapters and the plan of the whole of Genesis is that the present state of mankind comes, not from the powerlessness or indifference of God, but from the fault of the creature. Consequently the divine plan, begun by creation and compromised by sin, will nevertheless be brought to a good

[1] J. Coppens, 'Le protoévangile', in *Eph. Theol. Lov.*, XXVI, pp. 5-37, reprinted in the collective work, *Problèmes et méthodes d'exégèse théologique*, (1950), pp. 45-77, see p. 54. The author refers for this parallel to A. Schulz, 'Nachlese zu Gen. 3: 15', in *Bibl. Z.*, XXIV, (1939), pp. 343-46, and A. Lefèvre, 'Bulletin d'exégèse de l'A.T.', in *RSR.*, XXXVI, (1949) pp. 455-80. There is room for completing what I wrote in *Les Sages d'Israël*, (Paris, 1946), pp. 11 and 15.

end by an all-powerful and very good God.[1] As it continues the book leaves us in no doubt about what the beginning has allowed us to presume.

The passage describing the awakening of shame and the fear of God, then the curse pronounced on the serpent characterizes the most profound and important aspects of the spiritual situation arising from sin. The sentence pronounced on woman and man expresses the punishment properly so called. The woman is in future to give birth in pain and to be subject to her husband. Man is to cultivate a reluctant soil by the sweat of his brow, and it will produce thorns and briars. The situation that existed or ought to have existed before the Fall, childbirth, the subordination of woman to man, and work, is now burdened by suffering. It is not a completely new state of life that begins, but the happy harmony of innocence has been upset.

The supreme punishment of sin is death,[2] not simply the premature death to which a human legislator can sentence a criminal for a particular crime, but death as universal experience makes us know it. The story's position at the beginning

---

[1] L. Köhler, *Theologie des A. T.*, p. 200: 'We may also and justifiably ask whether, according to the sense of Old Testament revelation, this state of punishment is to last forever . . . is Paradise to be forever closed? . . . With this question that the Bible does not contain, but that it compels us to ask, these stories become half-uttered promises.'

[2] The history of the interpretation of this point has been written by W. Goosens, 'L'immortalité corporelle dans les récits de Gen., II, 4b-III', *Eph. Theol. Lov.*, XII, (1935), pp. 722-42; reprinted in *Sup. Dic. Bib.*, under 'Immortalité corporelle', Vol. IV, col. 298-313. The conclusion is 'that Gen. 3: 19 presents death as the consequence of man's constitution and at the same time as a punishment inflicted on his disobedience' (p. 735). 'The doctrine of the gift of immortality promised to the first man is an integral part of the biblical story of the earthly paradise; it is contained there implicitly but not equivocally' (p. 742). The problem has been taken up again recently by W. Vollborn, 'Das Problem des Todes in Gen. 2 und 3', in *TLZ*, LXXVII, (1952), pp. 709-14. Man is mortal by nature, but after his sin what had been the consequence of his nature becomes the reaction of divine holiness.

79

of the whole history and its significance demand this very full sense. The threat accompanying the divine interdict does not mean instant death, which God in his mercy did not wish to inflict; still less is it a trick to win the obedience of credulous children. The words 'in the day that you eat of it you shall die' imply not the immediate fulfilment of the punishment, but the certainty that it will be fulfilled. We meet the same words again in a case where the very nature of the transgression, flight, puts the guilty party out of range of any immediate sanction (1 Kings 2 :37). Death itself, not simply a too premature death, punishes sin. By expelling the couple from the garden of Eden, Yahweh means to prevent them from having further access to the tree of life and so living for ever. Man loses a possibility which was open to him till this point.

However there are various indications that call for a closer examination of the question. The divine sentence contains a phrase in which the dissolution of the body appears as a normal thing : 'you are dust, and to dust you shall return' (3 :19). This is the consequence of the earthly origin common to man and animals.[1] Later Israelite thought was to be struck by this idea, which was frequently developed. Apart from that, life and death in the Old Testament are frequently used in the sense of temporal happiness or unhappiness, which are the sanctions for good or bad conduct. It was a matter of courtesy to wish that kings, even on the day they expressed their last wishes (1 Kings 1 :31), might 'live for ever', the Hebrew word *'olam* having a much less precise meaning than the English word *eternity*, and sometimes meaning no more than a far off

[1]This is why Genesis can, without scandal, describe the serene death of the patriarchs, old and full of years, in a good old age (25:8; 35:29). It is true that these passages belong to the priestly code and not to the yahwist.

time of uncertain duration (Neh. 2 :3; Dan. 2 :4; 3 :9; 6 :7, 22; cf. Psalm 21 :5; 61 :7-8). According to this parallelism, by keeping man away from the tree of life in order to prevent him from living eternally, God would be depriving him of a state of royal happiness and making him subject to death and unhappiness.

Taken as a whole the story of the Garden of Eden shows us how sin damaged existence prior to it : social intercourse is hampered by a sense of shame : childbirth and work become painful; the help woman renders man turns into drudgery for her. But the author seems to have wanted to avoid too precise a definition of the state lost by sin and simply to show the consequences of man's fault in our actual experience.

Concerning the state before sin, it is the reader's mind that supplies what the text does not explicitly say. But, if we must speculate, we must do so consistently and say that the thorns and briars appeared on this earth only after the sin. Otherwise, in conformity with the sober restraint of the narrator, we must be content to say that the relationship of man to certain realities of his existence has been vitiated through his fault. The story confines itself to a comprehensive picture of death as we know it : the brutal end to our life and plans, the obscurity and anguish which accompany it : and it maintains that this fact results equally from a punishment and from our earthly origin.

In short, this chapter, by both its content and place in the whole plan of the book, means to assert the hereditary loss through sin of man's state at his creation : loss of confident access to God, loss of innocence and mutual confidence between individuals, and consequently an obligation to a difficult struggle against evil, and the appearance of servitude, suffering and death.[1] In a simple form, that all can understand, the essential elements of original sin are already present in this passage.

VII. THE ACCOUNT OF SUCCESSIVE FAULTS

We should be in danger of misunderstanding the evidence of Genesis on original sin if we considered only this one text in the third chapter, telling of the disobedience of the first couple and their expulsion from the Garden of Eden. In fact this is only the first in a series of stories in which the conduct and fate of an ancestor appear as a determining factor in the destiny of the race. From the time of the first man down to Joseph's sons, the law of a biological and moral heredity continues without interruption. Therefore it would be contrary to the thought of the biblical author to think of the original fault as an isolated fact whose consequences do not follow the same general law as the other sins committed in the course of time. This faculty for involving the fate of a whole race is something it has in common with many other events described by the book as it continues. Only, there is a unique gravity in the first disorder of the series, for it causes the loss of a perfect harmony, which cannot be entirely restored, even though divine mercy intervenes to remedy the evil.[2] But it does not lead to the loss of all possibility of a religious life or human development. After

[1] 'All the descendants of the first couple will suffer the penalty of their fault and will be born in the inferior state that succeeded the first: loss of familiarity with God, concupiscence, suffering and death' (M.-J. Lagrange, *L'innocence et le péché*, p. 361.).

[2] It is of course a question of the earthly condition, the only one considered by Genesis. St Paul will show the redeemed Christian always threatened by the sinful flesh, but, at the resurrection, sharing in the total triumph of Christ over all his adversaries, including death.

it, the heads of a line will be able either to better or to worsen its common fate.

Cain, the first murderer, is condemned to a life of wandering. Then there appears in his posterity, together with the different ways of life and the musical arts, polygamy and that skill in arms which will permit the satisfaction of an inordinate desire for revenge.

> If Cain is avenged sevenfold,
> truly Lamech seventy-seven fold (Gen. 4:24).

No doubt the author wants to show how the progress of profane culture is too often bound up with moral corruption.

The rather enigmatic episode of the sons of God and the daughters of men in Gen. 6:1-4 seems to be a passing reference to a more detailed tradition found in Jewish writings which are notably more recent and outside inspiration: the book of Enoch and the book of Jubilees. Wicked angels leave their heavenly abode, marry ordinary mortal women and beget a race of giants who begin to ravage the earth and destroy mankind. At the prayer of the faithful angels the Flood puts an end to their misdeeds. The author of Genesis seems to have been anxious not to omit all reference to a tradition concerning the corrupting intrusion of the superhuman world into mankind, but he does not insist on the nature of this intrusion.[1] Fidelity to his sources and a relative independence of mind with regard to the lesser details contained in them are the habitual characteristics of the editor to whom we owe the present combination. We should be no more surprised to find in the present text traces of a rather bizarre legend than to read a description of creation in six days in which not every detail bears a divine message. In both cases the final

[1] J. Chaine, *Le Livre de Genèse*, (1948), pp. 104-06.

author simply sees an all-embracing means of expression. [Wickedness, corruption and widespread violence provoke the Flood.] God's justice annihilates a wayward humanity but spares one just man, Noah, with his family. And so, in spite of his regret at making man, God could continue to pursue the execution of the first plan that he had conceived in his wisdom : to give the earth to man to fill and subdue. The more detailed legislation proclaimed at the end of the catastrophe is to prevent the recurrence of the evil which it had been necessary to exterminate. [The obligation of avenging bloodshed is meant to deter anyone tempted by the thought of murder. And the law against eating animal blood helps to impress upon man the inviolability of human life (9 : 4-6).

The blessing given to Noah, when he came out of the Ark, is very nearly the same as the initial blessing given to man (1 : 28-30). The two passages come from one and the same source, the priestly code, which tells of the great goodness of creation but does not mention the original Fall. However, this source, too, is aware of some deterioration by comparison with the first harmony. Instead of peaceful dominion over the animals which was promised to man in the first place, after the Flood we hear of the fear and terror inspired by man. Instead of the vegetarian but exquisite and substantial diet of cereals and fruit, first intended for man, it is now expressly recognized that he has the right to eat flesh (but not blood). These two changes of emphasis are not fortuitous : they show that some disturbance had entered into the divine order of creation, in spite of God's perseverance in his intentions of blessing everything.

One other detail confirms this sign that the priestly code, too, is aware of humanity's downfall. The duration of human life decreases by degrees in the course of the great historical

84

epochs which the story distinguishes. Up to and including Noah, the age of the patriarchs is more than seven hundred years (5:1-31; 9:29). After the Flood, it gradually lessens, from six hundred to two hundred years, until Abraham's father, Thare (11:10-32). Abraham, Isaac and Jacob do not live more than two hundred years. After the Exodus, the length of life is reduced to that of our present experience. The idea of a gradual deterioration is expressed by this artificial scheme. And that agrees with the picture painted by Genesis of a succession of falls, all of which more or less seriously condition the fate of a more or less numerous lineage.

Even among the sons of Noah a fault calls down a special curse on the posterity of one of them: Cham, failing in respect for his father, is punished for it by the enslavement of his son, Canaan, to Sem and Japhet (9:22-27).

Then the text lists the different peoples who came from this threefold stock, noting the diversity of their habitats and of their languages. In this picture (10:1-32) the author seems to see nothing amiss in the differentiation that accompanies the multiplication. In fact God had repeated to Noah the initial command to multiply and fill the earth. But just as the sin of the first couple had spoiled the goodness of the original condition, so a sin, this time collective, spoils the goodness of the numerical and territorial expansion of mankind. This episode has great importance in the general plan, for it involves all men and not, as in so many other cases, one particular branch; and the divine initiative in calling Abraham refers more directly to the situation created by the sin of Babel than to that which arose out of the sin in the Garden of Eden.[1]

---

[1] On this passage see chap. 1, pp. 35-8. Here it is enough to note the position of this passage in the plan of Genesis. Cf. E. Koenig, *Theologie des A. T.*, (1922), p. 53.

Men, now numerous on the earth, conceive the idea of building themselves a town and a high tower to serve them, so it seems, as a rallying point; for they seem anxious to avoid dispersal. Thus they conflict with the divine command to fill the earth. But Yahweh forces them to abandon their plan by confusing their speech. The salient fact of the division of mankind becomes an irremediable appendage to its separation from God, effected in the Garden of Eden. The author does not ask whether dispersal, without man's transgression, would have allowed the unity of language to continue. He is content to show the part played by sin in a state of affairs where hostility and inability to understand and collaborate with people are irretrievably part and parcel of the situation.

Extreme oversimplification has condensed into one clearly localized episode what actually happened as a result of a multitude of anonymous events, the details of which could no longer be ascertained. The simplification which results from the literary genre should not cause us to overlook the human and religious reality so profoundly described and analysed in this passage. Instead of considering division and incomprehension between peoples as natural, Genesis considers them abnormal. In its view, only unity would correspond to the intention of the Creator. If things are otherwise, it is because of a rebellion justly punished, with consequences reaching even those not personally responsible for it. 'Mankind today, with its barriers and divisions, never ceases to bear the sin of Babel, just as it is still a victim of the sin of Adam.'[1]

After the description of the dispersal, Genesis tells of the call of Abraham, as if it wanted to show the remedy immediately

[1] J. Guillet, *Thèmes bibliques*, p. 104.

after the perversion.[1] The patriarch receives from Yahweh the order to leave his country and his kin, as if it were essential to leave all that was most legitimate and natural for the work of gathering together the scattered peoples, which is what the redemption of fallen mankind entails, to be carried out. Abraham is to become a new centre. In him all the families of the earth will be blessed or will bless themselves (12:3). Even if we adopt the more limited original sense 'will bless themselves', we must understand in this promise a return to unity. The friend of God, loaded with God's blessings, will be so obviously happy that one could do no better than desire a similar lot. He will begin by realizing moral unanimity in his person.

The rest of Genesis is no longer part of the theme of original sin. But, in concluding this study of Genesis, we have established that Scripture treats original sin in the perspective of the salvation that frees men from it, even before St Paul.

---

[1]This is what the book of Wisdom seems already to have realized:

> (Wisdom) also, when the nations in wicked agreement had been confounded;
> recognized the righteous man. (10:5).

Echoing this, the Fathers of the Church frequently contrasted the confusion of tongues and the miraculous gift of tongues by which the Holy Ghost began, on the day of Pentecost, to show his influence on mankind regenerated by Christ.

3

Original Sin in the Wisdom Literature

Only two of the later Wisdom books incontrovertibly refer to the sin of Eden : Ecclesiasticus and Wisdom. This almost complete silence goes hand in hand with numerous references to the history of the patriarchs, as much in the two books mentioned as in the rest of the Bible. Even the early history is mentioned several times. Noah appears twice (Isaias 54 : 9; Ezech 14 : 14); and Jeremias (33 : 20-25) speaks of God's covenant with the day and night (cf. Gen. 8 : 22). Moreover, the dispersal of men is mentioned (Deut. 32 : 8).[1]

Before passing to an examination of the formal texts, it may be useful to review various passages which may provide some light or assistance in our assessment.[2]

---

[1]The tenor and the sense of Osee 6: 7 are very doubtful. The text of Ezech. 28: 12-19 is not a direct allusion to Genesis. The visions of paradise is Isaias 11 : 5-8 and 65: 25 refer to Genesis or to traditions that are very close.

[2]A very complete list of passages with a more or less remote connection with Genesis can be found in B. Brodmann, 'Quid doceat S. Scriptura utriusque Testamenti de indole historica narrationis de paradiso et lapsu, Gen. 2-3', in *Antonianum* XII, (1937) pp. 125-64; 213-36; 327-56. In spite of his distinction between evidence which is certain, doubtful or insufficient, the author often exaggerates the probative value of the texts.

I. LIFE AND DEATH

It was a long time before Israel came to dwell in the hope of a happy immortality. But at the same time they did use the words life and death to express what we should call happiness and misery.[1] This fact deserves to be mentioned briefly, for it can influence our interpretation of Genesis and also of the book of Wisdom.

The two words have not an exclusively religious meaning, just as today we speak of the life of grace and mortal sin. They indicate the long life, full of good things, which is the life of the just and the early end or the wretched fate of the impious and wicked.

The man who carries out God's commandments has life through them.[2] Deuteronomy sets out the fundamental choice between life and goodness and death and evil (30 : 15-20). The prophet Amos promises life to those who aim at goodness or seek Yahweh (5 :4, 6 and 14). Ezechiel announces that the just man will live and the sinner die (chapter 18). These examples could be multiplied. The essential point here is to note the biblical authors' strong conviction that there is some connection between sin and death, and at the same time be aware of the very undefined content of this idea.

The book of Proverbs takes up the traditional idea that fidelity to the divine law brings life[3] and sin brings death.[4]

[1] See for example G. von Rad, 'Leben und Tod im A. T.', in Kittel, *TWNT.*, II, 844-60; J. Guillet, *Thèmes bibliques*, (1951), pp. 145-49, 161-64; A. R. Johnson, *The Vitality of the Individual in the Thought of Ancient Israel*, (1949), pp. 88-107.
[2] Lev. 18: 5; Ezech. 20: 11; Neh. 9: 29; cf. Rom. 7: 10; 10: 5; Gal. 3: 12; Luke 10: 28.
[3] Prov. 3: 2; 3: 16; 4: 10; 9: 11; 16: 31; 21: 21.
[4] Prov. 3: 22; 6: 15; 10: 25; 29: 1.

These promises or threats involve a long and happy life for the just, an early death and a useless existence for the wicked. But nowhere does the hope of a providential retribution in an afterlife appear.[1] Even the expression, the tree of life,[2] does not embrace the idea of immortality, since it is used in contexts where there cannot possibly be any allusion to a hereafter: the 'fulfilled desire' and the 'gentle tongue' are both called a tree of life (Prov. 13 : 12; 15 : 4). In the same way, the expression 'fountain of life' implies no more than an earthly happiness.[3] The reference to one element in the story of the Garden of Eden is here a simple literary image signifying happiness of limited duration.[4]

II. ECCLESIASTES AND PSALM 49

One verse in Ecclesiastes at first sight recalls the story of the fall:

God made man upright,
but they have sought our many devices (7 : 29).

Elsewhere[5] the author affirms that God made everything beautiful in its time (3 : 11) which reminds us, in spite of the different words used, of the optimistic outlook which pervades the six days account of the creation.

In spite of a general resemblance, it is really not very likely

[1] On this point see A.-M. Dubarle, *Les Sages d'Israël*, (1946), pp. 48-50.
[2] Prov. 3: 18; 11: 30; 13: 12; 15: 4.
[3] Prov. 10: 11; 13: 14; 14: 27; 16: 22; 18: 4.
[4] In Prov. 23: 31-32 the tempting wine is compared to a serpent. But there is probably no reference to Genesis here; cf. Ecclus. 21: 2; 12: 13-14
[5] Eccles. 3: 11; 7: 23-24; 8: 16-17; 9: 1; 11: 5.

that this book of experiences, which plainly and repeatedly admits the failure of wisdom, underwent any profound influence from Genesis. Ecclesiastes does not know what God does from the beginning to the end (3 : 11); that is enough to distinguish it from the book which has so clearly outlined the history of salvation.[1] If there is any influence from Genesis, it would be in the abandonment of all historical interpretation, even in the widest sense, and the transference of what is said of the origins to present-day humanity. *Surely there is not a righteous man on earth who does good and never sins* (7 : 20). Often it is the woman who is the temptress (7 : 26). This is not the fault of the Creator, for

> God made man upright,
> and they have sought out many devices (7 : 29).

If the influence of an earlier work is to be recognized here, the change from the collective singular to the plural and the nature of the reproach would rather suggest the legend preserved in the non-canonical book of Enoch (6-8), according to which the perversion of humanity goes back to the practices handed on to men by the fallen angels.[2] In the opinion of Ecclesiastes, rationalizing the sense of the story, the enterprises of human activity are the source of many ills.[3] They are not condemned out of hand but we are invited to prefer mediocrity to the excitement of business.

[1] Cf. the negative conclusions of K. Galling on the question of the supposed influence of Genesis on Ecclesiastes, in *TLZ*, LXVIII, (1933) p. 274, à propos of the commentary of H. W. Hertzberg.
[2] This comparison with Enoch is obviously very conjectural. However it is corroborated by other indications: the description of the regular course of nature (Enoch 2:1-5:3; Eccles. 1: 5-9), the expressions 'since the beginning of time' (Enoch 2: 2; Eccles. 3: 11), 'all the days of life' (Enoch 5: 9; Eccles. 2: 3; 5: 17; 8: 15; 9: 9).
[3] Eccles. 2: 1-11; 4: 4-8; 5: 9-16.

In another connection Ecclesiastes sees in death not a punishment but a necessity common to animals and man (3 : 18-21); for both there is a time to be born and a time to die (3 : 2). What has come from dust returns to dust (3 : 20; 12 : 7). The spirit lent to all living beings is not different in man and animals;[1] and on the day of death it is taken back by God (12 : 7). Merit has nothing to do with it : the wise and the foolish alike will die (2 : 15).

This is an idea which does not envisage any connection with sin, but remains religious for all that; for death shows the weakness and wretchedness of man in relation to God, and it is in a certain way a judgement of God (3 : 17-18), who puts an end to injustice by this means.

The ideas of a psalmist (Psalm 49) can be compared with those of Ecclesiastes, for the psalmist consoles himself for the inequalities of fortune, the result no doubt of injustice (v. 6), by thinking of death :

> Man cannot abide in his pomp,
> he is like the beasts that perish (v. 13).

This levelling force strikes man and animal, the wise man as well as the fool (Psalm 49 : 11; cf. Eccles. 2 : 15). Wickedness, as well as the scandalous unfairness of fate, are only temporary. The psalmist does not rise to general considerations on the divine government, as Ecclesiastes does, but he does give proof of a far more religious feeling for, in contrast with the bitter remarks of the sage, he shows his confidence in God's

---

[1]Or at least nothing is known about it. Ecclesiastes uses a phrase expressing doubt, which is closer to a denial. Naturally this equality of body and breath between animal and man does not exclude the continued existence of the soul after death in the gloom of *sheol*.

special favour towards himself.[1] It is all the more remarkable that he should have considered death under this aspect of material objectivity without any reference to divine punishment.

Although original sin does not come into it, one undeniable sign of the influence of the story of the Garden of Eden deserves to be noted here. The late book of Tobias, in which some of the typical ideas of Wisdom literature reappear, recalls the creation of Adam and Eve and quotes God's words: *'It is not good that the man should be alone.'*[2] He opens the door to the use of the first chapters of Genesis, which from now on will be more and more developed.

III. The Origin of Death in Ecclesiasticus[3]

Ben-Sirach, the author of the book called Ecclesiasticus, is the first to allude without shadow of doubt to the sin in the

---

[1]Contrary to what I said in *Les Sages d'Israël*, (1946), p. 138, R. Tournay, 'L'eschatologie individuelle dans les Psaumes', in *RB*, LVI, (1949) pp. 481-506, has shown that Psalm 49 can be understood very naturally, without the introduction of the idea of belief in eternal life, simply by the confidence of being preserved from an untimely death. In the absence of unmistakable evidence in the text, it is better to interpret it in keeping with the general evolution of biblical thought, known from other sources, rather than demand an exception.

[2]Tobias 8: 6; cf. Gen. 2: 18. The Vulgate and the Old Latin version omit this quotation.

[3]On this question see F. R. Tennant, 'The Teaching of Ecclesiasticus and Wisdom on the Introduction of Sin and Death', in *Journ. of Theol. Stud.* II, (1901) pp. 207-23, an article that was reprinted in *The Sources of the Fall and Original Sin*, (1903); I. Levi, *Le péché original dans les anciennes sources juives*, (1903); J. -B. Frey, 'L'état originel et la chute de l'homme d'après les conceptions juives au temps de Jésus-Christ', in *RSPT*, V, (1911), pp. 507-45; W. O. E. Oesterley, *Ecclesiasticus*, (1912), pp. lviii-lxiv; J. Freundorfer, *Erbsünde und Erbtod beim Apostel Paulus*, (1927), pp. 52-65; J. -Bonsirven, *Le judaisme palestinien au temps de Jésus-Christ, Sa Théologie*, (1935), Vol. II, pp. 12-18; C. Ryder Smith, *The Bible Doctrine of Sin*, (1953), pp. 87-92.

Garden of Eden. The numerous passages in which he uses the story of the creation in Genesis do not allow us to think of anything else when he writes :

> From a woman sin had its beginning,
> and because of her we all perish.[1]

Ecclesiasticus refers to the biblical tradition that affirms the connection between sin and death, and to the particular form presented by the story of the original Fall, in which it is the woman who first gives in to the temptation and who involves her husband. The allusion to the consequences resulting from this transgression concerns only a penalty for sin : there is no question of a religious downfall or any separation from God, resulting from the disobedience and affecting all the descendants of the sinful couple. Nor is it simply that he keeps silent about an idea which is tacitly admitted. Ecclesiasticus does not even connect the evil inclination, on which the Jewish rabbis were later to speculate, with the original fault, if in fact this is the inclination whose existence he recognizes when he says :

> O evil imagination, why were you formed
> to cover the land with deceit ?[2]

Even if this text does imply an inborn tendency to evil

---

[1] Ecclus. 25 :24 (Author's translation). The hebrew word translated as 'perish' is synonymous with the word used for 'to die' in Gen. 2: 17. It occurs again in Ecclus. 14: 17.

[2] Ecclus. 37: 3. In the hebrew manuscripts the words corresponding to the 'evil imagination' of the greek are a doubtful reading. The translations allow them to be supplied. This reading is admitted by R. Smend. Other commentators correct it to 'evil friend'. It is possible to conjecture that the hebrew word *yeser* lies behind the greek, in the sense of an (evil) inclination in Ecclus. 21: 11; 23: 2.

94

and is not simply speaking of the evil decision of the
origin of such a tendency is left uncertain. Elsewhere
imagination' of flesh and blood, that is of this fragile being
man, is even compared to the eclipses of the sun. Weakness
and insufficiency are normal characteristics in a creature
(17:26).

Thus, of the consequences of the first sin, Ecclesiasticus retains only death. And it is legitimate to ask to what extent this
is the expression of a profound thought, or whether he has not
merely concluded his satirical comments on the wickedness of
woman in a pointed sally.[2] It is clear, for example, that in a
passage about the punishment of sin the mention of the
'ancient giants' (16:7) does not carry the weight of a historical statement or a categorical doctrinal statement.

In this representative of the Wisdom tradition, inclined
from its beginnings to exalt individual responsibility, there are
several references to a heritage of evil for the descendants of
sinners.[3] There is, then, nothing to prevent him from finding
in Genesis a wider application of the same idea. What is more,
Ecclesiasticus, thoroughly steeped in the general idea of providential retribution, sometimes uses the word *life* to sum up
the benefits promised to the just[4] and *death* to describe the

---

[1] In Ecclus. 15: 14, the same word *yeser* is used in the sense of freedom
without the addition of the adjective 'evil'. In Ecclus. 27: 6, the word
means moral character. See above, chap. 1 pp. 16-17.

[2] Ecclus. 25: 12-26; cf. 42: 13.—I. Levi, op cit., p. 3, sees in this text 'a
satirical shaft', a 'thrust' inspired by 'misogyny'. He does not think that
the sage 'attached any particular importance to these words'. This view
is fair enough, though a little exaggerated, both in the matter of misogyny
and the description of this verse as a satirical shaft. In *Les Sages d'Israel*
I did not pay sufficient attention to the fact that Ecclus. 25: 24 is isolated
in the book and exaggerated its resemblance with later doctrines.

[3] Ecclus. 23: 24-26; 41: 5-9; 47: 20.

[4] Ecclus. 4:12 (wisdom); 34:13 (fear of God). Elsewhere friendship
(6: 16), gladness of heart (30: 22), wine (31: 27) are called 'life'.

evils which threaten sinners.[1] So he is ready to understand the condemnation to which the fault in the Garden of Eden led.

But he spoke of it only once, in his description of feminine malice. Elsewhere, in a hymn on creation (16:22 to 17:27), full of biblical reminiscences, he celebrates the greatness of man, drawing his inspiration from the first chapters of Genesis, and passes directly to the giving of the mosaic law and then to the powerlessness of the dead in *sheol*, without the least reference to any heritage of punishment and without envisaging anything but individual freedom. In the same way, in his eulogy of the ancestors of Israel (44-50), he does not begin with the sin of the first parent, as, later, the book of Wisdom (10:1) does, but with Enoch and Noah. If at the end he comes back to Adam, it is only to honour him above Sem and Seth, both the first of a privileged line, and above every living being (49:16). While Jewish writings which are a little later than Ecclesiasticus add to the Genesis story various precise details about the state preceding the Fall or the benefits lost through it,[2] Ecclesiasticus maintains an absolute silence. If this silence is taken into consideration, the solitary passing allusion to the

[1] Ecclus 23:12 (sins of speech). In equivalent terms, the way of sin leads to Hades or *sheol* (21:10); sin is a lion which takes away the soul or life (21:2). It is a serpent that must be avoided so as not to be bitten (21:2; cf. 12:13). This image is not necessarily a reference to the serpent of Genesis; there is a parallel in Prov. 23:32. However an allusion to Gen. 3:15 in Ecclus. 12:13 is admitted by L. Ginsberg, *Journ. Bib. Lit.*, LXXIV, (1955) pp. 93-95.

[2] See the texts in J.-B. Frey, J. Bonsirven, op. cit. Vol. II, pp. 13-15. Also L. Couard, *Die religiösen und sittlichen Anschauungen der alttestamentlichen Apokryphen und Pseudepigraphen*, (1907), who notes, p. 112, the difference in tone in this matter between this literature and the Old Testament books. The remark does not concern Ecclus. in fact, even if L. Couard, who numbers it among the apocryphal books, has not made this exception.

fault in the Garden of Eden (25:24) appears as a sarcastic remark suggested by the context and not as a considered doctrinal statement.

Again, the same duality of tendencies is to be seen in Ecclesiasticus as in Genesis: on the one hand, death is the penalty for sin; on the other, dissolution is the normal condition of a body taken from the earth. But the second tendency seems the object of much more careful attention in the Wisdom writer. The phrase 'to return to earth' indicates the influence of Genesis.[1] But it is noticeable that, even when he draws his inspiration most obviously and most completely from his model, Ecclesiasticus has no place for original sin as the cause of death.

> After this the Lord looked upon the earth,
> and filled it with good things;
> with all kinds of living beings he covered its surface,
> and to it they return.
> The Lord created man out of earth,
> and turned him back to it again (16:29-17:1).

To a similar thought and expression in Genesis, Ecclesiasticus adds the explicit comparison between animal and man, which comes from Ecclesiastes (3:19). What he is claiming to formulate is a general law and he feels no need to go beyond this or to vary it at all. Elsewhere he returns to the point.

> All things that are from the earth turn back to the earth,
> and what is from on high returns on high (40:11).[2]

[1] Ecclus. 17: 1; 40: 11, with 'earth'; Gen. 3: 19, with 'ground, dust'; cf. Eccles. 3: 20, with 'dust'; Eccles. 12: 7, with 'dust', 'earth'.
[2] This is according to the hebrew text.

4

What is being discussed here is still the common lot of living beings. *All flesh, both man and beast* (40 : 8) is afflicted with sorrowful feelings described at great length. Finally the body dissolves into dust and the impersonal breath of life returns to God; as for man, his soul subsists in a state of inactivity in *sheol* (cf. Ecclus. 17 : 28). The thought is expressed again in a more radical way :

Whatever comes from nothing returns to nothing;
so the ungodly go from chaos to chaos.[1]

The earth, then, is *the mother of all* to which all return (40 : 1). It is remarkable to see this idea, which we find elsewhere in the Bible (Job 1 : 21) and in the ancient East, expressed here in terms so opposed to the sense of Gen. (3 : 20): the first woman was called Eve (life) because she was the mother of all the living.

So Ecclesiasticus does not ordinarily see in the dissolution of the body anything other than the normal consequence of its earthly origin. In that case, when he says :

All living beings become old like a garment,
for the decree from of old is, 'They must surely perish!'[2]

is Ecclesiasticus thinking of the divine sentence pronounced against the first couple as a punishment for their sin? This is neither expressly excluded nor formally stated. The parallel silence of 17 : 1-2 does not suggest that the idea should be

[1]Ecclus. 41 : 10, according to the hebrew. The greek has adjusted it according to parallel passages: 'whatever is from the dust returns to dust, so the ungodly go from curse to destruction'.
[2]Ecclus. 14 : 17. The hebrew has the third person plural; the greek has followed Gen. 2 : 17 by adopting the second person singular and the word 'to die'. For the idea, see also Ecclus. 41 : 3-4.

supplied. It is probable that the writer is thinking of death without considering its penal character.

If there is a connection between death and sin, then it is in the sense that evil things have been created for sinners[1] and that it is inevitable that the just should to some extent, though to a lesser degree, be affected by them (40 : 8). So it only remains to submit to the decree of the Almighty by resigning oneself to death (41 : 4). Man is not immortal any more than he is exempt from all moral failings.

> For all things cannot be in men,
> Since a son of man is not immortal.
> What is brighter than the sun? Yet its light fails.
> So flesh and blood devise evil.
> He marshals the host of the height of heaven;
> but all men are dust and ashes.[2]

From a more general point of view, Ecclesiasticus at times simply relates good and bad to the will of God without particularly laying the blame for evil on the sin of man.

> All men are from the ground,
>   and Adam was created from the dust (33 : 10).

And with the freedom of a potter, God has sanctified some and cursed others.

> Good is the opposite of evil
>   and life the opposite of death;

[1] Ecclus. 39: 25; 40: 10.
[2] Ecclus. 17: 30-32. The first two lines are translated from the greek. The hebrew is missing. The syriac version allows the following (with R. Smend): *For with God it is not as with man, and his mind is not as the mind of man.* It is not directly a question of immortality. On this point see also Ecclus. 37: 25.

> so the sinner is the opposite of the godly
> and the light the opposite of darkness.[1]

In the same way God distributes good things and bad things, death and life, poverty and riches; sin and righteousness come from him. But the just receive his gifts.[2]

> The Lord hardened Pharaoh
> So that he did not know him, . . .
> and he divided his light and darkness. . . .[3]

Naturally in these expressions, couched in the normal biblical style, Ecclesiasticus is not overlooking human freedom, which he stresses in other passages. God is not the author of sin : it would be blasphemy to attribute responsibility for it to him.

> It was he who created man in the beginning,
> and left him in the power of his own inclination,

that is to say, of his free will. He has placed before him water and fire, life and death. And each will have what he has chosen (15 : 11-20). Here again the passage moves without a break from the initial creation to the present state of man, which seems to be no different than it was in the beginning.

We cannot reach any but vague conclusions on this question. The scribe, anxious to collect the heritage of thought from the

[1]Ecclus. 33: 7-15; the hebrew presents some slight differences from the greek. It is the only one to add the couplet on light and darkness.
[2]Ecclus. 11 : 14-17. The hebrew text only contains the antithesis: sin and righteousness. It is not certain that the word 'sin' is authentic; it is perhaps a fault of the copyist. The greek omits it. The Vulgate translates it by 'love'.
[3]Ecclus. 16: 15-16. This passage is missing in the Vulgate and the main greek manuscripts.

biblical books, has more than once in his work set different pieces of information side by side without trying to give them logical organization.[1] Misfortune comes from the deliberate sin of man, and from the all-powerful decision of God. Misfortune, created for sinners, sometimes rebounds upon the just; men receive good and bad according to their merits. Suffering is a punishment and it is a trial.[2] Death is the condition of all flesh taken by God from the earth; and it is the penalty for the sin of the first woman.

These oppositions must be stated without making them contradictions of them,[3] for that would be asking of the Israelite writer a way of thinking foreign to him. Nor must we attempt to remove the difficulty by finding some explicit way to reconcile them,[4] for that would be to attribute to the author ideas he did not express and did not have.

Ecclesiasticus is a witness to the sorrowful reflections provoked by the thought of death;[5] he echoes Job and Ecclesiastes. He also bears witness to the attention that was beginning to be paid to the account of creation. He is at the meeting point of two currents of thought: the Wisdom literature's meditation on the facts of experience and the theoretical exploitation of the Genesis text.[6] As regards death, he only glimpses for a moment, in a flash of irony, the use that could be made of the story of the Fall. But we cannot regard this passing raillery

[1] W. O. E. Oesterley, *Ecclesiasticus*, (1912), pp. lvii and lxiv.
[2] Ecclus. 2: 2; 4: 17-19; 33: 1.
[3] As is done by R. Charles, *The Apocalypse of Baruch*, (1896), p. 44, quoted by J. -B. Frey, art. cit., p. 517, n. 2.
[4] 'There is nothing incoherent in stating on the one hand the universality of death . . . and in admitting on the other hand than man would have enjoyed immortality if Eve had not failed.' J. -B. Frey, art. cit., p. 517. That may be so; but Ecclesiasticus does not seem positively to have made the supposition this envisages.
[5] Ecclus. 14: 15-19; 22: 9-10; 38: 21-23; 41: 1-2.
[6] To be compared with Tob. 8: 6.

as doctrine without creating the paradox of inexplicable silence at the moment when a statement would be expected.

Rather, we must state that ordinarily Ecclesiasticus saw in the biblical story of the origins only the lesson relating to the present condition of man and did not fall prey to the speculations or imaginings of so many of the Jewish writings on the subject of man's original state. His matter-of-factness did not exhaust all that was implicit in the poetic passages of Genesis but it did have the merit of imitating its reserve in describing what went before the Fall. It was also a merit to add nothing to the word of God.[1]

IV. THE BOOK OF WISDOM[2]

Exegetes, early and late, have claimed to find in the book of Wisdom belief in original sin or in certain of its elements, such as hereditary mortality. The present study will begin by considering the texts by themselves, before we turn to interpretation on a wider scale.

The author is acquainted with the story of the Fall in Genesis and makes fairly detailed reference to it.

Wisdom protected the first-formed father of the world,
when he alone had been created;

[1]Prov. 30: 6; cf. Deut. 4: 2; 13: 1; Apoc. 22: 18-19.
[2]On original sin in Wisdom, see the works of F. R. Tennant, J. -B. Frey, J. Freundorfer, J. Bonsirven, C. Ryder Smith quoted above p. 93. n. 3 à propos of Ecclesiasticus. To these can be added H. Bois, *Les origines de la philosophie judéo-alexandrine*, (1890), according to whom Wisdom denies original sin, p. 276ff.; P. Heinisch, *Die griechische Philosophie im Buch der Weisheit*, (1908); *Das Buch der Weisheit übersetzt und erklärt* (1912); R. Schütz, *Les idées eschatologiques du livre de la Sagesse*, (1935), chapter 1. Many articles in dictionaries and reviews depend on J. -B. Frey. There is no need, therefore, to refer to them.

she delivered him from his transgression,
and gave him the strength to rule all things (10 : 1-2).

What this reveals is the merciful attitude attributed to God
throughout the whole of the biblical story and through the
sequence of events. In spite of his fault man receives or preserves his pre-eminence among creatures.[1] No allusion is made
to the dreadful consequences for the culprits' whole posterity.
Elsewhere the sage goes back beyond the human actors:

But through the devil's envy death entered the world
and those who belong to his party put it to the test (2 : 24).[2]

Normally the first line is taken to refer to the serpent, instigator of the sin of Eden which is punished by condemnation
to death,[3] and the second line to men in league with the devil,

[1] Clearly we must not look for exact chronological order in this poetic
passage. The sage does not ask at what precise moment man received
the gift or the confirmation of his superiority. He simply states that he
possesses it and that, apart from that, God has forgiven his sin. In
Gen. (3: 16), after the disobedience of the first couple, the woman is
condemned to be subordinated to her husband. If the sage thought of
this verse, he interpreted it optimistically; instead of seeing in it an enslavement detrimental to the woman, he saw in it the renewal of the
power already conferred at the time of creation (Gen. 1 : 28). Or the sage
may be thinking of the scene where God after the Flood, the punishment
of sin, renews to Noah the promise of domination over the animals
(Gen. 9: 2). But if this is the case the sequence of events is freely treated,
since further on (Wisdom 10: 4) the Flood is mentioned again. So it is
simpler to admit that there is no chronological intention in 10: 2.
[2] Author's translation of text.
[3] Another interpretation sees in the death mentioned here the first murder, that of Abel by Cain. It has taken two forms. Either the devil tempts
Cain out of envy (H. Bois, op. cit., pp. 296-97; J. A. F. Gregg, *The
Wisdom of Solomon*, (1909)), or the 'devil', the enemy, is Cain himself
(W. H. A. Learoyd, 'The Envy of the Devil in Wisdom 2: 24', in *Expos.
Times*, LI., (1939-40), pp. 395-96). This interpretation does not correspond with the solemnity and universality of the preceding verse, which

that is sinners, who experience death : so this is not to be confused with the universal fact of bodily decease. Individual freedom is what decides the fate of each man. However it is also possible to read the meaning as : evil spirits, who are on the devil's side, tempt the world.[1] In this case the propagation of death through one man's fault is neither denied by the text nor affirmed : the text concerns quite another matter.

In practice the second line of 2 : 24 can be left for further discussion and it is enough to state clearly what the death that entered the world through the devil's envy is and how it is propagated.

In the author's view man is destined to a life without end; in the secret plans of God, there is a reward for pure souls :

> For God created man for incorruption,
> and made him in the image of his own nature,[2]
> but through the devil's envy death entered the world
>
> (2 : 23-24).

Incorruptibility, or rather the fact that this is man's destination, would be the characteristic distinguishing man from

speaks of the first intentions of God. It leads to a stress on the death of an innocent person, while the following verses (3 : 1-3) declare that the decease of the just is only an appearance. Against this interpretation, see F. R. Tennant, op. cit., p. 128, n. 2.

---

[1] This new exegesis can quote in its support a parallel with the *Manual of Discipline*, discovered near the Dead Sea in 1947. In this the angel of darkness persecutes the children of the light. 'And all the blows that strike them, all their moments of distress are the effect of the power of his hostility. And all the spirits of his kind make the children of the light stumble' (*IQS.*, III, 23-24, trans, Dupont Sommer). Cf. A. -M. Dubarle, 'Une source du Livre de la Sagesse?', in *RSPT.*, XXXVII, (1953), pp. 425-43.

[2] A reading preferred by the edition of Rahlfs has 'eternity' in place of 'nature'. The only difference between the two words in greek is an α.

other earthly creatures and the effect of his dignity as the image
of God, if it is assumed that the parallel lines of verse 23 explain one another. This incorruptibility is seen not as a gift
possessed in the beginning and lost through sin, but as an ever
open possibility or better still as a possession already entered
into but precarious, and rendered more secure by observance
of the laws (6 : 18). Wisdom offers herself to all with benevolence (6 : 16). Those who accept her discipline will obtain
ultimate incorruptibility by reigning with God (6 : 19-20).
Thus, to know God is the root of immortality (15 : 3).

It is remarkable that in the description of eternal life
in Wisdom, there is no mention of bodily resurrection. The
most we can say is that it is not positively excluded. Perhaps
there is a passing reference to it when the homicidal power of
man is contrasted with the healing power of God. The former
can cause death but cannot restore life; the Lord, on the contrary, has power over life and death; he makes men go down
to the gates of Hades and brings them back again (16 : 12-14).
In this historical section, which recalls the events of the Exodus
in order to suggest through them the eschatological events, it
may be that the author wants to hint at a healing more wonderful than that of the Hebrews in the desert : namely the
resurrection of the body. But it is remarkable that nonetheless
the words he has used in the most explicit passages are only
vague : eternal life (5 : 15) and immortality (3 : 4).

However that may be, eternal happiness is described in exclusively spiritual terms : grace and familiarity with God,
knowledge of the truth, peace, kingdom. If the author had
thought that the first sin had caused the loss of bodily immortality, the obvious thing would have been for him to show
how this disastrous effect was repaired thanks to Wisdom : his

4*

silence here cannot be understood apart from a certain indifference to the fate of the body.

In fact the decease of the just is only an appearance to deceive the senseless. In the eyes of men they may have suffered, yet they hope for immortality (3:2-4). Love of the body and of its well-being, one of the traditional themes of wisdom literature, does not appear in Wisdom; in its place comes the loud complaint about the obstacles this corruptible earthly dwelling sets for the life of the spirit (9:15). The author admits that he is mortal insofar as he is descended from the first man, born of the earth (7:1). He echoes the explanation that death is due to the material composition of the body, which was developed by Ecclesiastes and Ecclesiasticus. He does not seem to see anything shocking in this. On the contrary, an early death in his eyes is a sign of God's care for a favoured person, who is removed from a corrupting environment (4:10-15). The prophet Daniel described the final retribution at the resurrection (12:2). The author of Wisdom did not use such expressions: to judge from his statements, it seems that life is the normal human existence, that is it is in accordance with God's justice and so with God's plan, life which begins here below in the precarious conditions of trial, and blossoms in eternity after the occurrence of natural decease, which has no real importance.

On the other hand death is the lot of the unjust or rather the unjust are the lot of death (1:16), as if it were a question of a personal power, of a chief surrounding himself with his followers. As in the Hebrew biblical books (Isaias 28:15; Hab. 2:5), death and *sheol*, which here becomes Hades, are used in parallel constructions (Wisdom 1:13-16). This death of which our book speaks is not the simple corporal dissolution, common to just and sinner alike; nor is it sin insofar as this is a deliberate act separating a man from God; it is the sad, shameful and useless existence of the sinner. Indeed lies take away life[1]: death and damnation are the result of bad conduct (1 : 12). Idolatry was the beginning of infidelity to God and the corruption of life (14 : 12).

There is no reason to distinguish between the earthly phase and the eschatological phase of this punishment: the author sees them as continuous with each other. The impious lead an existence which is often wretched. In this life they have only a precarious prosperity, which does not last. And finally, their decease is accompanied by no hope (3 : 11 and 18), unlike that of the just (3 : 4). The misfortunes which they may have to suffer are an image and a foretaste of the graver punishments awaiting them in the next world, as it is said about the plague of darkness in Egypt (17 : 13 and 20). Normally the author speaks of decease or end τελευτή (2 : 1 and 5; 4 : 7; 5 : 4) to indicate the end of the corporal existence called βίος However sometimes he does speak of θάνατος or death, when it is a question of a definite providential punishment, as in the case of the extermination of the first-born in Egypt (18 : 12 and 16), the plague which struck the Hebrews in the desert (18 : 20) or the drowning in the Red Sea (19 : 5).[2] For the author of Wisdom death is not the simple fact of decease: it is not simply the earthly misfortune which it is for many prophetic or Wisdom texts; it is not simply the 'second death', that is, the eschatological punishment; it is simultaneously the earthly misfortune and the second death destined for sinners, one being the continuation of the other.

[1]Wisdom 1: 11; cf. John 8: 44.
[2]The word *thanatos* also means, in the mouths of the unjust, the shameful death that they are preparing for the just man (2: 20), and in a stereotyped phrase, (corporal) death as opposed to life (16: 13). The adjective *thnetos* means physically mortal (7: 1; 9: 14; 15: 17).

In these circumstances it cannot be maintained that the author has connected bodily decease and sin. God made all things good, as the story of creation in six days said; he is not looking for the death of the sinner but that he should be converted and live, as the prophet Ezechiel (Ezech. 18:23; 33:11) had said. The sage echoes these words.

> God did not make death,
> and he does not delight in the ruin of the living.[1]
> For he created all things that they might exist,
> and the generative forces of the world are wholesome,
> and there is no destructive poison in them;
> and the dominion of Hades is not on earth (1:13-14).

This optimism does not necessarily indicate any assumption of an original bodily immortality. God made man to last without end and no creature can prevent one who practises justice from obtaining this eternal destiny. The decease of the just, even those killed by their persecutors, is death only in appearance (3:2).

Hades has no irresistible power over men : however, the devil can tempt and incite to evil those who consent to it and in this way he can let into the world death, that is the misfortune that sooner or later follows sin, as we read in 2:24. This text, considered in the light of individual responsibility on which the book is so insistent, gives an express indication only of the fact of the first human sin with its consequences for its author, or of the general law that connects deliberate fault to misfortune in every sinner. Verse 23, concerning creation by God, expresses a general law by referring implicitly to the case of this law's first realization, the first man of whom Genesis

[1]This line is the author's translation.

speaks. Verse 24, concerning the envy of the devil, probably also brings together the general law and the first case of its application, the Fall. The baneful influence of the tempter is mentioned here, but nothing gives any positive indication that there is solidarity in death between the first parent and his posterity.[1] There is, however, nothing to exclude this, and consequently this verse has been taken as a prelude to St Paul: *Sin came into the world through one man* (Rom. 5 : 12). The almost total resemblance of these expressions leads us to suppose a similar thought behind them.

But it is well to beware of too swift an equation between the thought of two biblical authors. As Christians, we may feel that they cannot really contradict one another, but we are not obliged to hold that their conceptions were identical. One might have been unaware of an aspect which the other revealed. When reading something which he holds to be inspired, a believer must not decide *a priori* what the Holy Spirit should or should not have communicated to men through the hagiographer.

Some interpretations are *exegesis* and bring out of the text what it really does contain and what is not evident at first sight. Other interpretations are *eisegesis* and introduce into the text an idea which it does not express. Without openly contradicting the obvious sense, it adds to it; and so it runs the risk of falsifying the meaning. It may sometimes be necessary for the complete explanation of the text, when the elements of doctrine positively contained in it have no intelligible meaning unless seen in terms of an overall idea which is

[1] P. Heinisch's careful commentary has nothing to say about 2 : 24 on the hereditary consequence of the first sin: he explains the meaning of the words 'incorruptibility' and 'death' and then speaks at length on the role of the devil.

not expressed. It may, then, be necessary to fill in the gaps in order to discover the author's real thought. But it is clear that one must be absolutely certain that such completion is demanded.

In the present case it has more than once been supposed that the author must have been thinking along the same lines as St Paul or the Jewish milieu of the time and that he must, therefore, have admitted a universal influence of the first sin on the whole of mankind. With this supposition in mind, writers have gone from Wisdom to other books or from one text to another for supplementary evidence in favour of the proposed interpretation. But it has not always been noticed in the second case that each text by itself suffers from the same obscurity and therefore cannot be used to explain the others.

If one is not to fall victim to a preconceived opinion the study of the problem must be resumed by consulting the book of Wisdom itself and being careful not to add anything to what the texts obviously contain.

Admittedly no marked violence is done to any passage by attributing to the author the idea that death and even corporal death are the first sin's consequence for all mankind. But there are two facts that immediately call for a prudent approach.

In the first place the author uses extremely forceful expressions to attribute the source of all sin and evil to idolatry.

> For the idea of making idols was the beginning of fornication, and the invention of them was the corruption of life (14 : 12).
> For the worship of idols not to be named
> is the beginning and cause and end of every evil (14 : 27).

Certainly such statements are not theoretically irreconcilable with belief in original sin. Genesis recounts the Fall and the proud enterprise of the builders of Babel, one after the other. An individual fault can in the course of time be followed by a collective and anonymous fault, such as polytheistic paganism. But, psychologically, it is not very likely that a writer with a lively belief in original sin would have used such categorical language on the subject of idolatry.

St Paul was to take up this same accusation against his contemporaries and reproach them with the same errors and crimes as the author of Wisdom. But he did not represent idolatry as the origin of all evil (Rom. 1 : 18-32).

In the second place, in the passage where he makes the clearest reference to the sin in the Garden of Eden, the sage insists exclusively on the mercy shown to the first parent. There is no denial of an original hereditary downfall, but complete silence on the point, while the following verses speak of the more or less far-reaching consequences of the crimes of Cain and the inhabitants of Pentapolis. It cannot be said : 'Adam was saved . . . from his personal fault by God's favour, but the general consequences remained, as can be seen at once in the murder of Abel,'[1] for nowhere has the author spoken of the general consequences of the first sin and there are no grounds at all for attributing such a thought to him.

St Paul's conviction follows clearly from a whole paragraph (Rom. 5 : 12-19), to which 1 Cor. 15 : 21-22 must be added. There is no doubt that in his eyes the fault of one man influenced the fate of all his posterity. But the most similar verse of Wisdom, which speaks of the devil's envy, has as its object

[1]This is what M. -J. Lagrange says in *Saint Paul, Epître aux Romains*, p. 115. J. Freundorfer, op. cit., p. 65, n. 5, rightly remarks that this is to introduce into the text an idea which is entirely alien to the context. The same must be said of the statement of R. Schütz, op. cit., p. 41: 'For the sage the Fall certainly exists, with annoying consequences for mankind.'

not to confront one individual and the multitude, but to contrast the work of God which is life, and the work of the devil which is death. So it can be understood quite easily, apart from any idea of hereditary causality, either as a general law (sin, the source of death, is committed among men at the instigation of the devil) or as a statement of a particular fact, the further consequences of which are not clearly stated but which has exemplary value as the first of a series. Probably the idea of a general law and the idea of its first illustration are united in the thought.

Even granting that this passage contains a reference to the Fall, it does not follow that the sage is in any sense whatsoever stating a hereditary and universal condemnation to death. On the contrary, the second line, as it is generally understood, reserves the experience of death to sinners.[1] And since the book as a whole suggests that the word 'death' should be given a very comprehensive meaning, it is all the more unlikely that we should see here the idea that corporal decease is the consequence of the first sin.

Strictly speaking *through the devil's envy death entered the world* could be taken to mean that death, in the wide sense of misfortune and moral indignity, depends on the merits of the individual, and at the same time that death, in the sense of physical decease, depends on the fault of one ancestor. This complex idea, which denies or maintains the role of solidarity, according to the case, is not in itself absurd; strictly speaking an author whose thought was already developed could contain the whole idea in one pregnant phrase, which would present all the various realities at once that the word 'death' can call to mind. But this cannot be done by one solitary statement,

[1] This seems to suppose an idea similar to that expressed in the syriac apocalypse of Baruch: 'Everyone has been an Adam for himself' (54: 19).

which is not really made more explicit anywhere else in the book. The arguments by which J. B. Frey has tried to maintain this compromise interpretation fail to convince.[1]

It does not follow from the fact that the author draws his inspiration from Genesis that he interpreted the threat of death that it contains in the precise sense of corporal decease. The general doctrine that God has not made death (1:3-14) does not make it any clearer that this means physical death. The echo of Ezechiel which we hear in the words: *he does not delight in the death of the living*,[2] leads us to think that the sage, like the prophet, understands death and life here in a wide sense and is not concerned with the universal fact of decease. The conviction shown that men are mortal by virtue of their descent from the first man, formed from earth (7:1), might equally well prove that the first parent was mortal because of his earthly origin. There is nothing to show that the author is thinking here of a mortality brought on by sin.[3] Nor can one invoke the parallel of contemporary Jewish apocrypha,[4] for the sober style of Wisdom is far removed from the copious information given by these writings about the circumstances of the Fall; and there is nothing to prove the identity of their views in regard to corporal immortality.

One other deduction is equally invalid. The general existence of certain difficulties in the exercise of the highest faculties

[1]See J. -B. Frey, art. cit., pp. 519-20.
[2]Wisdom 1: 13b; cf. Ezech. 18: 23; 33: 11: 'I have no pleasure in the death of the wicked, but that the wicked turn from his way and live.'
[3]J. Freundorfer, op. cit., p. 63, n. 8, has rightly noted that it would be necessary to prove from other sources that the sage is thinking of a penalty of hereditary death, before seeing it in this verse.
[4]As J. Freundorfer does, op. cit., p. 61. Apart from this there is evidence that complete unanimity did not exist on this point. J. Bonsirven, op. cit., pp. 14 and 17, mentions some discordant voices, notably those of rabbis maintaining that, as Elias did not sin, he lives for ever.

of the spirit is not indubitable proof of an initial deterioration of the whole human race. No doubt

> a perishable body weighs down the soul,
> and this earthly tent burdens the thoughtful mind (9 : 15).

Hence the discovery of earthly realities is not easy. The discovery of divine secrets must be far more difficult. In order to understand the exact meaning of this statement and the lessons that follow from it, certain antecedents must be kept in mind. Deuteronomy had already proclaimed the need for an educative discipline dispensed by God himself and had described it as a fatherly correction, on occasion severe, and as a trial designed to reveal hearts (Deut. 8 : 2-5).

The tradition of the Wisdom literature, in its turn, avoided considering any suffering or difficulty as a divine punishment. On the contrary it might well be a sign of a hidden favour.

> My son do not despise the Lord's discipline
> or be weary of his reproof,
> for the Lord reproves him whom he loves,
> and he afflicts the son in whom he delights.[1]

Job, the just man without reproach, had been subjected to the worst pains to try the sincerity of his attachment to God, as once before Abraham, God's friend, had also been tried (Gen. 22). Ecclesiasticus is likewise aware of the trials that anyone who serves God must expect (Ecclus. 2 : 1-6). It is a dark hour during which Wisdom disguises herself and hides from the eyes of her disciple, as if one of the conditions of the test were not to recognize it as a test (4 : 17-18).

[1] Prov. 3: 11-12. The last line is corrected from the Septuagint.

So when the sage represents the just as the sons of God (2 : 16), subject to discipline and painful corrections (3 : 4-5; 11 : 9-10), when he states the usefulness of this discipline as a means of finding favour with God (7 : 14) and the wretchedness of anyone who makes light of it (3 : 11), he may very well be explaining the need for it by saying that these are the conditions of a trial in which God recognizes those worthy of him.[1] There is nothing in his book to suggest that he has any idea that the psychological condition of man has been universally corrupted and that the difficulties of moral and religious life are to be explained in this way.[2] Man must acquire the eternal life that God has destined for him by his own efforts, inspired and guided by divine Wisdom.

On the other hand the book of Wisdom contains no direct denial of original sin. Occasionally, the way in which the author recalls his birth is quoted in this sense :[3] he was a child of natural goodness gifted with a good soul and a body without stain (8 : 19). But that is to give the text a meaning which goes far beyond it. The author merely wishes to say that the happiest qualities, even the rarest, are incapable of making up for the divine gift of Wisdom. He takes for granted the fact of

[1]Wisdom 3: 5. In 11: 9, the two ideas of trial and of discipline come together again.
[2]In *Les Sages d'Israël*, p. 194, I admitted that an expression such as the 'perishable body' (9:15) was a discreet antithesis to the incorruptibility for which God created man (2: 23), and therefore a possible allusion to the distressing consequences of the original fault. In this interpretation something is supplied which is not based on any positive evidence: there is nothing to prove that, for the author, the body is to share in the happy immortality. R. Schütz, op. cit., pp. 40-41, thinks that the inconvenience of the body for the intelligence of 'mortals' is a consequence of mortality, itself a punishment of the original fault (2: 24). But it has not been proved that, for the sage, the sin of the first man involved a penalty for his descendants.
[3]Thus H. Bois, op. cit., pp. 276ff.

experience, that all do not possess the same natural dispositions and that he has been favoured; but that does not prevent
him from saying elsewhere that he is like all men (7 : 1), that
is to say, his royal origin does not confer any divine dignity
on him. He states, then, that he had none of those special
blemishes that are to be seen on some children. But he is no
more thinking of denying the existence of that universal stain
that is called original sin than the book of Samuel, when it
said of Absolom, the heir presumptive to the throne and in
this way comparable to the pseudo-Solomon, that he had no
blemish in him from the soles of his feet to the crown of his
head (2 Sam. 14 : 25).

These expressions indicate the exclusion of defects known
to the two writers and not of defects of which they had
no notion at all.

Thus the book of Wisdom is not aware of the doctrine of
original sin, nor even of the doctrine of death, the hereditary
penalty for the first sin. Nowhere does there appear a statement of a universal deterioration of any kind. This silence is
not a denial; it is simply the absence of a question.

However there are several passages that already insinuate
the idea of a heritage of sin passing from one generation to
another. In one there is a powerful description of the fate of
illegitimate races in particular :

But the children of adulterers will not come to maturity,
and the offspring of an unlawful union will perish.
Even if they live long they will be held of no account,
and finally their old age will be without honour.
If they die young, they will have no hope
and no consolation in the day of decision.
For the end of an unrighteous generation is grievous.

(3 : 16-19).

A little further on, when the first picture gives way to a new one, its lesson is less harsh :

> For children born of unlawful unions
> are witnesses of evil against their parents when God examines
> them (4 : 6).

It is not just a punishment that passes from ancestors to their descendants, it is a moral perversity, which will reveal itself in the family of the unjust :

> Their wives are foolish and their children evil;
> their offspring are accursed (3 : 12).

However this idea, so close to biblical thought, never becomes an absolute determination. Freedom persists in the members of a criminal race and God's justice only strikes them by degrees so as to leave them room for conversion.

> But judging them little by little thou gavest them a chance
> to repent,
> though thou wast not unaware that their origin was evil
> and their wickedness inborn,
> and that their way of thinking would never change.
> For they were an accursed race from the beginning
> (12 : 10-11).

In this difficult passage and its immediate context some rather overcharged phrases describe the action of God and reject the mistaken interpretation that some might be tempted to give of them. Some people might be surprised at the delays observed by God in the extermination of the Canaanites, thinking that there was no chance of conversion in the case of a hereditary perversion, such as they concluded from the curse pronounced by Noah on Cham and Canaan (Gen. 9 :25-27). Without pronouncing on this opinion directly, the sage, in a complicated grammatical construction, states that God does not act out of ignorance any more than he acts out of powerlessness or fear of reproach. More positively he recalls that God spared the guilty Canaanites, because they were men (12 :8); that he gave them a chance to repent (12 : 10); that he takes care of all and does not judge unjustly (12 : 13) and that his power does not take pleasure in condemning anyone who does not deserve punishment (12 : 15). Thus, in spite of the relative obscurity of a very complicated sentence, the sage is far from thinking that descent from a stock that was cursed at the very beginning takes away all hope of change. On the contrary, he states that the Canaanites had time and opportunity to turn away from their malice (12 :20), in exactly the same terms that he used earlier for sinners in general (12 :2), terms that recall those of 12 : 10.

It is then remarkable that the author of Wisdom, while admitting the existence of limited, hereditary sins in particular cases (for example the posterity of the unjust and especially of the adulterous or the race of the Canaanites), did not make this a general idea extending to the whole of mankind. He recognized the sin of the first man and yet he stressed only the favourable points in the biblical account concerning the mercy of God towards the first sinner (10 :2) or the place destined for man in the world (2 :23; 9 :2). He wanted to emphasize above all the freedom of the individual, responsible in the last resort for each man's fate. It is possible, then, to speak of a preparation for the doctrine of original sin.[1] But it must also

[1]With F. R. Tennant, op. cit., p. 130.

be recognized that this doctrine is not taught, even if it is not excluded.[1]

In conclusion, the teaching of Wisdom on the questions discussed here can be summed up in the following way. Man was destined by God for an eternal life with him, a life in which the present life will find its continuation and fulfilment. The return of the body to the earth from which it was taken is not, then, the supreme misfortune that the unjust think : for the just it is only an appearance of death and a passage to a state of happiness. This happiness is the reward for a good life : but, tempted by the devil, man can fall into sin and bring death upon himself, that is, lose in the present time and for the time to come the life that God destined for him. In the period of actual trial the body is to some extent an obstacle to the highest activities of thought. This may go back to God's original intentions for man. All suffer from this limitation, but there may be organisms more or less pure, that is, favourable to a morally pure life, and malign influences of environment or race. However God, who shows mercy to sinners not yet hardened, judges all men with a perfect justice and does not punish those who do not deserve it. The eternal fate of each person, then, depends on the use that he makes of the gifts he has received although, as things are, these gifts are not of the same value.

It is not stated in a doctrine of the resurrection (nor is it excluded) that the body has any part in the incorruptibility promised to man. It is not stated that the body was originally to have been preserved from death and that this original immortality was lost by the sin of the first man. It is not stated

[1]With J. B. Frey, op. cit., p. 520, and A. Gaudel, in an article 'Péché originel' in *DTC.*, XII, col. 290-92. This was also F. R. Tennant's view, p. 130.

(nor is it excluded) that this first sin produced a general deterioration in the whole of mankind that in some way deserved the name of death : a separation from God or a moral difficulty or a greater weakness in the face of the devil's temptations. The author pays particular attention to the essential attitude of God towards men, namely that eternal life is given or refused to men according to their chosen conduct, and to the facts of present experience, namely the inequality of individuals and the malign influence of some faults on other people. A heritage of sin can be observed in some families. It is easy to see that temptations come in this way from the social environment. The attraction of idolatry is an example of this which is specially analysed by our author, and one that St Paul takes up (Rom. 1 : 18-32). The images of false gods have been a scandal, a net, a snare (Wisdom 14 : 11 and 21); they have led all peoples astray, apart from Israel (15 : 4). They have been the occasion of the corruption of life (14 : 12).

Thus the author of Wisdom has not neglected the malign influences amid which man has to live without having created them. He has noted the place in sacred history of the sin of the first man (10 : 2). But he has not taken the step that St Paul was to take, by associating death and the sinful state of all men with this sin.[1] Rather, he puts forward doctrines which complete that of original sin : the pernicious influence of successive sins, the reality of personal freedom and the ever-present possibility of reaching the eternal happiness designed for man by the Creator.

[1] Death: 1 Cor. 15: 21-22; the state of sin: Rom. 5: 19.

V. Conclusion

Scattered over the Old Testament one finds the elements that all appear together in the story of the Fall: the religious uncleanness of man, the heritage of sin passing from one generation to another, the connection between sin and death (including all human wretchedness) and the tendency to evil. But the influence of the Genesis story was slow to appear. It is to be found with certainty only in the books of Tobias, Ecclesiasticus, and Wisdom. Even then it is remarkable that the doctrine of original sin properly so called was not seen by the inspired authors of the Old Testament. They noted the other teachings contained in the first pages of Genesis, on marriage,[1] on the image of God in man,[2] on the dominion of man over the other creatures,[3] on the connection between sin and death[4] and on the connection between earthly origin and corporal dissolution.[5] But the two Wisdom writers, both of whom traced a sort of sacred history,[6] did not stress the effects of the first sin in the religious and moral sphere.[7] They did not represent mankind as separated from God or less able to do good and inclined to evil as a result of a universal heritage of sin. On the contrary they recall the freedom of man

[1]Tobias 8: 6; Ecclus. 36: 26; Gen. 2: 18.
[2]Ecclus. 17: 3; Wisdom 2: 23; Gen. 1: 27.
[3]Ecclus. 17: 2-4; Wisdom 9: 3; 10: 2; Gen. 1: 28.
[4]Ecclus. 25: 24; Wisdom 2: 24; Gen. 2: 17; 3: 22.
[5]Ecclus. 17: 1; 40: 11; Wisdom 7: 1; Gen. 3: 19.
[6]Ecclus. 44: 1 to 50: 24; Wisdom 10: 1 to 11: 4.
[7]It is not right to say: 'Implicitly, it is the *total sense*, the complete meaning of the downfall that emerges, since the author, by referring to Genesis, also speaks in the same spirit.' A. Verriele, 'Les textes bibliques sur le péché originel', in *Rev. Apol.*, XLIV, (1937), p. 12. Even granted the desire to be faithful, and author can only incompletely assimilate the work that he has read and to which he refers his own reader.

and offer to all the choice between good and evil, between life and death.[1] In so doing they were unconsciously faithful to the lesson that was to be drawn from the divine oracle when it announced an enmity between the serpent and the posterity of the woman.

Neither Ecclesiasticus nor the author of Wisdom saw that in this struggle everyone suffers a handicap or an initial and inevitable disadvantage on the level of religion itself, and in this way inherits sin. Nor should this surprise a Christian who knows that a veil prevented the reading of the Old Testament from being fully understood and that this was only removed by Christ (2 Cor. 3 : 14-16). Many of the prophetic oracles did not really strike home until the arrival of the one who fulfilled them. In the same way the sad plight of mankind described in the story of the Garden of Eden was not realized in all its fulness until the proclamation of the Good News of salvation.

The Wisdom movement, then, shows that there were fairly long periods of uncertainty in the full maturing of the doctrine of original sin. When they hit on the idea of explaining evil as the penalty for sin, the sages felt no need to look for causes apart from those that could be seen at the time, the faults of the individual or of his immediate forbears. Similarly they looked for the manifestation of providential retribution first of all in the events of the present life, before teaching, very belatedly, the existence of future sanctions. Together with the idea of punishment, the sages admitted the idea of trial, in order to explain the wretchedness of existence : and so they had no such pressing need for the doctrine of original sin to explain the universal characteristics of the sad human condition.

[1] Ecclus. 15: 14-17, explicitly recalls the origins. Wisdom 1: 1-15, with reference to Gen. 1: 31.

The care not to go beyond the realm of experience too soon and the use of the idea of trial together with that of penalty are lessons which should not be forgotten. Although it offers only a passing and very incomplete allusion to any original deterioration,[1] the Wisdom literature has something to say and we must take note of it. It ought to forestall formulas that make things excessively simple, reducing all the ills of mankind to the first Fall. The Wisdom writers can be considered as the precursors and guarantors of the theological movement which, from the time of Augustine, was at pains to show what remained of good in human nature in spite of the ravages of sin.

[1] Ecclus. 25: 24.

4

Original Sin
in the Suggestions of the Gospel

Exegetes generally think that the Gospel does not speak of original sin.[1] However Jesus' words do contain various references to the first chapters of Genesis (Matt. 19 : 4-5; Mark 10 : 6-8; John 8 : 44). And once attention has been aroused in this way it can be seen that there are in the Master's teaching suggestions rich in substance if not in systematic elaboration, which would not be in keeping with his method.

A passage from the synoptics turns our thoughts to the story of the creation in Genesis. Jesus is asked by the Pharisees about

---

[1]F. R. Tennant, *The Origin and Propagation of Sin* [2], (1906), pp. 152-53 ; J. Weinel, *Biblische Theologie des Neuen Testaments* [4], (1928), p. 151; A. Gaudel, 'Péché originel', (1933), in *DTC*, Vol XII, col. 305; H. T. Powell, *The Fall of Man. Its Place in Modern Thought*, (1934), p. 1-15; H. J. T. Johnson, *The Bible and the early History of Mankind*, (1947), p. 63; A. Feuillet, 'Le verset 7 du Miserere', in *Science religieuse*, (1944), p. 22. 'Le plan salvifique de Dieu d'après l'épître aux Romains', in *RB*, LVII, (1950), p. 361; J. Haas, *Die Stellung Jesu zu Sünde und Sünder nach den vier Evangelien*, (1953), pp. 91-96. Some authors express the same view but with slight modifications: A Verriele, 'Les textes bibliques sur le péché originel', in *Rev. Apol.* LXII, (1936), p. 672; J. Bonsirven, *Les enseignements de Jésu-Christ*, (Paris 1946), p. 100; A. Gelin, in *L'Ami du clergé*, LXIII, (1953), p. 372; E. C. Rust, *Nature and Man in Biblical Thought*, (1953), p. 167. On the other hand A. G. Hebert recognizes very positive indications in Mark 10: 5-9 and 7: 14-15: see *The Throne of David*, (London 1941), chap. 7.

the lawful reasons for divorce and raises the question above the juridical level, on which the rival schools of Hillel and Shammai confronted one another. He is not concerned to favour a wide or narrow interpretation of the law on divorce (Deut. 24:1) but to take account of the whole of God's will as revealed by the parts of Scripture which are not legislative. It is the Creator who made man male and female, as the story of creation in six days stated (Gen. 1:27); and it was his intention not only to ensure the propagation of the human species by the union of the sexes as in the case of animals, but to establish between man and woman a stable society, which would take precedence over all other bonds. The account of the formation of the first woman ended by showing her as the fitting helpmate, who was able to remedy man's loneliness and whom man received from God's hands with enthusiasm. For Genesis it was not a question of an impossible ideal but of a fact that was repeated to some extent in each new union: 'Therefore a man leaves his father and his mother and cleaves to his wife, and they become one flesh' (Gen. 2:24).

Jesus quotes this last line and he sees in it an expression of the divine will to unite the spouses, a will that begins to be realized every time a marriage is contracted. It is not for man to frustrate the Creator's intentions, by separating what has been united by him.

The procedure of divorce foreseen by the Law is a concession to men's hardness of heart. But it was not so in the beginning (Matt. 19:8). The contrast indicated between the original state and the tolerance shown by Moses must be understood in the light of the unreserved approbation which Jesus gave to the law of Moses. No part of this law must pass away until the end of the world (Matt. 5:18; Luke 16:17). It is to the law that Jesus refers when he wants to define the commandments of God (Matt. 19 : 18-19; 22 : 37-39). Moses and Elias, the law and the prophets, appear at the transfiguration of Jesus (Matt. 17 : 3). And Moses is the ever-living authority imposed on the Israelites (Matt. 8 : 4; 23 : 2; Luke 16 : 29; John 5 : 45; 7 : 19-22).

When he attributes the law on divorce to a tolerance of men's hardness of heart, Jesus has, therefore, no intention of condemning Moses for a weak connivance towards an evil which he ought to have fought energetically. He does not present 'the work of Moses ... as a temporal, human intermediary between two manifestations of the divine will, at the beginning ... and now'.[1] He makes no claim to decide, by a prophetic charisma, where the true revelation of God lies between two opposed messages contained in Scripture, both claiming to be revelation.[2] He does not resort to a juridical principle, according to which a prior law would take precedence over a later law :[3] such a legalistic statement is not in keeping with Jesus' very liberal attitude towards the smaller points of the law's letter. For him, the decalogue and the double commandment of charity are the essentials of the Law (Matt. 22 : 40); although these were promulgated by Moses, they take precedence over the Sabbath, which goes back to creation, over the vengeance of murder and the abstention

[1] I join issue here with the opinion expressed by L. Cerfaux, 'Simples réflexions à propos de l'exégèse apostolique', in *Eph. Th Lov.* XXV, (1949), p. 569.
[2] Here I join issue with J. Hempel, 'Der synoptische Jesus und das A. T.', in *ZAW*, LVI (1938), pp. 10-11.
[3] A principle supposed on very weak evidence by H. J. Schoeps, 'Restitutio principii als kritisches Prinzip der nova lex Jesu', in *Aus frühchristlicher Zeit*, (1950), pp. 271-82; the same position in 'Jésus et la loi juive', pp. 13-14, in *Rev. Hist. Ph. Rel.*, XXXIII, (1953), pp. 1-20; a less clear formula in *Gottheit und Menschheit*, (1950), p. 65.

rom blood, which go back to the flood, and over circumci-
ion, which goes back to the patriarchs.

The words 'but from the beginning it was not so' directly
:ontrast not a law in the strict sense of the term, but a primi-
ive state of things in conformity with the divine ideal of
narriage, and a later law, which made concessions to men's
aardness of heart. The blame, if there is any blame, falls not
on the fact of the concession itself but on the dispositions of
nen that made it necessary.[1] Genesis showed God himself, after
he Flood, modifying the laws of eating, promulgated at the
ime of creation, as if taking account of the new situation
:reated by men's violence.[2] Jesus himself is the master full of
kindness, who does not break the bruised reed nor extinguish
he smouldering wick (Matt. 12 :20).

Indirectly, then, Jesus suggests that the hardness of heart,
on which Moses quite rightly avoided imposing too heavy a
ourden, did not exist in the beginning. It is not a normal
attribute of man as he left God's hands : it is the result of
sin, a result so irremediable and general that the Law took
note of it.

The reply to the Pharisees, then, contains a fleeting refer-
:nce to a lost state of original innocence. At the same time
Jesus implicitly promises its restoration. From now on a man
will no longer be allowed to send his wife away; in fact to
lo so will make him guilty of adultery. If an act tolerated by
:he law and an act strictly forbidden by it are now put on the
same footing, it is because the situation has changed, as it had

---

[1] Here I am following E. E. Tilden, 'The Study of Jesus' Interpretative
Methods', in *Interpretation*, VII, (1953), pp. 45-61: 'From the intent of
God he (Jesus) then explains the sinful character of divorce. . . . What
Moses' legislation does is to express the will of God *within* a sinful situ-
ation, which conditions man's life' (pp. 54-55).
[2] Gen. 9: 1-4; cf. 1: 28:30.

changed—although in the other direction—between creation and the Law. It is understood that the gift of a new heart docile to God's will, will be made to man.[1]

The prophets had described the messianic era as the restoration of the peace of paradise.[2] Jesus insists on the accomplishment of God's will in the era that he is inaugurating. Tolerance towards what is imperfect does not completely disappear:[3] but when talking to his disciples Jesus proposes and imposes the divine ideal of the beginning.[4] This passage, then, suggests the idea of salvation as the re-establishment of an original innocence. It is a prelude to Paul's doctrine of the two Adams, for which it might be the source.

The Greek word *sklerokardia*, used by the evangelists, was already to be found in the Septuagint version, where it translated 'stubborn heart' (Ezech. 3 : 7) and was a euphemistic substitute for 'the foreskin of the heart' (Deut. 10 : 16; Jer 4 : 4). Ezechiel spoke also of a hard heart (2 : 4) and a heart of stone, destined to be replaced by a heart of flesh, given by God (11 : 19; 36 : 26). And our thoughts are turned to this same prophet by the hidden reference in a text of St John 'unless one is born of water and the Spirit, he cannot enter the kingdom of God. That which is born of the flesh is flesh and that which is born of the Spirit is spirit' (John 3 : 5-6).

This pregnant text leads to a distinction of two elements: a carnal state, passed on by natural birth, and the absence of a higher life, caused by God's Spirit. In this condition man is affected by an uncleanness, since he must come out of it

[1] H. J. Schoeps, 'Jesus und das jüdische Gesetz', in *Aus frückristlicher Zeit* (1950), pp. 212-20.; see pp. 213-14'
[2] Isaias 11: 5-9; 65: 25; cf. Gen. 1: 29-30; 2: 19-20.—Isaias 55: 13; cf Gen. 3: 18. In a more general fashion, Osee 2: 20; Ezech. 34: 25-29.
[3] For example in the episode of the temple tax (Matt. 17: 26).
[4] As St Mark (10: 10) shows more clearly than St Matthew.

by a rite of ablution.[1] It is not merely a question of receiving a gift better than the purely human life hitherto possessed : for this effect gestures such as the imposition of hands or anointing with oil, which are mentioned in the Gospel, would be more appropriate. The contrast established here between the flesh and the spirit has, as in Matt. 26 :41, a pejorative nuance, on which St Paul was to insist.[2] However this carnal state is not expressly called a state of uncleanness : it is the total situation, including also the deprivation of the life of the spirit, which is seen as uncleanness. A new birth, a regeneration which is going to add to the effects of carnal birth the possession of a higher life, will at the same time effect a purification.

All this is very delicately suggested. But a striking analogy with a passage from Ezechiel brings a very satisfying confirmation :

[1]There is no serious argument from palaeography to suppress the mention of water in the text. The Fourth Gospel is obviously interested in the sacraments, as O. Cullmann has shown, *Les Sacrements dans l'Évangile johannique*, (Zurich 1951). On John 3:5, see p. 46, n. 4. Marcus Barth *Die Taufe, ein Sakrament ?*, (1951), pp. 434-53, studies this passage at some length and gives a very full account of the history of its exegesis. His conclusions: the non-sacramental character of the baptism with water, as Jesus wanted it, and the quasi-identity between water and spirit in v. 5, have only an indirect bearing on original sin and cannot be discussed at any length here. These conclusions are based rather unsoundly on the use in the Fourth Gospel of couplets such as to see—to believe, etc., in which the two terms, in spite of their necessary connection in view of a salutary effect, are by no means the same, whatever M. Barth may say. However, even supposing his thesis to be true, the fact would remain that in John 3: 5 what Jesus (or the evangelist) is identifying with the Spirit is not an anointing (as in 1 John 2: 20, 27) but the water, that is to say a purifying element, as the parallel with Ezech. 36: 25-27 (quoted by Barth p. 448) makes clear. Strictly speaking that would be enough for the conclusion we are defending here, namely that there is a connection between the new birth and purification from an uncleanness.
[2]In John 6: 63, the opposition seems to involve no more than the contrast between what is human and limited and what is divine and exceptional, as in so many passages of the Old Testament.

'I will sprinkle clean water upon you, and you shall be clean from all your uncleanness, and from all your idols I will cleanse you. A new heart I will give you, and a new spirit I will put within you : and I will take out of your flesh the heart of stone and give you a heart of flesh. And I will put my spirit within you' (36 : 25-27).

Beneath the difference in vocabulary we can see a remarkable likeness between the two texts. Corresponding to the two parallel phrases, heart of stone and heart of flesh, we have the parallel, flesh and spirit. On both sides there is an inward renewal produced by a rite of purification and the communication of the divine Spirit.[1] Jesus makes no reference to personal sins committed by the baptized, but the objective analogy with the prophecy seems intentional : this is suggested by the words : 'Are you a teacher in Israel, and yet you do not understand this?' Consequently it is not arbitrary to see in this passage the assertion that carnal man, born of the flesh and still deprived of the Spirit, is tainted by an uncleanness. Anyone who has known only the birth of the flesh is in a state of uncleanness, which remains as long as the regeneration of the spirit is not completed.[2] The Gospel is here richer than St

[1] We may note here a text that came from a milieu fairly close to that of John, the Qumran community, near the Dead Sea. In the *Manual of Discipline (Rule of the Community)* it is a question of lustrations that are quite real, but ineffective of themselves without the intervention of the Spirit: 'in an upright and humble spirit his sin will be atoned . . . that he may be sprinkled with water for impurity' (*IQS.*, III, 4-9: trans. M. Burrows, *The Dead Sea Scrolls*, Vol. II, (1951)).

[2] This exegesis is no longer the one most current among catholic authors, especially modern ones. The majority do not even mention it; some explicitly reject it. This passage would express nothing more than the superiority of a life according to the spirit over a purely human life. However, unanimity is far from complete. In antiquity, St John Chrysostom (whose object, no doubt, was not exegetical precision but the most complete instruction of his listeners) makes a clear allusion to an

Paul: the role of natural propagation in the transmission of original sin begins to make itself seen in the words: 'that which is born of the flesh is flesh'.[1]

However St John's Gospel does not explicitly trace the

---

original downfall. It is impossible, he says, that one who has not been begotten of water and the spirit should enter into the kingdom of God, because he is wearing the garment of death, of the curse and of corruption (*Hom. 25 on St John, PG.*, 59, 148). On v. 6 he has a fairly long discussion of the original benefits that we lost by our sin in paradise and the greater benefits that are conferred on us by regeneration (Hom. 26, col. 153). St Augustine did not use this text in support of original sin in the *Tractatus in Joannem*, but in *De peccatorum remissione*, in the course of the pelagian controversy (I, xxx, 58; II, ix, 11; *PL.*, 44, 143 and 158). In support of an explanation of this text of John by the idea of an uncleanness, the commentaries of St Albert the Great, Jansen, Cornelius a Lapide, Calmet, Schanz (1885), among the catholics, can be quoted, and, among protestants, those of Meyer (1869), F. Godet (1885), J. Weiss (1902), A. Plummer (1913) and W. Bauer (1913). Jansen (whose *Tetrateuchus* is not on the index) expressed the meaning of this text very accurately, when he said that original sin *'indirecte significatur'*. Titus 3: 5 can be compared with John's text.

---

[1]However, care must be taken not to give this suggestion too precise a value. Today we distinguish physiological generation and the influence (even the very early influence) of the social environment, and we know that the second is absolutely indispensable to awaken a psychological human life. Biblical thought takes these things in a summary fashion. In Israel, the family regularly formed the first social unit and wider groups could quite naturally be called the extension of the little family community, so there was less scope than we have to distinguish, in the human patrimony received by the child before he could exercise his free activity at all, the part played by strictly physiological origin and that played by society. And so Genesis often spoke of a people as the race of one ancestor. The prophets, modifying this picture slightly, often personified a town or a nation as a mother with many children: Isaias 47: 8-9; 49: 17-22; 50: 1; 51: 18-20; 54: 1, 13; 60: 4, 9; 66: 8-13; Jer. 5: 7, 17; 50: 12; Ezech. 16: 20, 36, 45; 19: 1-5; 23: 4, 10; Osee 2: 4-25; Micheas 1: 16; Zach. 9: 13; Lam. 1: 16-20; Baruch 4: 5 to 5: 9. St Paul took up this picture in Gal. 4: 24-31. He contrasts Ismael and Isaac as begotten according to the flesh and according to the spirit and makes them a symbol of two alliances, or two peoples. Such is the mental context of these words of Christ in St John.

origin of this congenital stain to the fault of the first man, just as the origin of men's hardness of heart was left in an impersonal vagueness by the synoptics. And this is all the more remarkable since some words spoken on another occasion name another father of sin. It is wrong for the Jews to call themselves sons of Abraham : 'You do what your father did,' Jesus said to them, and this guilty ancestor, whose perversity they imitate, is not Adam as might have been thought. 'You are of your father, the devil, and your will is to do your father's desires. He was a murderer from the beginning ... for he is a liar and the father of lies' (John 8:41-44). The simultaneous reference to murder and lying leaves no doubt that this is a reference to the serpent tempter in the Garden of Eden, who had deceived the woman and brought down the sentence of death on mankind.

These words about the devil, the father of the Jews, were probably provoked by personal faults. But it is remarkable that this clear reference to the Genesis story does not draw attention to the first parents themselves and simply serves to reveal the perfidious character of the tempter.

So the evil goes beyond the limits of mankind. It is not without interest to note that in the synoptics too the baneful influence of the devil is brought to light. The historical parable of the weeds, describing the destiny of the kingdom of God from the sowing season to the harvest, shows us the enemy (the Satan of the Old Testament) sowing weeds among the good seed. From then on the two plants are mixed and cannot be separated before the last end; only the angels will be capable of making this separation (Matt. 13:24-30, 36-43). And there is a remarkable parallel with John 8:44, in that the weeds are the sons of the evil one (Matt. 13:38; cf. Acts 13:10; 1 John 3:10).

This reference to the devil, a murderer from the beginning (John 8:44), recalls the phrase in the book of Wisdom: 'through the devil's envy death entered the world' (2:24). This raises the question of the relationship between bodily death and original sin according to the Gospel.

In this passage it is not simply a question of the spiritual death which separates the soul from God. The idea of bodily death is not entirely absent, for it is the intention which his enemies have of killing him that leads Jesus to speak of the devil the murderer. But it would be too hasty to draw the conclusion: the devil provoked corporal death through sin; therefore man, if he had remained innocent, would not have been subject to corporal death, according to presupposition of the text.

If we take a broad view of the Gospel lesson on life and death, we shall see that in the problem envisaged here, the wide scope of the idea of life does not allow any clear conclusion on the well-defined fact of corporal dissolution, considered independently of the human significance which it assumes in a climate of sin.

In the controversy with the Jews, when he reproaches them for imitating the murderous intentions of their father the devil, Jesus continues: 'If anyone keeps my word, he will never see death' (John 8:51). Obviously the Saviour is not promising here that his faithful will escape corporal dissolution, but that they will possess and no longer be able to lose a life which is not necessarily connected with the material organism. Parallel passages leave no doubt on this subject. Through faith, through the flesh of the Son of Man, we possess eternal life and the assurance of resurrection (John 6:39-40, 54), which supposes the dissolution of the body first of all. And, similarly, through the flesh of the Son of Man, we possess eternal life and the assurance of not dying (John 3:16; 6:49-50, 58; 10:28; 11:26). Comparison of these various statements shows clearly that corporal decease is merely an incident of no importance compared with the true life that Jesus gives to his own.[1]

There is a total human life, of which bodily life is only the less precious part and of which the highest manifestations, spiritual and religious activities, are only achieved through faith in Jesus. Anyone who attacks this life, even in its least noble parts, anyone who wants to kill a man, is imitating the devil, the murderer. But the term *life* in the Gospel is too rich for the word murder to be simply the equivalent of the word assassination. The devil was a murderer from the beginning. He struck a blow at the integrity of the life possessed by man. Was it materially, by being the origin of bodily dissolution, from which innocent man would have been preserved? Was it, in a wider sense, by giving, through sin, the character of death to the dissolution by decease, normal in itself? Was it by causing the loss, partly or wholly, of the spiritual and religious life? The Gospel does not allow an affirmative answer to the first hypothesis and indeed scarcely suggests that we confine ourselves to it. The small importance attached to the simple fact of decease does not agree with the gravity which seems to be attached to the murderous action of the devil. But nor does the Gospel give a clear and exact picture of the damage caused by the seducer.

Briefly, then, the Gospel offers the essential outlines of the

---

[1] This idea of the Fourth Gospel can be compared with the passage in the synoptics according to which the dead patriarchs are not dead but living in anticipation of the resurrection (particularly Luke 20: 38: 'for all live to him', that is to God). The simple fact of decease is not really to be feared: 'do not fear those who kill the body, and after that have no more that they can do' (Luke 12: 4; cf. Matt. 11: 28).

doctrine of original sin between the lines rather than on the surface of the text. Through the action of the devil a primitive state of innocence has been lost. Now, by receiving life from a race that has become carnal, man contracts a certain uncleanness, he is affected by the hardness of heart, he is subject to death in a vague sense. St Paul was simply to express the same teaching in clearer language and add the explicit reference to Adam which is missing in the Gospel.

True, it might be asked if these conclusions are not weakened by various sayings of Jesus which we must now examine, for it is quite clear that an inference drawn from the text would have little weight in the face of a direct statement to the contrary.

First of all there comes to mind the occasion when the little children are put forward as an example to the disciples.[1] The relationship between these passages in the synoptics and John 3:3-5 has very often been pointed out:

'Unless you turn and become like children, you will never enter the kingdom of heaven. Whoever humbles himself like this child, he is the greatest in the kingdom of heaven' Matt. 18:3-4).

'Let the children come to me, do not hinder them; for to such belongs the kingdom of God. Truly, I say to you, whoever does not receive the kingdom of God like a child shall not enter it' (Mark 10:14-15; Luke 18:16-17).

[1]This is not the place to enter into the question, so much discussed today, of the baptism of children according to the New Testament, in spite of its possible connection with the question of original sin. It will be enough, then, to see whether the Gospel asserts the total innocence of little children, as H. Windisch, in order to reject the practice of infant baptism, wrongly claims: 'Zum Problem der Kindertaufe im Urchristentum', in *ZNW.*, XXVIII, (1929), pp. 118-42.

In fact these words do not necessarily imply a passive or negative innocence, consisting in the absence of voluntary sin or of congenital uncleanness. They give, as an example to be followed actively by adults, an attitude which is spontaneous in young children, the trusting openness to all that their surroundings have to offer them. The child readily believes what it hears and imitates what it sees done. By this very fact it is also more open than others to corrupting influences, and that is what makes scandal given to little ones so grave.[1] Jesus asks for faith in the Good News and condemns the proud assertion of self. By their eagerness to receive what comes from outside, by this instinctive feeling of their own smallness, children can show adults the way in which the kingdom of God must be received, with docility and humility. The resemblance between Matt. 18:4, appealing to the example of children, and Matt. 23:12; Luke 14:11; 18:14, all passages which call for self-abasement, shows that it is not only the negative innocence which Jesus is considering in children but rather a certain psychological attitude.[2] He has not, then, excluded a state of uncleanness contracted by carnal birth.

---

[1]Matt. 18: 6. For his part, Paul was also to note the ease that children experience in believing and that can make them the easy victims of the most varied influences, Eph. 4: 14. This is the distressing consequence of a disposition of which Jesus stresses the favourable side.

[2]This impression, which comes from the texts, has not escaped H. Windisch. In the same article where he insists on the innocence of children, he writes: 'The words of the Lord only want to assure children of access to the kingdom of God, because of their natural innocence, their natural openness and their capacity for putting themselves totally in the hands of another, on the one hand, and to tell adults on the other hand that they will only gain entrance if they regain this childlike state of mind', p. 119. Similar ideas will be found in A. Oepke, in the article ' παῖς ' in *TWNT*., Vol. V, pp. 647-48: 'Jesus never speaks of the innocence of the child, even in a relative sense, still less in an absolute sense, but rather of the modesty, etc.'.

Another difficulty might arise from the decisive importance, one could almost say the unique role, attributed by the Gospel to the action of the heart in the matter of sin. Anger is as serious as actual murder (Matt. 5:22). A lustful look at a woman is adultery committed in the heart (Matt. 5:28). The intimate and necessary connection of sin with the free and personal will, independently of the material actions, emerges clearly from phrases such as these. And that is what creates in the mind of the believer a certain reluctance to recognize, apart from this, a sin received by contagion or inheritance, and therefore prior to any decision of the person concerned. The mind feels inclined to reject such an eventuality out of hand by generalizing the principle enunciated by Jesus about food : 'Not what goes into the mouth defiles a man, but what comes out of the mouth, this defiles a man ... but what comes out of the mouth proceeds from the heart' (Matt. 15:11-18; cf. Mark 7:14-23).

In fact such a statement should be understood according to the style of the Gospel, which is so fond of strongly contrasting phrases,[1] not as an absolute affirmation and negation but as a forceful insistence on the real hierarchy of values, in the manner of the prophets. Inevitably ritual purity was frequently compromised by profane contacts. The tradition of the Pharisees

[1]In the Gospel, as in the Old Testament, formulas that are most decidedly negative in appearance should often, above all when followed by a correlative affirmative formula, be understood as a statement of a hierarchy of values, rather than antithetical negation and affirmation. 'This illness is not unto death; it is for the glory of God', said Jesus of Lazarus, who was soon to die (John 11: 4). There are many examples of this sort: Matt. 7: 21; 10: 20; 10: 28; Mark 9: 37; Luke 14: 12; John 6: 32; etc. To judge the exact meaning of the turn of phrase in each case, the immediate and remote context must be taken into account. Cf. A. Guillaume, *Prophecy and Divination*, pp. 369ff. Blass-Debrunner, *Grammatides nt. Griechisch* [6], 448, 1, (trans. *A Greek Grammar of the N. T. and other Early Christian Literature*, 1961). The absence of the comparative in semitic grammar led to marked oppositions.

tended to raise the anxiety to regain this purity before meals to the level of an obligation, when the Scriptures imposed nothing of the sort. In the presence of this exaggeration, Jesus tries to raise the minds of his listeners above the idea of outward cleanness, left optional by the Law and sometimes even involuntarily lost, to the idea of an inward cleanness of infinitely greater importance in God's eyes, which can only be lost by the free action of the heart. He does not even explicitly condemn the tradition of the Pharisees in itself but only the precedence that it takes over the observance of the commandments (Matt. 15 : 1-9; Mark 7 : 1-13).

Still less does he make any pronouncement on the categorical prohibitions of the Law concerning various kinds of food.[1] He who showed himself so careful to respect the rules of purification for lepers,[2] does not, by his words on what does and does not make a man unclean, reduce all the levitical legislation on uncleanness to a superstition lacking all value in truth or life. He simply points out its secondary importance.

Therefore Jesus, who was so profoundly convinced of the lasting value of the whole of Scripture, does not strictly speaking reject the reality of religious uncleanness not proceeding from

[1]This interpretation is very close to that of H. J. Schoeps, 'Jésus et la loi juive', in *Rev. Hist. Phil. Rel.*, XXXIII, (1953) pp. 1-20: 'By substituting a moral purity for a ritual purity, these words of Jesus . . . almost suggest the idea that the whole of the levitical legislation has thus become out of date. However it is a conclusion that Jesus himself has not yet drawn . . . He only wants to give the ethical laws of the Torah precedence over those that concern ritual about food' (p. 12).

[2]Lev. 13: Matt. 8: 4; Mark 1 : 44; Luke 5: 14; 17: 14. This respect for the law appears even more if the reading 'he grew angry' for Mark 1: 41 instead of 'he was moved with pity' is adopted, as is suggested by C. Masson, 'La péricope du lépreux', in *Rev. Th. Phil.*, (1938), pp. 286-95, and L. Vaganay, 'Marc 1: 41. Essai de critique textuelle', in *Mélanges Podechard*, (1945), pp. 237-52.

the heart.[1] All the various situations, lying between ritual uncleanness and deliberate sin, (of which the Old Testament had
such a strong feeling, never, however, clearly thought out) are
to be considered not as illusory but as relative.

The words about food not making a man unclean ought, then,
to help us define the idea of original sin which we may legiti-
mately infer from the Gospel. In short, it is personal sin that
causes the most serious uncleanness. A sin received as an inheritance can only leave a stain of lesser responsibility and one
of a different nature.

Once clear references to the stories of creation and the Fall
in the Gospel have been noted, we find our attention drawn to
passages in which at first sight this idea does not appear.

The parable of the weeds among the wheat gives us in brief
the whole history of the kingdom of God from the beginning to
its consummation.[2] The father of the family sowed good grain in
his field. The appearance of the weeds, then, raises a problem
for the servants who know what was sown. In the same way, evil
is a problem for those who believe that creation is very good
and that evil cannot come from God. The reply of the master is
that the enemy alone is responsible for the weeds. In the same
way, the serpent is the instigator of the disobedience in the story
of the Garden of Eden. But where does the enemy or the serpent

---

[1]Attention to the style of the Gospel and the consideration of the inci-
dental character of many of the sayings permit us to interpret this statement about food without seeing in it a radical opposition with the general principle of the permanence of the Law (Matt. 5: 17-19; Luke 16: 17).
It is useless to deny its historicity, as W. Brandt or C. Montefiore do, or
even to hesitate on this point, as H. J. Schoeps does; cf. art. cit., pp. 12-13.
There was, however, in these words a suggestion about the relative
character of the legislation regarding food, which helped to justify its
abandonment in the eyes of apostolic Christianity, given the new circumstances (cf. Rom. 14: 14-20; Titus 1: 15; Heb. 9: 10).
[2]Matt. 13: 24-30, 36-43.

come from? The texts do not even ask this question; they simply indicate the intervention of a superhuman evil principle in the destiny of mankind.

Once they have taken root in the field, the weeds cannot be pulled out until the end of the world. Here again the lesson of Genesis appears, in a new guise. The fault committed by the first couple has its repercussions in every generation, just as the destiny of each ancestor continues in that of the particular race which takes its origin from him. The Gospel parable underlines the fact that they can no longer be separated. This is also the lesson to be drawn from the sentences pronounced by Yahweh on the guilty. The blessing of fecundity is not withdrawn, but childbirth is henceforth to be painful. The union of the two sexes is not suppressed, but the wife is to be subject to the husband. The earth will continue to give food, but it will be at the price of hard labour. So at the heart of everyone's life good and bad are inextricably mixed.

This reading of the parable in parallel with the story of the Fall certainly goes beyond the immediate sense of the text, which is the simultaneous presence in the world of good individuals and sinners and not of good and bad in each person. But the two things are connected. And a broad interpretation is not illegitimate, for the parables are designed to make us think. We have here an answer to the problem of evil which should not be neglected, since the doctrine of original sin is itself an answer to this problem and since, besides, Christ appealed to the teaching of Genesis.

What is more, the parable of the weeds unites the two ideas of a perversion of the initial work and of a development.[1] And

[1]The most striking point of the parable is the mingling of good men and sinners. But only the ripening of the two crops permits the final distinction on the day of the harvest. It is no exaggeration, therefore,

this calls to mind once more the description of a simultaneous growth of mankind and of sin in the stories of primitive history. St Paul will reap the fruits of this legacy, for in his eyes the religious destiny of mankind consists not only in the spread of sin from one person, but in the growth of a son to the time of his majority.[1]

---

to see here the idea of a development that is essential to various parables about the harvest: the sower (Matt. 13: 3-23), the grain of mustard seed (Matt. 13: 31-32) and the seed scattered on the ground (Mark 4: 26-29).
[1]Rom. 5: 12-21; Gal. 4: 1-5.—The parable of the good Samaritan (Luke 10: 30-37) has been interpreted by several Fathers of the Church as representing the Fall of man and the salvation brought by Christ. This explanation seems to me to come from the accommodation and not from the true sense of the parable and, in consequence, has not been taken into account in this chapter. It would have been superfluous here to develop the reasons that rule out this exegesis. Recently J. Daniélou has taken up and defended the christological interpretation of certain Fathers; see *Mélanges Bibliques . . . A. Robert,* (1957), pp. 457-65. After the French edition of this present book the following work appeared: L. Ligier, *Péché d'Adam et péché du monde. Bible, Kippur et Eucharistie, II: Le Nouveau Testament,* (1961). The author has brought out the ideas of the Gospels on the collective and hereditary faults (pp. 117-54), but only within the history of Israel and without dealing directly with Jesus' allusions to the sin in the Garden of Eden.

5

Original Sin in St Paul

To the Christian mind Paul has always been the great doctor of original sin. Hence the interest in examining his testimony. And this is the object of the present chapter, first of all following step by step the passage from Rom. 5:12-21, which forms the basic text, then grouping together the evidence scattered in the epistles, in order to answer more comprehensive questions: the relationship of death and the flesh with the sin of Adam.[1]

[1]Here, in alphabetical order, are the commentaries and general works that I have consulted and that will be quoted simply by the name of the author in the course of this chapter: *E. B. Allo, *Saint Paul. Première épître aux Corinthiens*, (1934); H. Asmussen, *Der Romerbrief*, (1952); *R. G. Bandas, *The Master-Idea of St Paul's Epistles, or the Redemption*, (1925); *J. Bonsirven, *L'Évangile de Paul*, (1948); R. Bultmann, *Theologie des Neuen Testaments*, (1948) (trans. *Theology of the New Testament*, London, 1952); *L. Cerfaux, *Le Christ dans la théologie de saint Paul*, (Paris, 1951), (trans. *Christ in the Theology of St Paul*, (Nelson, Edinburgh, 1959)); P. Feine, *Theologie des Neuen Testaments*, (1910); *J. Freundorfer, *Erbsünde und Erbtod beim Apostel Paulus*, (1927); M. Goguel, *L'apôtre Paul et Jésus Christ*, (1904); H. J. Holtzmann, *Lehrbuch der neutestamentlichen Theologie* [2], (1911); A. Juncker, *Die Ethik des Apostels Paulus*, (1904); *M. -J. Lagrange, *L'Épître aux Romains*, (1916); H. J. Lietzmann, *An die Römer*, [4] (1933); *M. Meinertz, *Theologie des Neuen Testaments*, (1949); *F. Prat, *La Théologie de Saint Paul*, Vol. II, [6], (1922), (trans. *The Theology of St Paul*, (London, 1957)); G. Quell and Grundmann, article 'ἁμαρτάνω', in *Theol. Wört. zum N. T.*, Vol. I, (1933); Sanday-Headlam, *Romans* [4], (1900); A. Schlatter, *Die Theologie des Neuen Testaments*, (1910); C. R. Smith, *The Bible Doctrine of Sin*, (1953); E. Stauffer, *Die Theologie des Neuen Testaments*, (1941, 3rd. ed. 1946); Strack-Billerbeck, *Kommentar zum*

But, in order that we may understand the apostle's personal contribution better, it will be useful to see it briefly in the framework of contemporary Judaism. From the time of Ecclesiasticus (25:24), the story of the Garden of Eden had attracted the attention of religious minds, anxious to penetrate and justify the ways of Providence with regard to man. Several examples of this reflection are preserved, either in Wisdom (2:24) or in the non-canonical writings. It was classical to attribute death and the ills of life to the sin of the first father: sometimes the pathetic tone shows how great and tragic the original catastrophe appeared.[1] Nevertheless individual freedom remained, and eternal damnation was attributed only to individual faults. 'If Adam was the first to sin and has brought untimely death on all those born of him, each has prepared the future punishment for himself.... Adam is the cause of ruin for himself alone: but each of us is an Adam for himself.'[2]

Paul does not recall these assertions in order to contest them: on several occasions he repeats that God will judge each one according to his works.[3] But he is not content to preserve a picture of God's justice that is true in itself but could easily give

---

N. T. aus Talmud und Midrasch, Vol III, (1926); F. R. Tennant, The Sources of the Doctrines of the Fall and Original Sin, (1903); *E. Tobac, Le Problème de la Justification dans s. Paul, (1908); H. Weinel, Biblische Theologie des Neuen Testaments 4, (1928). One could also consult N. P. Williams, The Ideas of the Fall and Original Sin. A Historical and Critical Study 2, (1929); H. T. Powell, The Fall of Man, (1934), pp. 17-32. *Catholic authors.

[1] Jub. 3: 17-31; 4 Esdras 3: 7; 7: 118; Apoc. Bar. 17: 3; 19:8; 23: 4; 54: 15; 61: 6. It is easy to find more detailed information about the doctrine of judaism concerning the original downfall, for example in F. R. Tennant, chaps. 6-10; J. Bonsirven, Le judaïsme palestinien au temps de Jésus-Christ, (1935), Vol. 11, pp. 12-18.
[2] Apoc. Bar. 54: 19; cf. Enoch 98: 4; 4 Esdras 8: 56.
[3] 2 Th. 1: 6-9; Rom. 2: 6-11; 2 Cor. 11: 15; 2 Tim. 4: 14. This is a general axiom not only of Paul's thought, but of biblical belief in general.

rise to a too simplified and individualist theory of the conditions of salvation. In the story of the Garden of Eden he sees not only what the sentence of Yahweh clearly expressed, the hereditary penalty of death and various sufferings, but also what was insinuated much more obscurely, a state of sin transmitted to the whole of mankind.

I. THE TEXT OF ROMANS 5:12-21

The most important pauline text for the doctrine of original sin is obviously Rom. 5:12-21. It will be the object of a detailed examination, which will first of all consider fully the difficult problems raised by verses 12-14, in order to be able to comment more rapidly on what follows. But in the first place, the passage must be set in its context.

The parallel between Adam and Christ follows an enthusiastically expressed recognition of the extraordinary love that God has shown us. For Christ died for us, but not for the benefit of men who were good, a gesture that would appear strictly possible. It was when we were sinners, and therefore God's enemies, that he reconciled us to himself by the death of his Son (Rom. 5:1-11). We must bear these thoughts in mind in order to understand what follows, as the rather vague connecting word '*therefore*', placed at the beginning of verse 12, suggests. Paul's object is to extol God's way of ensuring salvation and he takes this opportunity to give a new insight into the origin of sin and the need of salvation for all.

The Gospel of God's love announces that all now receive life and justification because of Jesus Christ. To prove the efficacious role of one man on behalf of all, Paul turns to that passage of the Old Testament in which appears, in the most striking if disastrous way, the law of solidarity of which justification by Christ is the supreme favourable example. The story of the Garden of Eden showed the first couple bringing on themselves by their sin a condition that was wretched in all respects and that was to be handed on to all their descendants. The lesson to be drawn from the sacred text allows us to state that the act of one man can influence the fate of the multitude : it provides a point of comparison in which, besides, the superiority of Christ will clearly emerge. If all men are in a state of sin and death as a disastrous consequence of Adam's transgression, they are freed from them by Christ.

Since the text that he uses was set in Genesis at the beginning of human history, Paul is led to stress that all men have need of redemption. The first chapters of the epistle trace the history of the moral corruption of the pagans and the Jews (Rom. 1-2). When Paul wants to describe the benefits of salvation, he normally does so by comparing them with the present ills and sins of men.[1] Here he goes beyond the limits of his experience and lays down a general doctrine, based on Scripture.

Finally, this leads to a very important piece of information about the depth of the evil which afflicts the multitude of men even in their relations with God : through the fault of the first man not only misery and death came into the world, but sin also.

In two statements, which scarcely differ except in form, the passage from Rom. 5:12-21 repeats the same ideas : the actions of the two heads of mankind leading to ruin and salvation are parallel (5:12-14, 18-19) and the work of Christ is superior to that of Adam (5:15-17, 20-21). He is seeking the best form of expression for the idea.

[1] Eph. 2: 1-6; 2: 11-13; 4: 17-19; Titus 3: 5-7.

The difficulties of verses 12-14

The meaning of verses 12-14 has been the subject of much discussion. A certain number of alternatives can be listed:

1. Is verse 12 a regular construction in which the two terms of comparison (the protasis and the apodosis) are stated one after the other, or does it end with an anacoluthon (that is, is grammatical sequence lacking)?

2. What is the meaning of the expression ἐφ'ᾧ? Is it 'because' or 'in whom'?

3. Does the phrase 'all sinned' refer to personal sins, committed by all, or to a state of sin spread to all through the one sin of Adam?

4. Does the phrase: 'Sin is not counted where there is no law' refer to God's judgement or man's conscience?

5. Do verses 13-14 prove the reality of original sin by the universal fact of death, or do they, on the contrary, explain death by the personal sins of each man?

6. Do the words 'those whose sins were not like the transgression of Adam' mean children incapable of responsible acts or men (sinners possibly) who have not, like Adam, transgressed any formally promulgated precept?

The answers to these questions vary according to the author. Logically one often follows from the other. It is sometimes supposed that Paul's thought forms a perfectly coherent system. But this supposition may not be accurate. Without accusing the apostle of any real contradictions, we may think, with several exegetes, that he is to some extent groping, that he is putting forward some ideas, not indeed false, but secondary in comparison with his main plan. Those who admit an anacoluthon at the end of verse 12 (and these are in the majority) have less reason than the others to reject such a possibility *a priori*. If we consider the possibility of a mind hesitating a little, searching for exact

146

expression, rather than formulating a chain of faultless arguments, it is more prudent to determine briefly the ideas that are clearly contained in this passage, before explaining the meaning of the controverted parts.

[Adam's sin is a cause of death for all men.] 'Many died through one man's trespass' (5 : 15). 'Because of one man's trespass, death reigned through that one man' (5 : 17). The sin of Adam makes all men sinners. 'By one man's disobedience many were made sinners' (5 : 19). Therefore Paul thinks that Adam's sin has produced in mankind not only a penalty, death, but a real state of sin. And in this he differed from contemporary Jewish thought, which admitted only a hereditary penalty.

This liability to death depends on the state of sin in which all men find themselves; no doubt it is this link between sin and its penalty that is meant by the word 'condemnation' in verses 16 and 18. Paul, who affirms a general connection between sin and death, normally applies this principle to the sin and the death caused in all men by Adam's fault and does make them the result of the same fault not simultaneously, but independently of one another. [In all probability, then, he thought that every man has to die on account of Adam's sin, because every man has himself contracted sin in consequence of this first sin.]

On the other hand personal sin is itself also a cause of death. In verses 20-21 we read that (through the law) sin increased and reigned in death. And further on similar ideas appear : the end of sinful actions is death (6 : 21) : the wages of sin is death. Sinful passions are at work in our members, to bear fruit for death (7 : 5). When the commandment came 'sin revived and I died' (7 : 10). But this does not prevent him from stating that by one man's trespass death reigned through that one man (5 : 17).

Thus, in this parallel between Adam and Christ, different ideas emerge. Apart from the one sin of the first man, which

brings condemnation, death and sin on all men, Paul mentions
the other sins which were committed before and after the law
and over which the grace of Christ also triumphs. Clearly, then,
the sole point of this passage is not to draw a comparison between Adam and Christ, two individuals who both determine
the fate of the multitude but, more widely, to emphasize the
superabundance of justification over the abundance of sin of
any kind : original or personal. Neither the one nor the other
should be eliminated from this passage.

We can now return to the obscure and controverted verses
at the beginning. It will be noticed that often the terms of the
alternatives facing the reader can each claim some support from
the sense contained in other verses of this passage. However the
commentary that follows will not refuse to make a choice. By
looking sometimes for points of confirmation from afar, it will
succeed in finding an answer to the questions put earlier.

First Question.—'As sin came into the world through one man
and death through sin. . . .' It is possible to see here simply a
statement of the strictly personal fault and death of Adam,
which are the beginning of a long series; but such an interpretation is a little flat coming at the beginning of a parallel between
the disastrous influence of Adam and the justification worked
by Christ. So it is more probable that these first words of the
verse are to be understood in another way : through one man
exercising an influence on his race the power of sin began to
reign in the world, that is to say, in mankind, and the same is
true of death.

According to the majority of exegetes the protasis or first
term of the comparison continues : '. . . and so death spread to
all men, because all men sinned . . .', and then the phrase breaks
off, leaving the parallel unfinished, for it is not to be taken up

again expressly till verses 18 and 19. Others[1] feel that the phrase does have a regular conclusion, introduced by καὶ οὕτως although in parallel cases it is οὕτως καὶ which introduces the second term of the comparison.[2] Paul, according to this interpretation, draws attention successively to two complementary aspects of mankind's destiny [one man is the origin of the fate of all, and there is a universal diffusion of this fate.] This difference of syntactic construction, however, does not make any great difference from the point of view of doctrine.

Second Question.—The two little words ἐφ᾽ ᾧ provide material for further discussion.[3] Should they be understood as a phrase abbreviated by attraction, equivalent ἐπὶ τούτῳ ὅτι *for this reason, that,* or *because*? Or should we rather understand, with St Augustine and a few modern writers :[4] *in whom*?

[1] F. X. Patrizzi, *Commentationes tres de scripturis divinis.* . . . 'Commentatio secunda: De peccati originalis propagatione a Paulo descripta', (1851), and recently, L. Cerfaux, p. 231, n. 41 (Eng. trans.).

[2] Rom. 5: 15, 18, 19, 21; 6; 4; 1 Cor. 15: 22; 2 Cor. 8: 11; Gal. 4: 29.

[3] A detailed history can be found in S. Lyonnet, 'Le sens de ἐφ᾽ ᾧ en Rom. 5: 12 et l'exégèse des Pères grecs', in *Bibl.* XXXVI, (1955), pp. 436-56. Thorough lexicographical enquiry comes to the conclusion that the meaning of the phrase in Greek may vary a good deal, but that the most plausible sense here is 'on this condition, that'. In our text, which concerns not the future but the past, where the condition is therefore considered as actually realized, only a shade of difference separates this meaning from the fairly common translation: 'because', and it is a satisfactory way of expressing 'a real causality, but subordinate to and not simply placed side by side with the causality of Adam's sin' (p. 456). The considerations that follow on the 'eternal damnation' seem to me to be beyond the scope of this passage. S. Lyonnet has taken up more briefly the same grammatical explanation in a longer article: 'Le péché originel et l'exégèse de Rom. 5: 12-14', in *RSR.*, XLIV, (1956), pp. 63-84. I point out my agreement particularly on the point that in Rom. 5: 12ff. Paul is thinking principally of the case of adults and not specially of children at an early age.

[4] L. Cerfaux, p. 232 understands 'because of the one by whom' all sinned. According to him, the parallel between Adam and Christ demands that the thought should come back to the one who is the origin of the sin. To this one can reply that this passage speaks of other things apart from

The relative pronoun would refer to Adam, in whom all have sinned, not by sharing in his voluntary decision but by contracting a state of sin on account of him. The expression would be similar to the phrase about dying in Adam or being made alive in Christ (cf. 15:22); except, however, that the preposition ἐν is not the preposition ἐπί But the actual expression: to sin in Adam, is not found anywhere else in St Paul. And, what is more, in this case the antecedent would be placed rather a long way from the relative and separated from it by other words, *world* and *death*, that could themselves also play the part of antecedents. We must, therefore, abandon the construction: Adam . . . in whom all sinned, for it would in this case do violence to the normal course of the sentence, and accept the meaning 'because' or rather 'on this condition that'.

Some modern authors have tried to refer the relative pronoun which they insist in seeing in ἐφ' ᾧ to the death: 'to (deserve) which all have sinned'[1] or again to the whole preceding phrase: '(circumstances) in which all have sinned'. But the sense obtained in this way is rather far-fetched and artificial.

Third Question.—Now that problems of construction and translation have been settled, how are we to interpret the words: committed after Adam by all men? It was seen earlier (p. 146) that Paul sometimes attributes death to actual sins. It may be, then, that he is doing the same here without contradicting himself, for in verses 20-21 he speaks of multiple sins, committed after the law, which have reigned in death. And the

Christ and Adam: the law, the many transgressions of men.—It is clear that the quotation of Rom. 5: 12 according to the Vulgate text 'in quo' by the Council of Trent (Sess. V, can. 2) is not the equivalent of a decision on exegesis.

[1] Thus T. Zahn, quoted by S. Lyonnet (cf. supra p. 149 n. 3). And recently E. Stauffer, p. 248. n. 176, where he quotes the parallels of Wisdom 2: 23; Phil. 4: 10; 2 Tim. 2: 14.

ordinary meaning of the word 'to sin' ἁμαρτάνω, which is actively to commit a fault, confirms the probability of this interpretation.[1] But conversely, in this passage contrasting the influence of Adam and that of Christ, if not exclusively at least principally, it would be less likely for the sinful conduct of all men to be mentioned. Not only is this idea a secondary, or even alien, element; it upsets the flow of the thought.[2] It is not surprising, therefore, that the interpreters of Paul are very divided on the meaning of these words.

Some remark that Paul uses verbs that normally indicate an individual and momentary act in an unusual sense, in order to signify the entrance into a state in consequence of an action, whether personal or even of another person. 'When the commandment came, sin revived and I died', says St Paul, putting himself in the picture as the representative of every sinful man (Rom. 7:9-10). To die is not in this case to decease but to undergo that diminishment of life, notably by separation from God and moral debasement, that the Old Testament often calls death. Elsewhere 'to die' denotes a condition determined for the Christian by the death of Christ: the past tense of the verb is used in order to show that the new state is acquired in principle by the death of Christ and the baptism which unites the believer to him. From then on the Christian is dead, either because he is now dedicated to give his life for others like Christ (2 Cor. 5:14) or because the old man in him has lost the power of controlling his conduct.[3] According to this analogy it would be

[1] H. J. Holtzmann, Vol. 11, p. 47; M. Meinertz, Vol. II, p. 27.
[2] As H. Lietzmann notes, p. 62.
[3] Rom. 6:8; Col. 2:20; 3:3.—All these texts are referred to by R. G. Bandas, p. 35.—Protestant authors giving a similar interpretation of 'all sinned' in the sense of a state of sin are quoted by J. Freundorfer, p. 208. Recently L. Ligier, *Péché d'Adam et péché du monde, I: L'Ancien Testament*, (1960) pp. 273-66, has maintained that ' ἁμαρτάνω ' could mean 'to be (or enter) in a state of sin', according to Septuagint usage.

possible to understand these words 'all sinned' as a reference to a connection between all men and Adam's sin, by a participation not in his free act but in the separation from God resulting from it. Paul would here be making a few preliminary remarks to the idea which he was to express more clearly in verse 19.

In a different way M. Meinertz[1] also sees an assertion about original sin in the words 'all sinned'. The word always refers to an act and cannot mean 'to become a sinner'. But Paul could not have introduced an idea here without any connection with the context. 'The solidarity of the whole human race is the basis for the possibility that the descendants are in some way included in the first sin of the ancestor.' The manner of this participation is not clearly indicated by the context. And so all sinned in Adam.

Many authors maintain that it is a question here of individual sins.[2] What is expressed here in passing is an explanation of the universality of sin and death, distinct from the theory of original sin. In chapter 1 Paul described the idolatry of the pagans without going back to Adam; in chapter 7 he sees the psychological cause of sin in an irresistible urge to evil. Even in chapter 5 he cannot help referring in passing to these ideas. According to the circumstances, the interpreters of Paul's thought reduce the opposition between these two tendencies or stress it, sometimes going so far as to make almost a contradiction out of it.

If sides must now be taken, it will be useful to note first of all how much our exegesis can unconsciously be influenced by categories worked out by an earlier epoch. When the Christian theologians were speculating on original sin, they instinctively

---

[1] M. Meinertz, Vol. II, p. 29. Besides, he admits that ἐφ' ᾧ must be translated 'because' and not 'in whom'. This is more or less the exegesis of J. Freundorfer, p. 254.

[2] This is what J. Freundorfer, pp. 181-85, calls the individualist interpretation.

took the case of quite young children into consideration. The practice of infant baptism led to the examination of original sin in a pure state, in cases where there was no question of personal sins as well. But Paul is thinking of adults in the first place. The religious stain, produced as a result of Adam's sin, has not remained in them in a purely virtual state. It has shown itself in acts, so much so that, in Paul's eyes, one can die for one's own sins and at the same time die on account of Adam's sin. Thus the solidarist view of this passage taken as a whole does not exclude mention of individual acts.

The state of the child, who is already in a state of original sin, is called life by St Paul, because it does not yet include the inward struggle of the subject torn between desire for evil, coming from the flesh, and at the same time desire for good, coming from his intelligence enlightened by the law. Sin, which exists already, is dead without the law. With the awakening of moral consciousness it comes to life again, leads to transgression and consequently the death of the person, who was up to that point living (Rom. 7:8-10). This act, which brings on death, though related to sin may in certain cases involve no inward culpability. Just as the author of Job, in order to discuss the problem of the innocent man's suffering, had taken a blameless man as his hero, so Paul envisages the borderline case of a young Jew, deeply and sincerely attached to the commandments and giving in reluctantly. Such a man can say: 'it is no longer I that do it, but sin which dwells within me' (Rom. 7:17 and 20). In the eyes of men there is responsibility; in the eyes of God there may be none. And yet it brings with it the tragic consequence of death, not immediate decease but division of conscience, the prelude to the final dissolution.

It is not necessary to discuss here the exact relationship between the sin dwelling in the flesh of chapter 7 and the sin which results in all men from the sin of Adam. It is enough to note that Paul does not stop to consider virtualities, faculties or powers which are not active; he is concerned with the acts that result from them.[1]

In Rom. 5 : 12, when he says: 'death spread to all men, because all men sinned', [Paul may very well be speaking of evil deeds, actually committed by all men as an inevitable consequence and manifestation of original sin.][2] What follows fits in very naturally : 'sin indeed was in the world before the law was given'; in other words, [evil actions on the part of individuals did exist before the law.] This is the assumption of the principle which is immediately formulated : 'but sin is not counted where there is no law'. For such a principle would have no application, if there were no sin apart from Adam's sin. Besides, in verse 16, Paul speaks of the numerous trespasses followed by justification. And it is improbable that he is thinking here exclusively of the trespasses which have been committed since the gift of the law.

The most usual sense of the word 'to sin' remains that of the individual act; and yet the thought unfolds in the same perspective of solidarity without any inflection that would lead to confusion. There is no conflict between two different theories, nor any alien element not fully part of the whole. The thought is similar to that expressed in Eph. 2 : 1-5 : 'when you were dead through the trespasses and sins in which you once walked, following the course of this world, following the prince of the power of the air, the spirit that is now at work in the sons of

acts as manifest gos.

[1] 'Saint Paul never leaves the firm ground of history to speculate on abstract metaphysical notions': A. Feuillet, in *RB.*, LVII, (1950), pp. 359-60, n. 2. The whole phrase is underlined. When Rom. 7: 8 speaks of the sin that 'lies dead', it is only to describe at once how it revived (7: 9).
[2] This is more or less the exegesis of St Cyril of Alexandria, as S. Lyonnet remarks, art. cit., p. 449; see *P.G.*, 74, 784 C and 789 A.

disobedience. Among these we all once lived in the passions of our flesh, following the desires of body and mind, and so we were by nature children of wrath, like the rest of mankind . . ., even when we were dead through our trespasses. . . .'

However one difficulty could be raised. In Rom. 7:8-10 it is due to the Law that sin exercises its pernicious influence : in Rom. 5:13-14 it is in the absence of the Law. It seems that there is a contradiction between the intervention of the Law that is shown as necessary on the one hand and the actual absence on the other. But the point of view is not the same. In both cases it is a question of evil deeds committed by people conscious of what they are doing, and leading to death. In both cases Paul ends by showing the influence of a principle of sin in these acts, independent of the will of the person. He stresses anything that can bring out the importance of the particular aspect that he is studying. When he wants to describe the interior struggle between a will desiring good and a carnal desire enslaving a person to evil, he takes the case of a young Jew, to whom the Law gives a firmer and wider knowledge of good and evil. When he wants to show the existence of a power of sin in non-Christians, distinct from their personal culpability, he takes the case of men who lived before the mosaic law and who could not have any responsibility, because of lack of knowledge.

All those who lived between Adam and Moses underwent death, which was the result of sin. Since the necessary condition for personal fault was lacking, namely knowledge through the law of the divine will, these men could not have undergone death as the just penalty for a blameworthy decision of their will. This must have been due, according to the point of view adopted, either to a fully conscious transgression, that of Adam (5:5), or to the objectively sinful acts of men, which were not

155

the imitation but the ultimate consequence of the first sin. 'Death spread to all men, because all men sinned.'

And so in chapter 5 as in chapter 7 Paul envisages the existence in man of a power of sin, which leads him, once the stage of childhood is past, to commit evil deeds and which thus shows all its maleficence. [When the Law is not known, death cannot be the punishment for any personal malice determining the transgression : death is the objective effect of evil acts taken in themselves.] When the Law is known, there is added to the effect of death a distressing feeling of interior struggle. Paul always takes examples to illustrate his ideas. He does not move in a world of abstract notions : nature, grace, concupiscence etc. Constantly he applies these ideas to the case of adults, which lends itself either to collective observation or to introspection.

But if we admit that the words 'all sinned' refer to actual sins, we must see in this phrase a general consideration (as in Rom. 3 : 23) of mankind, in which sin is universally spread, whatever may be the case with children who are not yet capable of evil actions. Generally speaking, mankind (including all young children) dies because, generally speaking, it is sinful. If Paul can attribute, as he certainly does in verses 15 and 17, the death of all to the downfall of one man, he can, by virtue of the same idea of solidarity, attribute the death of all (without exception) to the sin of all (with some negligible exceptions).

But it is objected that Paul cannot have given the phrase 'all died' a wider extension than the phrase 'all sinned'. And as he could not have overlooked the very frequent case of children dying at an early age, he must have included them in the first phrase as in the second. Perhaps, however, this objection comes from a Christian feeling, formed by a long practice of infant baptism : whereas [many biblical stories show little children sharing the penalty for the faults of their parents.] Thus, in Num.

16:27-33, the whole families of Dathan and Abiron, without distinction of age, are swallowed up as a punishment for murmuring against Moses.[1] It is known that Paul referred to these episodes in 1 Cor. 10:10. At the moment when he is showing that a law of heredity continues to make its effects felt even on adults, Paul would not find the case of very young children specially worthy of mention. He does not exclude them from the consequences of Adam's sin, but he is not thinking particularly of them, when he says: 'all men died because all men sinned'. This passage contains approximations, which do not lay claim to absolute accuracy and, when Paul wants to show that the state of sin of which he is speaking does not involve personal responsibility, he appeals not to age but to the absence of law.

Fourth Question.—'Sin is not counted where there is no law' (Rom. 5:13). This sentence has been referred either to the conscience of men or the judgement of God. For some,[2] it means

[1] See also Num. 31:17; Deut. 2:34; 3:6; Joshua 8:24-25.
[2] Various authors, medieval and modern, cf. J. Freundorfer, p. 249, n. 3. Similarly Augustine and the Reformers; cf. G. Friedrich, ''ἁμαρτία οὐκ ἐλλογεῖται, Röm. 5:13', in *TLZ*, LXXVII, (1952), col. 523. In this article there are various pieces of information about the exegetical history of this verse. The author himself understands ἐλλογέω of divine justice, not in the vague sense of imputed, but in the precise sense of written in the heavenly book, to be recalled at the day of judgement. According to him, Paul meant to say that up to the law individual sins were punished immediately by death but were not taken into account for the judgement to come. This exegesis involves an opposition between verses 14 and 17, where death is referred to the fall of one man, and moreover is not easy to fit in with Rom. 2:16, where the judgement of men (expressly including the pagans) is expected in the future. It is not very likely that in these few verses Paul is alluding to a very complicated theory about the future judgement, establishing a difference between the pagans living before the mosaic law and those that lived afterwards. This juridical formalism on the part of divine justice is startling. If death continued to reign after the supposed inauguration of a new regime of justice, it would be an unexplained anomaly; it is dangerous to admit this construction on the mere combination of texts that are foreign to Paul.

157

that men do not pay attention to sin or do not judge it according to its real gravity except under the mosaic law, although this does not mean that it does not exist and bring death in its train. Against this interpretation there is the fact that on two earlier occasions Paul spoke of the knowledge of good and evil that the pagans have (1:32; 2:14-15), although this does not destroy the privilege the Jews have of knowing the will of God better on account of the law (2:18). Such a clear inconsequence in the same epistle should not too readily be presumed.

It seems preferable, then, to keep more closely to the obvious sense of the word ἐλλογεῖν to take count. This implies the intervention of the one to whom a man must account in the matter of sin, that is God. But to admit that this short sentence concerns the divine judgement is not itself without difficulty, for God is earlier said to have condemned the pagans by delivering them up to shameful passions (1:26). Applied to divine justice, the principle formulated in verse 13b implies an extremely formalistic and juridical idea of it. The supreme judge would punish only those sins that transgress a law that has been positively promulgated, just as would a human judge, who has only a limited knowledge of the conscience of others and at least avoids being arbitrary by formal precautions. How could Paul have attributed such an attitude to the one whom he represents as the searcher of men's hearts (Rom. 8:27) and the judge of men's secrets (Rom. 2:16), bringing to light things hidden in darkness and disclosing the intentions of hearts (1 Cor. 4:5), giving to each the praise that he deserves (Rom. 2:29; 1 Cor. 4:5)?

Besides, Genesis, to which Paul refers in this passage, gives quite a different picture. Not only does God punish sin by the Flood or the rain of fire on Sodom, without any law being promulgated beforehand, but he also issues laws containing a threat of death : after the measure of protection afforded to Cain (Gen. 4 : 15), this is what happens in the law against murder promulgated immediately after the Flood, and consequently imposed on all mankind descended from Noah (9 : 5-6).[1] This is probably the case too with the precept of circumcision imposed on Abraham's family (17 : 14). What is more, in the episode of Sarah (20 : 3-7) or of Rebecca (26 : 10-11) in the court of Abimelech, when the prohibition of adultery is at stake, a pagan seems quite conscious of the existence of a moral law. The divine revelation in his case is not to make him aware of a law which he would not otherwise have known, but to tell him that he is in danger of breaking it without knowing. Conscience has no need here of the apparatus of legal formalities to judge what is good or bad. At the beginning of his epistle Paul expressed in abstract terms the lesson to be drawn from these stories. Pagans have the law written in their hearts (2 : 15); they are aware of God's judgement declaring those who do evil to be worthy of death (1 : 32.)

The difficulty of reconciling Rom. 5 : 13b with Genesis can be overcome in the following way : when he takes, as a premiss of his argument, the fact that a law must be in existence before sin can be counted, Paul is thinking of the law of Moses and the situation of the Israelites. From this point of view his thought becomes clear. It is valid for all men, due to the implicit generalization of a principle, evolved in the first place with Israel in mind.

In accordance with Jewish thought, the law had to be promulgated regularly for the Israelites to be subject to

[1] Paul could scarcely ignore or neglect this passage from Genesis, which has already attracted the attention of the author of Jubilees and was to give rise to rabbinic speculation; cf. E. L. Dietrich, 'Die "Religion Noahs", ihre Herkunft und ihre Bedeutung', in *Zeitschr. Rel. Geistes-Gesch.*, I, (1948), pp. 301-15.

penalties.[1] So Paul states that sin is not imputed when there is no law. This proposition, which would be opposed to the sense of several biblical stories, if it involved pagans, becomes tenable if it is limited to the ancestors of the Chosen People. The drunkenness of Noah, the lies of Abraham and Jacob, the cruelty of Jacob's sons towards their brother Joseph are not the object of any divine blame. It is only the incest of Ruben and the merciless massacre of the Sichemites by Simeon and Levi that are condemned in the words of the dying Jacob (Gen. 49:3-7); furthermore, what is announced is not an immediate penalty but a distant downfall. During the exodus from Egypt, the murmurs at Mara (Exod. 13:23-26) and at Raphidim (Exod. 17:1-7) and the violation of the sabbath (Exod. 16:27-30) do not provoke any sanction but only a warning and steps to meet the people's needs. On the other hand, after their stay at Sinai and the gift of the law, similar faults are severely punished :

[1]J. Freundorfer, pp. 248 and 250, n. 1, and G. Friedrich, art. cit., col 526, think that Paul is borrowing here from Jewish theological thought but they do not quote any text in support of their claim. Nor is there anything to be found in Strack-Billerbeck, Vol. III, on Rom. 5: 13 Some parallels can however be quoted. According to the book of Jubilees (33: 15-16), Ruben, though guilty of incest, was not put to death because the law had not yet been promulgated. The *Damascus Document* (CDC, V, 2-5) gives as an excuse for the polygamy of David the fact that he had not read the book of the law, which had been sealed and placed in the ark and which was not opened from the death of Joshua till the coming of the priest of Sadoc; the king might therefore have been unaware of the law against having more than one wife (Deut. 17: 17). In the same way the Rabbi Eleazar (3rd cent.) declared that Israel was not subject to any penalty for breaking the law, as this had not been promulgated in the Tent of Reunion (Midrash of the Canticle, II, 3). These last two texts have been compared to Rom. 5: 13 by M. Delcor *RB.*, LXII, (1955), pp. 71-72. In this passage, where he is not attempting to write polished phrases, as the anacoluthon of verse 12 shows, Paul made use of these Jewish ideas, which gave a simplified expression of the reality but one that was sufficient for his purposes.

murmurs (Num. 11:1-3, 32-33) and the violation of the sab-bath (Num. 15:32-36).[1]

Paul, basing his remarks on Scripture, showed earlier that the promises were made to Abraham on account of his faith and not on account of the law, and he applied the truth thus acquired to the case of pagans also. In 1 Cor. 10:1-11 he has drawn from the events of the Exodus the conclusion that sin brings punishment with it even for those who have received an abundance of divine favours, among which, however, the gift of the law is not mentioned. Here again he draws the rules for divine judgement from the biblical story. Simplifying things for the sake of a clear comparison, he acts as if external sin did not involve real internal responsibility until the Mosaic law, be-cause of lack of knowledge. For the law gives a knowledge of sin (Rom. 3:20). Where there is no law, there is no transgression either (4:15). But it is the law that has made sin abound (5:20), because it has given a clearer knowledge of God's will than ever before (2:18).

Of course Paul is well aware that even the pagans are culp-able, for they know God (1:21) and the moral law (1:32; 2:14) without the help of the Mosaic revelation. He lets it be understood that the responsibility of each is in proportion to the knowledge that each has of good : 'All who have sinned without the law will also perish without the law, and all who have sinned under the law will be judged by the law' (2:12). By contrasting Adam's transgression, committed with full knowledge, and the

---

[1]This differing severity towards similar faults was already brought out by St Cyril of Alexandria, *Commentary on St John* (6: 32); *PG*, 73, 505.—Of course some actions are sometimes followed by annoying conse-quences: thus Jacob is punished by the tricks of Laban; Joseph's brothers see their misfortune as a punishment for their past cruelty (Gen. 42:21), but there are none of these divine reproaches that are so frequent in the rest of biblical history.

sins committed by Israel before the law, which would have been faults of ignorance, Paul gives a simplified outline of a fact whose complexity he makes us feel in other texts. In any case this passage allows a lack of precision to remain which is not removed. Does he mean that the absence of law meant a universal ignorance? That would not be in keeping with what he says of pagans and would be quite out of place even if confined to the ancestors of Israel, but at least in this hypothesis one can understand how divine justice did not impute sin before the law. Does he mean, on the other hand, that God did not impute sin, although the absence of law did not always prevent a certain knowledge of good and so a certain responsibility? But then divine justice is too like imperfect human justice, reduced to acting on general presumptions and rules and adjusting itself with difficulty to the variety of particular cases. Paul does not consider this dilemma. It is enough for him to have recalled the existence of a special type of sin : an objectively evil act, leading to a real separation from God, and therefore having death as a consequence, and yet not involving subjective culpability and so not falling under the weight of divine judgement. The text does not say to what extent, wide or restricted, this type of sin existed in the world before the law.[2] It simply states that it did exist, without contradicting other texts according to which there were also sins involving a real culpability.

Fifth Question.—Insofar as what we have just said is not already an answer, it remains now to ask what Paul meant in these verses 13-14 : does he refer death to Adam's sin or to individual sins?

Many protestant exegetes see in these two verses the idea that

[1]Cf. infra, p. 122 and n. 28.
[2]Sanday-Headlam, p. 135, insists on the lack of precision in the statement contained in verse 13.

personal sins caused the death of all men from Adam to Moses.[1] These personal sins are an undeniable fact but, for lack of a law, men had no realization of them or were not concerned about them. However, in spite of this ignorance, the fact of death (the wages of sin) shows clearly the reality of these sins, which differed from the sin of Adam, in that they did not break a law that had been expressly promulgated. So, far from providing a proof of the existence in each man of a state of sin passed on by Adam, this passage would on the contrary support the existence of personal sins that could by themselves explain the mortal condition of mankind.

This interpretation scarcely fits in with the whole of the passage. No doubt one must not insist too much on the fact that Adam is represented on several occasions in this passage as the cause of sin and death; for it is quite certain that various ideas adventitious to the main idea do slip into these verses. But the more important fact is that verse 17 reproduces the formula of verse 14: 'death reigned', adding the detail: 'because of one man's trespass ... through that one man', immediately after reference to the numerous trespasses from which grace justifies us (v. 16). The explanation of the difference in meaning that might exist between verses 14 and 17, according to the interpretation that we are examining here, cannot lie in a difference of point of view. In verse 17 Paul brings to our attention the numerous faults by which, so it is said, he explains death in verse 14. And yet he does not dwell on that, but attributes the cause of death to one sin alone. It is difficult to believe that two such different ideas should have been expressed a few lines apart, with the divergence underlined by similarity in the words used. Verse 14 must, therefore, be interpreted in the terms of verse 17:

[1] J. Freundorfer, p. 253, n. 1, quotes Mangold, Pfleiderer, Sabatier, Clemen.

it is through the fault of one man that death reigned from Adam to Moses.

Thus we are led to see in these two verses (13-14) an argument demonstrating the existence of a joint legacy of sin and death. It is tacitly supposed that death is the wages of sin (Rom. 6:23); but the reign of death from Adam to Moses cannot always be explained by the personal culpability of the men of this time, because of the lack of any law giving sufficient knowledge. Nevertheless death, the sanction for sin, has reigned over all. Therefore this can only be because of something other than this non-existent or diminished culpability.

Here the commentators are divided. A good number attribute death either to the sin of Adam alone[1] or to the state of sin that he caused in his posterity.[2] Others do not separate this state of sin from the sinful acts which are actually committed and which are its consequence. It is not essential to add 'as the cause of death' after the words 'sin is not counted'. It may be the same sin which on the one hand is not counted and, on the other, leads to death. Divine justice does not take into consideration an act not involving subjective malice, but this does not cease to have its objective nature and its proper effects of separation from God and eventually death.

All sinned, showing by their conduct that they were under the domination of sin which came into the world through one man. Sin did exist in the world before Moses, not only as a virtual power but as a reality, the sum of the many evil deeds committed by all. These actions were not, however, always sins as the transgressions of Adam were : the difference lay in the

[1]For example St John Chrysostom, in his commentary on this verse, PG, 60, 475.
[2]The majority of Catholic exegetes, so it seems. Among the protestants, F. R. Tennant, p. 257, for example.

fact that they had not contravened a law imposed on the conscience of those who performed them] In this state of childhood, mankind, or a part of mankind, was in a situation similar to that of the ancestors of Israel or again of the young Jews who were not held to the practice of the law before the age of puberty and so were not responsible in its eyes. So if evil deeds brought on death, this was not necessarily because of the voluntary malice (sometimes there was none) of those who did them but because of the objective perversity of these actions, the ultimate effect of Adam's disobedience in the human race.[1]

'Death spread to all men because all men sinned.' Paul, having put forward this idea, immediately sets out to illustrate it and abandons the scarcely begun parallel between Adam and another, who is Christ, as we see from the end of the passage. The words: 'Sin indeed was in the world before the law was given' refer to the evil deeds actually committed. They take up the statement: 'all sinned' and make its meaning clear.

The result of the present exegesis is, therefore, to recognize in verse 12 not a double cause of death: on the one hand Adam's sin causing the announcement of the penalty of death and on the other the individual sins determining the application of this penalty to each man, but a <u>single cause, Adam's sin</u>,

Single cause of death = Adam sin

---

[1] The exegesis adopted here draws inspiration from St Cyril of Alexandria and H. Preisker. The first writes: 'Those who are caught up in sins are, so to speak, murderers of their own souls, and they have fallen into this misfortune, not voluntarily, but as if constrained to break the law and offend God, because man's spirit is turned towards evil from his youth and because the law of unrestrained evil desires, which dwells in the members of the flesh, reigns tyrannically' (*Adoration in spirit and truth*, Vol. VIII; *PG*, 68, 581 B: the passage does not comment directly on Rom. 5: 13). See also the commentary on Rom. 7; *PG*, 74, 808-13. H. Preisker writes: 'When they sinned, they did not do so after the manner of Adam's transgression; it was by virtue of the collective state of sin included in the fall of Adam, not through a conscious enmity towards God' (*TWNT.*, article on 'ἐλλογέω', Vol II, p. 514, ll. 21-23).

leading to evil conduct in all men and in this way to death. 'All sinned' does not indicate an invisible inclusion in the sin of Adam,[1] nor directly a state of sin, but quite visible acts, objectively bad and causing a real separation from God, although perhaps lacking subjective malice.

Paul does not form any systematic theory on the origin of sin. According to the object that he has in mind at the time, he draws attention to this or that aspect of the reality. He is not unaware that there remains in every man a real personal responsibility; and in Rom. 1-2 he shows the culpability of pagans and Jews by which they merit death. But there is also a collective downfall in mankind, a state of sin which would be enough to bring death with it. Rom. 5:12-19 considers this, abstracting for the moment almost totally from the idea of individual responsibility. There is an element of artificiality in these descriptions, which in each case show only one side of the reality. But no doubt this inability to take a comprehensive view and above all to make a sure judgement of responsibility is the condition of our humanity.

Sixth Question.—The last of the questions mentioned earlier remains to be answered. Of whom is Paul speaking, when he mentions 'those whose sins were not like the transgression of Adam'? As we have already said, we are not specially concerned here with children incapable of sinful deeds, but with adults who have in fact sinned, that is, committed objectively evil acts without, however, going against a divine law recognized as such. They sinned, but not in all cases with the same responsibility in God's eyes as Adam. What excuses them is not lack of age but absence of law. Naturally it may be argued from analogy

[1] Contrary to the exegesis defended by J. Freundorfer, pp. 240-47, and M. Meinertz, Vol. II, pp. 27-29. On the relationship between death and sin, see infra, pp. 129 and 135-37.

and maintained that the case of the children, who were not subject to the yoke of the Law until the age of puberty according to the Jewish mind, is to be compared with that of these adults, victims of their ignorance. But that is to insist on a case left in obscurity by Paul.[1]

The end of the passage: Romans 5 : 15-21

After the end of the parenthesis of verses 13-14 the text presents less difficulty. The comparison is taken up again in verse 15 without any attempt to finish the interrupted phrase of verse 12. Between Adam and Christ there is far more than a likeness on equal terms. Expressions of the superiority, in quality as well in extent, of the role filled by Christ abound. The grace of God and the gift abound (5 : 15): grace superabounds (5 : 20). Paul repeats himself as if he could not restrain his admiration and as if still looking for the most accurate way of expressing his thought. Such formulas can only be understood properly if we admit something that is not expressly said, namely that the divine gift made in Christ surpasses the state lost by sin in richness or, in other words, if justification is more than the simple restoration of the life destroyed by Adam's fault, the life which St Paul does not think of describing clearly.

The wording of the phrase 'if . . ., much more . . .' repeated in verses 15 and 17, shows that this superabundance of grace corresponds to what God has already shown us of his love: it is an implicit reference to the ideas expressed in the preceding paragraph (particularly 5 : 8-10). Grace comes from God but it

[1] On the different interpretations of the words: 'those whose sins were not like the transgressions of Adam', see J. Freundorfer, p. 250, n. 2. Recently C. R. Smith, p. 173, has seen the difference between Adam and his descendants in the fact that these, when they sin, are already weak because of the flesh, which was not the case with Adam. This idea is alien to Rom. 5.

is given on account of Jesus Christ, just as death (the only effect of the first fault mentioned in this verse) spreads to all through one man. The parallel is continued between the two states of mankind and at the same time the two heads of mankind. The abundance of grace is stated without further explanation. The following verse will apply it to the pardon of sins. The verb is in the past in verse 15 to show that the gift of grace is already an accomplished fact; naturally that does not mean that it should not continue afterwards, hence the future in verses 17 and 19. The words οἱ πολλοί literally 'the many', in verses 15 and 19 should be translated not by 'the great number', which might be taken to mean that it is simply a question of an important majority, but by 'the multitude', which stresses the greatness of the number without denying that it does in fact mean the whole. For verses 18-19 expressly state that the Fall concerns all men just as the reparation does.

Concens all

Verse 16 reveals a new aspect of the superiority of the gift compared with sin : the judgement, provoked by one fault, ends in condemnation, but grace, after countless trespasses, ends in a sentence of justification. The redeeming power of Christ reaches everywhere where there is evil. It includes the pagan corruption described in chapter 1 as well as the faults committed by the Israelites under the rule of the law (5 :20). The words condemnation and acquittal add a nuance to the idea of death in verse 15. They insinuate, but less clearly than in verse 12, that the fault of Adam put all men in a state of sin.

In verse 17 the formal symmetry of the parallel is sacrificed to the vigour of the thought : the second part of the phrase has real persons corresponding to the abstract subject of the first part. 'If, because of one man's trespass, death reigned through that man, much more will those who receive[1] the abundance of grace and the free gift of righteousness reign in life through the one man Jesus Christ.' The situation is completely reversed: the slaves become kings.

In verse 18 a new development of the ideas previously stated begins, with the same succession of a parallel properly so-called (vv. 18-19) and a stress on the differences (vv. 20-21). Two sentences speak first of all of the condemnation and justification then of the men made sinners and afterwards justified. If it is assumed that these two verses 18-19 cannot be purely and simply repetitive, it must be granted that the word 'condemnation' in verse 18 draws attention particularly to death, the punishment for sin, and that verse 19 clarifies the idea by stating expressly the fact that sin too is passed on. The phrase points to its object without taking too much account of the rules of syntax: verse 18 has no verb. 'Just as through one man's trespass (things resulted) for all men in condemnation, so through one man's act of righteousness[2] (things resulted) for all men in justification.' Verse 19 makes it clear that the term justification or acquittal is to be taken in all its fulness: not only exemption from a penalty that has been extended to all

[1] According to Sanday-Headlam, p. 141, the words used show that it is a question of an external gift, coming to man, imputed, not worked or infused within him: this is drawing a disproportionate conclusion from an image: to receive.

[2] Grammatically it can also be translated: 'through one trespass . . . through one act of righteousness'. This second translation can claim some support in the fact that verse 19, whose meaning admits of no ambiguity (the disobedience, the obedience of one man), makes use of a different form from that of verse 18. In place of an act of righteousness, it can be translated 'sentence of righteousness'. But the word δικαίωμα can have the meaning of a righteous act (cf. Baruch 2: 19; Apoc. 19: 8). If it is understood in this way, the parallelism of the two terms of verse 18 is better preserved and points the way better for verse 19, which is so close in meaning.

Adam's posterity, but the purification granted to all those who have been contaminated by the sin. It is now the clearest expression of a doctrine that, until this verse, was seeking its best formula.

'As by one man's disobedience many were made sinners, so by one man's obedience many will be made righteous.' It would be quite wrong to understand 'made sinners' in the sense of 'treated, considered as sinners', appealing to 2 Cor. 5 :21, where it says that God 'made him to be sin who knew no sin'.[1] Paul cannot mean to establish any profound parity between the condition of Christ who redeemed us by his suffering and that of all men in the grip of perdition. On the one hand there is the appearance of sin (or sacrifice for sin, according to one possible meaning of the word); on the other hand the reality of sin.

Verse 19 considers the result of the moral attitude of Adam or of Christ without asking how far men's personal acts are necessary for the effect indicated to take place. In fact faith is the means by which justification is given : but for the moment that can be left out of the discussion. Nothing is said about the necessity of personal acts for the sin of Adam to make all men sinners.[2] Nor can it be maintained that here we have a question of a purely ideal state of sin, as the righteousness that is to be communicated to the multitude is purely ideal.[3] If the future tense is used here, it is because from now on salvation is to succeed damnation and because this effect is only to be realized in the future, on the occasion of the eschatological judgement. If all men do not in fact receive justification, that may be due either to their wilful obduracy or to delay in preaching (cf. Rom. 10 : 14). But this does not justify any conclusion which

[1]As H. Weinel does, p. 244.
[2]Contrary to the assertion of H. J. Holtzmann, Vol. II, pp. 49-50.
[3]Contrary to the assertion of K. Stier, quoted by H. J. Holtzmann, p. 49.

would deny the real influence of the first act of disobedience on the condition of all men.

After the parallel between the two heads of mankind, Paul returns to the idea of the superiority of Christ. The gift of the law has led to an increase of sin, either because its malice is henceforward graver, being conscious, or because the prohibition, arousing desire for freedom, has multiplied the transgressions. Evil seems to have triumphed over good, then, since sin has led men astray by means of a good thing (cf. Rom. 7 : 13). But the last word is to remain with goodness : grace, that is the pardon granted by God and the effect produced in man by this pardon, has superabounded where sin abounded. The reign of sin and death has given way to the victorious reign of righteousness and life. The passage concludes with the prospects of a universal redemption, having opened by stressing the effects of a definite sin, that of Adam.

The biblical origin of Paul's thought

Chapter 5 of the epistle to the Romans, therefore, teaches the spread of sin from one man to all men. Paul does not quote any biblical text to prove his statements, although that is frequently his method. He simply puts forward statements, as if this were a doctrine that could be taken for granted. The name of Adam was enough to bring Genesis to mind and in those days it was commonplace to seek an explanation of human destiny in the first sin. What is new, compared with Judaism, is the parallel between Adam and Christ and the idea that we all receive sin from the common ancestor. The parallel appeared quite natural in the framework of Christian faith in the Saviour. But is the doctrine of original sin and not merely of an original downfall or state of wretchedness a new revelation?

It is sometimes said to be so.[1] But perhaps Paul simply brought out and gave abstract formulation to what Genesis described in a concrete way. If the literary genre of the story of the Garden of Eden is taken into account, it will be recognized that the sentence passed on the first couple is, in the mind of the narrator, to reach all their posterity, that the expulsion from the Garden conditions the fate of this posterity, that even before sin the attitude of man in front of the helpmate brought him by God is shown as the model of every marriage. In the history of the ancestor the author is outlining the situation of his race. Thus it is quite in keeping with the intention that inspires this page to see in the reaction of fear and flight before God immediately after the disobedience not a purely individual fact but the prototype of a reaction and of feelings described more than once in Scripture,[2] fear and an attempt to hide when in contact with God. The episode suggests that on account of a deliberate sin, all mankind and not just the first couple is now incapable of approaching God with confidence and experiences in his regard a feeling of shame and unworthiness, which makes it keep at a distance.

Thus the early narrator had an inkling of a doctrine that Paul was the first to be able to express clearly. Before him Ecclesiasticus and Wisdom had seen death in this section of Gen. 2-3; but in their optimism they had passed the rest by. The non-canonical authors had suspected a much deeper mystery and had recoiled in front of what seemed to them an insoluble enigma. Meditating more profoundly than his predeces-

---

[1] Thus J. Guillet, *Thèmes Bibliques*, p. 102.
[2] The account of divine apparitions, granted even to favoured people, rarely fails to stress the fear, either immediate or retrospective, that seizes a man, when he recognizes a manifestation of God: Gen. 32: 31; Exod. 20: 18; Joshua 5: 15; Judges 6: 22; 1 Kings 19: 13; Isaias 6: 5. It is a discreet echo of Genesis.

sors and contemporaries, in the light of the good news of salvation, Paul was able to distinguish firmly and without risk of despair what had previously remained hidden. Perhaps the parallel between Adam and Christ was the determining factor : by antithesis, sin had to correspond to justification.

Such an idea easily shocks our modern minds, because we associate free individual responsibility with the word sin. But its meaning in Paul must be understood in terms of the Old Testament, where it does not necessarily denote free will. The simple breaking of a ritual regulation, whether unconscious or even deliberate and justified by some sufficient reason, can upset or prevent good relations with God and demand expiation or purification before acts of worship.[1] Such a usage helps us to understand the expression of Rom. 5:19: 'by one man's disobedience many were made sinners'. Men are separated from God, not worthy to approach him, in a state of religious impotency, which is profound without being absolutely radical (cf. Rom. 1:19-21). It goes without saying that Paul goes beyond the sphere of ritual uncleanness with its idea of gratuitous contingency. He is thinking of an objective separation from God, which reveals itself in evil conduct without, however, entailing a total corruption of each man's will, congenitally rooted in revolt; he admits the possibility of moral goodness for the pagans. This state is the result of a deliberate fault of our first father. It is not an incomprehensible necessity, a condition of our human nature.

These are the conclusions that can be drawn from Rom. 5:12-21, without encroaching too much on the lessons provided by the other epistles. It remains to consider these others in a more synthetic way in order to make as clear as possible the effects of original sin and the method of its transmission.

[1] Cf. G. Quell, p. 281.

II. Death

With Paul the word death θάνατος admits of a great flexibility. In the passages, which concern the death of Christ, the term clearly includes bodily decease and only that, in fact, together of course with the bodily sufferings accompanying it.[1] The meaning is very much the same where the decease of the faithful is concerned, whether this is considered as a theoretical possibility (Phil. 1:20) or a really threatening danger.[2] But already in 2 Cor. 4:11 a gradual change of meaning can be noticed. The death to which the living (who are faithful) are subject may in certain cases be not decease but a limited, precarious, threatened existence, full of suffering.[3] It is a process whose normal conclusion is decease, but it does not end in that immediately. In verse 10 Paul also calls it the death or mortification νέκρωσις of Jesus, because it makes us resemble Jesus dying and also makes me share in the fruits of life produced by his death. Baptism has buried us in death (Rom. 6:4), by it we are incorporated in Christ by his death (6:5); the resemblance is acquired in principle when the ceremony is performed. But it must be increased and confirmed by a continual putting to death of the deeds of the body (Rom. 8:13).

Finally he shows the relationship of death to sin, either the sin of Adam (Rom. 5:12-17) or sin in general. The sinner is worthy of death (Rom. 1:32) and is the slave of sin, which leads to death (Rom. 6:21, 23). The sinful passions bear fruit for death (Rom. 7:5); sin, provoked by the law, ends in death (7:10, 13). The sting of death is sin (1 Cor. 15:56). And so

[1] Rom. 5: 10; 6: 3, 5, 9; 1 Cor. 11: 26; Phil 2: 8; 3: 10; Col. 1: 22.
[2] 2 Cor. 1: 9, 10; 4: 11; Phil. 2: 27, 30.
[3] Cf. 1 Cor. 15: 31; 2 Cor. 6: 9.

it can be understood why the work of redemption accomplished by Christ should have consisted in the destruction of death (1 Tim. 1 : 10).

Certainly the idea of decease is not completely absent from a good number, at least, of the passages quoted. However some texts speak clearly of death in a different sense. In Rom. 7 : 7-25, where Paul says 'I' in the name of all the Jews subject to the Law, the child is seen as living at first without law. 'When the commandment came, sin revived and I died' (7 :9-10). It is here a question of separation from God, of a decay in the spiritual order, perhaps also of a distressing state of conscience, and all this existing at the same time as the continuation of physical life. In the same way the woman who gives herself up to pleasure is dead while yet living (1 Tim. 5 :6). The pagans are dead νεκρός in their trespasses and sins.[1]

Elsewhere the expression is less radical, 'if you live according to the flesh you will die' (Rom. 8 : 13), which cannot mean corporal decease alone, from which the just would then be preserved. In the same way the apostles, according to the attitude adopted with regard to their message, are for some a fragrance from death to death, for others a fragrance from life to life (2 Cor. 2 :16). Worldly grief produces death (2 Cor. 7 :10). The aspirant to salvation is asleep or dead as well.[2] It is quite obvious that in these texts the thought goes beyond simple decease.

Therefore it is legitimate to ask what exactly Paul means by these words. 'Physical death or spiritual death? Death now or eschatological death? In certain cases one or another of these

---

[1] Eph. 2: 5; Col. 2: 13. This does not prevent Paul from speaking further on of the vices in which 'you have lived' (Col. 3: 7).
[2] Eph. 5: 14. Concerning texts of this nature, C. R. Smith rightly remarks that for the Old Testament death is not total annihilation, but a state of torpor, weakness and inactivity in *sheol*.

meanings is obvious. [More often it is better not to choose but to include all the various shades of meaning in one fundamental reality, often personified by Paul.] This phenomenon of a word's meaning being widened is natural where the apostle's thought is richest: the same word then, includes the same range of meanings that Paul gives it and brings a whole complex to the mind of readers familiar with the whole of the doctrine'.[1]

Thus the correlative ideas of life and death undergo the same extension of meaning as in the Old Testament and the reader often finds himself confronted with the same difficulty, sometimes the same impossibility, when he wants to fix a definite position in the movement of oscillation between the two poles: simple decease and the total misery of enmity or separation from God.

What increases the difficulty is that when Paul was speaking in one passage of the resurrection, he contrasted it with the condition of the first man and with death, the ultimate enemy, in the same context. The distinction between what is the result of the will of the Creator in the present state of humanity and what is the result of the corruption of sin, between what is a remnant of the good creation of the beginning and what is a disastrous innovation of guilty creatures, is not easy to make: that is the conclusion of a passage in the first epistle to the Corinthians (15 : 20-57).

This text provides a partial parallel to Rom. 5 : 12-21, since it too contains the antithesis between Adam and Christ, but

---

[1] J. Nélis, 'L'antithèse litteraire ΖΩΗ-ΘΑΝΑΤΟΣ dans les épîtres pauliniennes', in *Eph. Th. Lov.*, XX, (1943), pp. 18-53; see p. 45. The first sentences as far as 'Paul' are a tacit and almost unmodified quotation from P. Benoit in *RB.*, XLVII, (1938), p. 489. In the same sense, J. Freundorfer, p. 229, n. 3; F. Prat, Vol. I, p. 305; R. G. Bandas, p. 29: 'what in Scriptural use is a compendious term for all the penalties and consequences of sin, namely death'.

restricted to the idea of death without any question of the diffusion of sin. 'For as by a man came death, by a man has come also the resurrection of the dead. For as in Adam all die, so also in Christ shall all be made alive' (1 Cor. 15 :21-22). [Death is here considered as something abnormal] the resemblance with Rom. 5 : 12-21, the fact that further on death is treated as an enemy (1 Cor. 15 :26) and connected with sin, which is its sting, can scarcely leave any doubt on that score.

However, between these two extremities of the passage, different considerations are introduced. Death, followed by the resurrection, is compared to the normal process of sowing and germination, which supposes the decomposition (the 'death') of the seed. The difference between the state of the body before and after the resurrection is comparable to the difference that exists between the grain sown in the ground and the plant that emerges, or again between the various categories of animal life, between the earthly bodies and the heavenly bodies. The list drawn up here repeats the list given in the story of creation in Genesis. The series: man, quadrupeds, birds, fish, is a slight simplification of Gen. 1 :20-27; earth and heaven, sun, moon and stars correspond to Gen. 1 :6-7, 16. Paul's thought moves here to the picture of the excellent world begun by the creation, a world including hierarchies of value and stages of progressive development.

There is a physical body and it was this that was created at the beginning, as Paul establishes by a quotation from the story of the origins in Genesis: 'The first man Adam became a living being'.[2] This body taken from the earth must give way to a spiritual body : for 'it is not the spiritual (which is) first, but the physical, and then the spiritual' (15 :46).

[1] Cor. 15: 35-36; cf. John 12: 24.
[2] Cor. 15: 45; cf. Gen. 2: 7.

So we find in this passage the following pairs of opposites:

Corruption	—	incorruptibility
dishonour	—	glory
weakness	—	power
physical body	—	spiritual body
first Adam	—	last Adam
living being	—	life-giving spirit
first man	—	second man
terrestrial	—	celestial

And there is nothing to indicate that the first list of terms involves any disorder that is contrary to the will of God; the reminiscences and quotations from Genesis suggest that this concerns the order of creation.

However, a little further on there does appear an opposition between two pairs of contraries, which are declared incompatible:

flesh and blood	—	kingdom of God
corruption	—	incorruptibility

Although the word 'flesh' often has a morally pejorative sense, the binomial 'flesh and blood' has not this sense and it simply means man left in his native weakness and not transformed by the spirit of God.[1] However, the statement: 'flesh and blood cannot inherit the kingdom of God' (1 Cor. 15:50) does remind us of the list, drawn up earlier, of the vices which 'will not inherit the kingdom of God' (1 Cor. 6:9-10), and the comparison may suggest that 1 Cor. 15:50 is to be seen as a condemnation.[2]

[1] Cf. E. B. Allo, p. 431.
[2] However we must not insist too much on the cogency of this comparison. For, in Paul's eyes, the fact that a condition is destined to disappear does not mean that it is bad: this is true of the need for food (1 Cor. 6: 13).

Finally, some verses further on, a new grouping of two pairs of contraries is found, one of which was mentioned previously :

| corruptible | — | incorruptibility |
| mortal | — | immortality |

This time there is an explicit connection with the victory over death, whose sting is sin.

Thus it is quite clear that there is a difference between the condition of our bodies that we experience now and that of the risen body. The thought on this point does not change and there is not the least uncertainty. But is the present condition different from the one inaugurated at the creation ? That is a question to which Paul does not propose to give a direct answer and which receives only an occasional ray of light from statements concerning some other subject. Reasons for thinking that our present condition corresponds to a divine institution are put forward and then the relationship of this condition with sin is suggested (it is no more than a suggestion). Paul seems equally convinced that our present state preserves the characteristics of the original creation and that it is suffering from a partial change for the worse on account of sin. But his attention is centred on something else and he does not undertake to make it clear to what degree the action of the Creator and the deforming action of sin, respectively, determine our condition. He recognizes the existence of two opposed factors and does not fix their proportion in the sphere of common experience.

body + risen body

In the same way marriage does not involve sin (1 Cor. 7: 28, 36), it is a gift of God (1 Cor. 7: 7; cf. Matt. 19: 4-6). Yet, because of the present necessity, it is better to abstain from it (1 Cor. 7: 26, 31; cf. Luke 20: 34-36). Strictly speaking, it could be understood that flesh and blood will not inherit the kingdom of God because of certain delays in development and certain conditions made by the will of the Creator; such an interpretation would not contradict any formal text.

These different ideas have sometimes been considered almost irreconcilable. So H. J. Holtzmann speaks of an antinomy in the pauline conception between a pharisaic element and a hellenistic element: (the first explaining universal death by a historic fact; the second explaining it by a natural necessity)[1] These simplifications are attractive: there is something pathetic in seeing Paul's mind divided between two exigencies (cf. Phil. 1:23): that of the Jewish and biblical tradition and that of Greek culture. But one fact, noted by Holtzmann himself, should show the doubtful nature of this explanation.

In Ecclus 14:17 (natural law) and 25:24 (the woman's influence) there is the same duality and the same is true of Wisdom 2:24 (the devil's envy) and 7:1 or 9:15 (earthly perishable body); so we find it both in a traditional Jew, on whom hellenism had no great influence, and, on the other hand, in an Alexandrine writer, who is not so impregnated with Judaism as Paul. So the duality of tendencies to be observed in Paul is not necessarily the result of the clash of two cultures; it is rather loyalty to a patrimony, present equally in two books, both of which he used.[2] The idea of death as a necessity of

[1] H. J. Holtzmann, Vol. II, p. 56. In principle it is legitimate to beware of trying to make Paul's thought too systematic. But, conversely, R. Bultmann seems to be multiplying the divergencies at will, when he suggests that there are two ways of presenting the connection between death and sin in Paul that are not in harmony with one another: 'the juristic conception of death as the punishment for sin and the conception of death as a fruit organically growing out of sin' (op. cit. p. 249). They are only two expressions of the same thought, stressing at one moment the causality of God and at another the secondary causes. R. Bultmann continues in a less artificial manner and rejoins H. J. Holtzmann when he mentions the lack of harmonization between these two forms of the connection between death and sin, on the one hand, and the idea of the first man, earthly and corruptible, on the other. He does not make this lack of precise elaboration into a real antinomy.

[2] Compare Rom. 9: 17-21 and Ecclus. 16: 15 (Hebrew: the hardening of Pharaoh); 33: 13 (the freedom of the divine potter).—2 Cor. 6: 14-17 and Ecclus. 13: 2, 16-17 (the incompatibility of the just and the unjust).

nature, that is suggested by Holtzmann as the hellenistic factor, can equally well come from the oldest Israelite sources of the Bible : 'We must all die, water spilt on the ground; there is no bringing back the dead' (2 Sam. 14 : 14).[1] Rather than an antinomy we must speak here of lack of precision, or a completion of the sense. The analysis of our present condition allows us to understand death, with the tragic frustration of our plans that it involves, but also with the beneficial return of a worn-out organism into the great reservoir of all life that it brings about, as a consequence of sin at the same time as a normal phase of life's cycle.

The inequalities of these two ways of looking at death cannot be made less by a distinction, which is not expressly made by the epistles, between decease, as the termination of physical life, and death in the full sense, that is, the distressing human significance that decease assumes in a world of sin.[2] The biblical way of thinking, which Paul adopts, dispenses with these explicit conciliations and simply states one partial truth after another.

There is one other interpretation that attempts to establish explicit harmony in pauline thought by the ideas of nature and supernatural privilege.[3] But this depends on theological explan-

—1 Cor. 6: 16 and Ecclus. 19:2 (the man who consorts with harlots).—2 Cor. 11: 3; 1 Tim. 2: 13-14 and Ecclus. 25: 24 (the sin of Eve).—1 Cor. 7: 36 and Ecclus. 42: 9 (daughter passing the age of marriage).—Rom. 1: 19-32 and Wisdom 11: 15; 13: 1 to 15: 19 (the punishment of idolatry by immorality).—Rom. 2: 4 and Wisdom 11: 23; 12: 10; the patience of God and repentance).—Rom. 9: 19 and Wisdom 12: 12 (one does not resist God).—1 Cor. 10: 1-11 and Wisdom 16: 1 to 19: 13 (the lessons drawn from the punishments of the Exodus).—1 Cor. 15: 34 and Wisdom 13: 1 (lack of knowledge of God).—2 Cor. 5: 1, 4 and Wisdom 9: 15 (the body, the earthly tent of the soul).

[1] According to the Knox version.
[2] As R. Bultmann rightly remarks, p. 251.
[3] R. G. Bandas, pp. 135-36.

ation and is beyond the scope of the exegesis of these epistles. If it can be assumed from 1 Cor. 15 : 42-48 that the terrestrial and physical body of the first man was subject to corruption, if it is understood from Rom. 5 : 12 that death entered the world through one man's fault, yet it is not certain that these two ideas have exactly the same content. For what Paul calls 'death', the human, religious, moral and physical affliction, goes far beyond the idea of decease, with the tragic and distressing circumstances by which it is surrounded. So the problem of reconciling two statements that did not deal with exactly the same topic was not so urgent for St Paul that he felt obliged to offer at least an implicit solution.

To return to the principal theme, the relationship between death and sin, we may remark at the outset that, when Paul speaks of it, he almost always mentions personal sins, committed by those whom death claims (Rom. 1 : 32). Even in the passage concerning Adam's sin, he writes : 'If many died through one man's trespass, . . . if, because of one man's trespass, death reigned through that one man . . .' (Rom. 5 : 15, 17), but soon adds that 'sin reigned in death' (5 : 21), à propos of the faults that abounded since the law.[1]

Therefore the question arises as to the connection that St Paul sees between the sin of Adam and the death of all. According to some,[2] the sin of Adam was the occasion of a sentence of death being passed on sin. Since then those who sin feel the weight of the penalty that was then decreed. But it is not difficult to see the exaggerated juridical character of this inter-

[1] Not to mention Rom. 5: 12, in which many exegetes see personal sins.
[2] R. G. Bandas, p. 31, quotes G. A. Fricke and P. Feine. H. J. Holtzmann, Vol. II, p. 55, can be added. H. Weinel, p. 224, speaks of the sentence of death passed once and for all on sinners, but he does not say explicitly that this was on the occasion of Adam's sin. And the context rather suggests the second theory (see below).

pretation of Paul's thought. According to others,[1] Adam has passed on to his descendants a flesh that is subject to desire (lust); he is thus the cause of sins committed by them and of the death punishing them. But to see in sin nothing more than the satisfaction of carnal desire is to restrict the notion of sin too much. There are various passages that show this satisfaction rather as the consequence of a blameworthy indifference towards God, which is the real sin.[2]

Paul does not form any such clearly constructed theory. Following biblical tradition, he simply states the connection between sin and death. He finds no difficulty in presenting, one after the other and sometimes both together in the same context, the sin of the individual or the sin of Adam as the cause of universal death, because he sees their continuity. The sin that came into the world through one man is a power that reveals itself in fact through external actions. Paul is not particularly interested in considering original sin in young children, before it has given rise to sinful deeds.

Whether all men die on account of their own sin or on account of Adam's sin, the difference is not very clearly brought out by Paul in Rom. 5 : 12-21, where he reveals the influence of the first fault. As for very young children, they are included in the fate of sinful adults, and this creates no special difficulty for a mind brought up on the Bible and used to the collective punishments that it recounts.

These conclusions are rather vague. But to say more would

[1] R. G. Bandas, p. 32, quotes M. Goguel and C. Clemen. A. Schlatter, Vol. II, p. 226, notes that Paul connects the carnal nature of man and his mortality, as he connects death and sin. It might be supposed, then, that according to Paul Adam's sin was the origin of this carnal nature of the body. But, in fact, there is no theory of this sort in Paul, says A. Schlatter. It is admitted in A. Juncker, p. 43, that there is no explicit statement.
[2] Rom. 1 : 19-32; Eph. 4 : 17-19; less clearly Titus 2 : 12; 3 : 3.

be to run the risk of attributing to Paul our own frame of mind, categories and doctrines that have only been worked out since his time.

The idea of the corruption of the material world is connected with the theme of death, the penalty for sin. In Rom. 8 : 19-22 Paul recalls, as a doctrine already known, the fact that creation was subjected to vanity against its will but that it preserves the hope of being delivered from it in order to share the glorious freedom of the sons of God. More than once this has been seen as a commentary on Gen. 3 : 17-18, where Yahweh, after the Fall, curses the soil because of man. But there is no indication in the epistle of such an idea and everything in this text can equally well be explained by the idea of a normal condition, entailing a provisory imperfection, destined to disappear.[1] The human body (cf. 1 Cor. 15 : 42-46) and all other beings are at the present time in a state of humiliating servitude. The present situation of the material world can be compared to the state of mankind described in Gal. 4 : 1-5 : the son, before he has reached his majority, is in a condition similar to that of the servants; once the time fixed by his father has come, he gains his freedom and the enjoyment of his inheritance. It is not possible to quote Paul with any confidence in support of an idea of a visible deterioration of the world as a consequence of original sin.

[1] For a more detailed examination of this text, which has really no contribution to make to the doctrine of original sin, see A. -M. Dubarle, 'Le gémissement des créatures dans l'ordre divin du cosmos (Rom. 8 : 19-22)', in *RSPT.*, XXXVIII, (1954), pp. 445-65.

III. THE FLESH

On many occasions Paul spoke of the flesh as something infected by sin. The word 'flesh' should not, however, be understood in a narrow bodily sense, since sometimes it may be a carnal wisdom that is meant (2 Cor. 1 : 12), or the intelligence of the flesh (Col. 2 : 18). Flesh means the whole of the old man, not yet renewed and purified by Christ.[1] Flesh is contaminated by sin : it is a flesh of sin (Rom. 8 : 3), which renders ineffective the moral light brought by the law. Man, torn between the law of sin that reigns in his members and the attraction that the divine law still exercises on his mind, remains powerless to put into practice the good that he loves (Rom. 7 : 14-25). Paul has described this interior struggle, which seems to be the first moral reaction when the conscience awakens, in moving terms.[2]

Elsewhere he suggests that it is on account of their sins of idolatry that God has delivered the pagans to the lusts of their

[1] The analysis of the notion of flesh can be consulted in R. Bultmann, pp. 232-46. In particular, for Paul the word 'flesh' is ambivalent: it denotes a natural reality, created by God, and therefore good, but also a perverse will on the part of man, who wants to find his life exclusively in this transitory reality and thus separate himself from God (pp. 230-31).

[2] This passage has been the object of a well-known diversity of interpretations: for some (the Greek Fathers and a good number of modern writers), it is a question here of man before his conversion to Christ; for others, not so numerous (Augustine, Luther, Calvin, A. Nygren), it is a question of the baptized Christian. A discussion between the modern holders of these two opinions can be found in P. Althaus, 'Zur Auslegung von Röm. 7: 14ff. Antwort an A. Nygren', in *TLZ.*, LXXVII (1952), col. 475-80. Against A. Nygren, who favoured the second interpretation, P. Althaus maintains that in Rom. 7: 14-25 Paul is speaking of the unbaptized man, not from the point of view of the psychological consciousness that such a man may have of his state, but from the point of view of the Christian faith looking back towards the time when it did not yet exist. C. Leslie Mitton, 'Romans VII reconsidered', in *The Expos.*

hearts, to shameful passions and to their base mind.[1] It would be too much to conclude from these expressions that God directly roused the passions that from time to time make themselves felt in the heart; taking into consideration the biblical way of expressing divine causality, it is enough to understand that God let the idolators give way to their passions, whether these already existed or whether they were the immediate result of their religious error. So what we have here is not a lesson on the origin of evil desires, but simply a statement that passions do exist which lead to actual sins.

According to H. J. Holtzmann,[2] sin dominates every man by reason of a natural condition of the flesh. It already existed in the first man and present trespasses only repeat the story of the first temptation and the first fall. This is what Paul insinuates when he describes in Rom. 7 :7-12 the way in which sin seduces him, with expressions recalling the story of the Garden of Eden (Gen. 3). There is a divergence in pauline thought between a Jewish view of the flesh and a hellenistic view. According to the first, Adam's sin is the cause of universal sin and brought about a transformation of human nature:

Times, LXV, (1953-54), pp. 78-81; 99-103; 132-35, adds a third interpretation to the two main ones already existing: it is a question of man relying on himself and not on God, which is a possible danger before baptism as well as after. He gives the following equivalents for the Greek words αὐτὸς ἐγώ: 'entirely on his own', 'on his own', 'left to himself', 'relying on his own resources', 'when I rely on my own resources, and cease to depend on God' (p. 134a).

---

[1]Rom. 1: 24, 26, 28, and again: 'the Gentiles . . . alienated from the life of God because of the ignorance that is in them, due to their hardness of heart; they have become callous and have given themselves up to licentiousness, greedy to practise every kind of uncleanness' (Eph. 4: 17-19). In 1 Thess. 4: 5: 'the passion of lust like heathen who do not know God', it seems clear that the ignorance of God is the cause of the debauchery.
[2]This view of Holtzmann is criticized by A. Juncker, Vol. I, pp. 42-45.

according to the second, sin has its origin in the fact that man is composed of flesh, and revealed itself for the first time in Adam (cf. 1 Cor. 15:45-47). The idea of a contingent historical origin of sin is sometimes expressed, but it does not fit in well with the rest of the teaching; a coherent construction can only retain the view, formulated also in 2 Esdras 3:21, that a principle of sin precedes and gives rise to all actual sins with compelling force.

This interpretation, which has the merit of not *a priori* trying to transform the occasional teachings of the apostle into a rigid system, finally runs into a radical difficulty: the suggestion that Paul held a doctrine that would make sin the necessary consequence of a principle of human nature. But what he has shown of his faith in creation is incompatible with any dualist conception that would make of matter a reality more or less independent or antagonistic towards God. In Paul's eyes man is the image of God (1 Cor. 11:7), and the human body, in the arrangements of its parts, is the work of divine Providence.[1] All that exists apart from God is a creature of God and therefore a good thing. 'The earth is the Lord's, and everything in it.'[2] 'Nothing is unclean in itself ... everything is indeed clean' (Rom. 14:14, 20). 'Everything created by God is good' (1 Tim. 4:4).

No doubt Paul admits the possibility of sinning to be inherent in rational creatures, but without entering into profound speculation on the subject. And this is quite different from the necessity of sinning postulated by H. J. Holtzmann. The factual state described by the epistles must come from a contingent

[1] 1 Cor. 11:15; 12:14-20. Here it is a question of the universal effects of the divine action, realized in all men, and not of the effects of the redemption in Christians, such as the dwelling of the Holy Spirit as in a temple (1 Cor. 6:19), or the promise of resurrection that it contains (Rom. 8:11).
[2] 1 Cor. 10:26, quoting Psalm 24:1.

cause, but what this is is not described with absolute precision.

It would sound quite plausible to say that Paul connected the hold that evil desires have on man with Adam's sin. But again it must be stated that he did not do so expressly. Considering the lack of precision that he displays on the subject of the incorruptibility of the body in 1 Cor. 15:42-52, we should avoid any statements concerning evil desires or concupiscence that are too clear-cut. Before forming any opinion we must examine various passages carefully.

[The struggle between the flesh and the spirit is not formally presented as the consequence of sin.] Strictly speaking, one could see in it the inevitable, even fruitful (cf. 2 Cor. 12:9) condition of human nature. The predominance of the flesh, then of the spirit, characterizes the normal stages of religious and moral life : men of the flesh are babes in Christ (1 Cor. 3:1). Clearly this would not rule out the possibility that in certain cases there might be culpable negligence, delaying the transition from one stage to another, which is what Paul seems to be saying here about his correspondents.

But elsewhere it is a question of sin dwelling in the flesh, in its members, and irresistibly making man captive to the law of sin (7:18, 23). The flesh neutralizes the effect of the law and makes it powerless (Rom. 8:3). The thoughts of the flesh lead to death, for they are hostile to God and cannot submit to his law (Rom. 8:6-7). The Jews themselves once lived like pagans, 'in the passions of their flesh, following the desires of body and mind, and so we were by nature the children of wrath, like the rest of mankind'.[2] The old man is corrupt through

[1]Gal. 5:17; cf. James 4:1; 1 Peter 2:11.
[2]Eph. 2:3. These words: 'we were by nature children of wrath' have been seen by Augustine and others as an expression of original sin. St Jerome, St John Chrysostom and the majority of the ancient Greek commentators understand that it is a question here, by reason of the

deceitful lusts (Eph. 4:22; cf. Col. 3:5-9). This opposition between the new man and the old reminds us of the contrast between Christ and Adam, but no express comparison is made in the texts. The old man is the one in need of redemption and, in the case of pagans, must be crucified with Christ, or, in the case of Christians, has already been crucified, so that the body of flesh may be destroyed and the dominion of sin cease (Rom. 6:6). The new man is, in these times, a predominantly interior reality and is renewed from day to day (2 Cor. 4: 16).

The old man, bound up with sinful desires, cannot, in Paul's eyes, be the work of God. The strong evil desires to which man is subject at present, in spite of any desire he may have to observe God's law, can scarcely be anything but the consequence of an earlier sin. This is not explicitly stated. However the description of the tyranny of these desires, coming between the description of pagan corruption and the recollection of Adam's fault on the one hand (Rom. 1, 5) and the triumphant assurance of the liberation brought by Christ on the other (Rom. 8:1-3), cannot leave much doubt. Evil desires are not simply an annoying result of our complex nature, they belong to that reign of sin, which was brought about by the malice of men, and from which Christ has come to save the redeemed.

context, of the actual sins to which natural concupiscence leads. Cf. J. M. Vosté, *Commentarius in epistolam ad Ephesios*, (1921, pp. 133-34 and Appendix I, pp. 253-60). F. Prat maintains a similar position, Vol. II., pp. 60-61. These two authors admit an indirect allusion to original sin, insofar as this is the origin of concupiscence.

[1] In spite of the absence of quite explicit texts there is nothing unreasonable in finding in Paul at least the basis of a doctrine equivalent to St John's: 'For all that is in the world, the lust of the flesh and the lust of the eyes and the pride of life, is not of the Father but is of the world' (1 John 2: 16). Christ himself said on the subject of the permission for divorce, granted by Moses because of their hardness of heart: 'from the beginning it was not so' (Matt. 19: 8). This implies that the hardness of heart itself did not exist in the beginning.

But any attempt to claim that evil desires, to the extent that they are an affliction that preys on men, come exclusively from Adam's sin[1] and not also from the corrupting influence of the world surrounding a child from birth, prior to any possibility of personal reaction on his part,[2] would be going beyond the letter of the very sketchy teachings of Paul, who did not pause to describe the psychological and moral state of the first man before the Fall.

To what extent did man, at his creation have easy mastery over his passions? Or did he, on the contrary, gain the upper hand laboriously, with an effort which yet was not that struggle doomed to failure experienced by the pagan, as well as the Jew, today? Paul does not answer this question clearly, any more than he tells us what was the original condition which corresponds to bodily decease, which for us today appears in the guise of death. The lack of precision in 1 Cor. 15:20-56 ought to lead the exegete to respect his silence on the origins of concupiscence.

On the one hand Paul does not consider the present state of mankind, in which sin comes from the flesh by a sort of necessity, entirely normal. He would not, therefore, need to define our state of corruption, if he thought of it, in the light of an initial free elevation; it would be enough to do this in the light of the good conditions established by God at the time of creation. On the other hand he does not consider that every difficulty or need for struggle is the result of sin. The troubles from which we suffer may, in part at least, be part of the Creator's

[1] A. Schlatter, Vol. II, p. 226, puts forward this idea as a likely supposition of an interpreter of Paul, while recognizing that there is no explicit theory on this point in the texts. Similarly A. Juncker, Vol. I, p. 43, where he develops various arguments in favour of supplying this point.
[2] A text such as Eph. 4:14 draws attention to the ease with which children allow themselves to be carried away by any influences around them.

plan and may be explained from the religious point of view not by the idea of punishment but by that of divine pedagogy or trial. To understand Paul's thought we need not attribute to him the idea of a privileged state enjoyed by man before his sin.[1] 'St Paul does not tell us what man's conditions would have been if he had not sinned. He does not like, any more than do his colleagues, to explore the nebulous regions of possibilities and hypotheses, and he rarely directs his gaze beyond the actual horizon.'[2]

So there remains a certain lack of precision in Paul's thought. The body with its physical functions is in a normal, though provisional, state : ' "Food is meant for the stomach and the stomach for food"—and God will destroy both the one and the other' (1 Cor. 6 : 13). At the same time the body offers the possibility of sin, from which the Christian can escape (ibid.). But the state of enslavement with regard to sin in which the non-Christian part of mankind lives at the moment on account of the flesh is, in Paul's eyes, too tragic to be considered as normal, and as the equivalent of the state that would have resulted from creation, had there been no sin. No such pessimism can be attributed to the apostle with regard to human nature, neither in its radical form with H. J. Holtzmann nor, with R. G. Bandas, in a form mitigated by the idea of a corrective privilege given at the beginning.

Thus, to state what is not expressed with such precision in the texts, the condition that we now experience in this body of sin (Rom. 6 : 6) is determined both by the creative will and by

[1] It is not very easy to decide in R. Bandas, p. 42, or in F. Prat, Vol. II, p. 75, whether the idea of a privileged state is attributed to Paul himself or simply used to account for his various teachings.

[2] F. Prat, Vol. II, p. 94. It is curious that, when he wrote this, the author did not think of correcting what he wrote earlier, p. 75 (cf. preceding note), when he forgot to make the necessary distinction between the thought of Paul and a later speculative systematization.

the corrupting influence of sin. Paul did not attempt to calculate
the respective roles of either of these two factors in the equi
vocal effect that springs from their meeting, nor to point ou
precisely which sin or sins have produced in us the law of the
members.

The handing on of original sin

Finally Paul admits that Adam's fault has some universa
influence on mankind, into which it introduced sin and death
The transmission of a spiritual heritage in a family or race is a
fact frequently mentioned by the Bible. The choice of Israel
is explained in this way. And, even if Paul does add some limitations to this law of heredity, he admits its fundamenta
validity.[1] It was not particularly hard for him to believe that this
had its disastrous counterpart in the propagation of sin from
the time of the first man. Paul could have accepted this as a
fact, without asking himself how it worked.

However the interpreters of his thought have felt themselves
able to offer explanations, which we must now examine.

Some have thought the comparison drawn between Adam
and Christ capable of extension beyond its explicit content. Just
as the justification conferred by Christ supposes, in order that it
may spread, that each makes it his own by a personal act of
faith, so Adam's sin is to be understood as a collective act, in
which his descendants have a part. Men make their own, by
their own sins, the sin of their ancestor.[2]

[1] Validity: Rom. 9: 4-5; 11: 28-29; 15: 8. Limitation: Rom. 9: 6-8;
Gal. 3: 6-7; 4: 22-32.
[2] H. J. Holtzmann, II, pp. 49-50. It will also be remembered that
Holtzmann sees in Paul several divergent conceptions of sin: apart from
the historical explanation (Rom. 5) there is the psychological explanation. J. Freundorfer, p. 244, refers to C. Clemen and A. Sabatier for
the same line of reasoning based on the parallel between Adam and
Christ.

But the comparison of the two heads of mankind does not make this conclusion necessary. For a positive effect to be produced each partial cause must play its part. For a negative effect to be produced it can be sufficient if one partial cause does not fulfil its function. Thus, for justification to work, the action of Christ and, in dependence on this, the action of the justified faithful are both necessary. For a state of sin to be handed on from the first father to his posterity, it is not necessary that each should sin personally. The *a priori* reasons cannot here make up for Paul's silence; this is all the more true as the whole of the comparison shows clearly enough that not only is there a parallel between Christ and Adam but also from various points of view a disproportion. When he says that 'death spread to all men because all men sinned', Paul is indeed thinking of objectively sinful deeds but not of malice resulting from a personal decision. In his opinion it is not a question of entering a society which it would be possible to remain outside of by a free refusal, but of belonging inevitably to a sinful race and of showing this by one's conduct.

Nor is it certain that Paul thought of physical heredity to account for the existence of sin in the whole human race. In Rom. 5 : 12-19 he does not explicitly mention it. In 1 Cor. 15 : 49 he says, speaking of Adam and Christ : 'Just as we have borne the image of the man of dust, we shall also bear the image of the man of heaven.' This is an echo of Gen. 5 : 3 : 'he (Adam) became the father of a son in his own likeness.' But the similarity of expression, which was probably conscious, does not necessarily mean complete similarity of thought. The parallel

[1]A. Schlatter, II, p. 221, stresses all the uncertainty of attributing to Paul too precise a notion of heredity. The idea of the divine decree was enough for the apostle. E. Stauffer, p. 52, speaks of a historical heritage, including and surpassing the biological heritage.

7

between Adam and Christ shows clearly that physical generation is not the only means by which one man's image is passed
on to another. Paul certainly considers generation as the cause
of the general resemblance between the first father and his race.
But there is nothing to prove that he considered this specially
for this particular characteristic of sin, which is mentioned in
Rom. 5 : 12-19, but is not envisaged by the immediate context
of 1 Cor. 15 :49. There is no systematic theory. In Gal. 4 :29
he mentions the two sons of Abraham, one begotten according
to the flesh, the other according to the spirit : the wording,
which means to contrast a birth about which there was nothing
exceptional and one that came from the divine promise, when
the parents' age allowed them no further hope of children,
shows clearly that Paul does not understand the word
generation with the precise limits of meaning that it has in
modern biology. It means the propagation of mankind in
general.

Some exegetes have proposed a combination of the explanation by personal sins and the explanation by physical heredity.
Adam's sin has produced a weakness in the flesh which com-
municates itself to his posterity by heredity. Inevitably, therefore, each individual is himself led to sin by the evil desires he
feels. His sin is indirectly determined by that of his first ancestor.[1]

This reconstruction is not sound. Paul did not connect the
desires of the flesh clearly with the sin of Adam.[2] Even supposing
that he did admit a causal connection between the two, this

[1]Sanday-Headlam, pp. 134, 136, 146, 147. A. Juncker, op. cit., I, pp.
43, 58, does not mention the word, heredity, but states as the conclusion
of a long discussion that the flesh is sinful not because of any necessity of
nature, but because of Adam's sin. C. R. Smith, pp. 172-74, simply
appeals to heredity in a paraphrase of Rom. 5: 12-13, which provides no
argument at all.
[2]Cf. supra, pp. 188-90.

new power, recognized in carnal desires, should have appeared to him rather as an excuse for the inordinate actions that they provoked, just as ignorance of the law means that sin is not imputed. And finally, several passages in the epistles tell of men giving in to their guilty passions because they are already sinners and not of men becoming sinners by giving in to their passions. It seems impossible, therefore, to present this explanation of the universal diffusion of sin by means of a hereditary weakness of the flesh as part of Paul's thought.

Consequently several interpreters of Paul come to adopt a solidarist view. Mankind forms a whole and the action of the ancestor is at the same time that of all his posterity. In this way all sin in Adam, when he breaks the divine commandment.[2] Perhaps it is wise to be satisfied with formulas of this nature, if it is realized that really they do nothing but repeat in different words the assertion of Rom. 5 : 12, 19.

It is the theologians more than the exegetes who sometimes speak of a juridical imputation of Adam's sin to his descendants by a free decree of God. There is no word of this in Paul. He does strongly emphasize the transcendent freedom of God, which man cannot resist (Rom. 9 : 20), but he also asserts God's justice. And it would scarcely be following the direction of Paul's thought to allege the imputation to a whole race of the guilt of its first father, in order to explain a passage that stresses the delicacy of God's retributive justice by stating that sins of ignorance are not counted (Rom. 5 : 13).

In conclusion, Paul teaches a handing on of sin from Adam

[1]For example Rom. 1: 24-28; Eph. 4: 17-19.
[2]J. Freundorfer, pp. 242, 257, 263; M. Meinertz, p. 29. F. R. Tennant, while using similar expressions, finally reduces the mystical realism recognized in Paul to a simple manner of speaking (p. 262) and grants that others would use the word forensic for the state of sin that he calls mystic.

to all men without explaining how it operates. He is content to take up the thought of Genesis, making explicit the idea that the heritage of the first man contains not only death but also sin. He is concerned, not to develop a theory on the origin of sin, but to show the Saviour's power over sin, to show that this influence of one man on the fate of all, which is the essence of the Christian faith, is in harmony with the content of God's word. He does not feel the need to ask how exactly sin was passed on, any more than he bothered to explain how the temptation of the devil (a fact that was quite certain) acted on the mind or heart of men to provoke them to evil.[1]

The sum of all the sins of mankind

If we want a true picture of original sin according to St Paul, we must at least summarily restore it to the context of the general corruption and the sins of mankind. For it is so far from occupying the whole stage, that it has been claimed, in rather an overstatement, that 'it only has an episodic part to play in Paul'.[1]

Already the classical passage of Rom. 5, recalls the sins before the Law (v. 13) and those that the law bred in profusion (v. 20). Here the attention is drawn in the first place, to the Chosen People. But various texts consider the pagan world. 1 Cor. 6:9-11 reminds the faithful of the vices from which they were purified by baptism. Titus 3:3-5 draws a similar picture and ends with a reference to the 'washing of regeneration'. According to Eph. 2:1-5 pagans and Jews were dead in their sins when God's grace brought them to life.[3] Ignorance of God is

[1] 1 Cor. 7: 5; 2 Cor. 2: 11; 4: 4; 11: 3, 14; Eph. 2: 2; 4: 27; 6: 11-12; 1 Thess. 3: 5; 2 Thess. 2: 9; 1 Tim. 3: 7; 5: 15; 2 Tim. 2: 26.
[2] J. Bonsirven, p. 114.
[3] Cf. also Eph. 5: 6-12; Col. 3: 5-7.

what lies at the root of evil conduct.[1] This theme is treated with
great vigour in Rom. 1 : 18-32, where the free responsibility of
men is stressed. A culpable repudiation of God, culminating in
idolatry, brought down the punishment of the most shameful
immorality, particularly sexual aberration.[2] Already the book of
Wisdom (13-15) had developed this stern indictment of pagan
corruption at some length. It is noteworthy that both these
texts referred elsewhere to death coming into the world, through
the envy of the devil (Wisdom 2 : 24) and by the sin of one man
(Rom. 5 : 12). The difference of the actual wording must not
obscure the identity of the allusion to the account of the Fall
in Genesis.

However Paul does not stress the baneful role of example and
the corrupting pressure exercised by society in the spread of
idolatry as much as Wisdom does.[3] He considers the pagans in
general and denounces their guilt without asking if it admits
of degrees according to the individual or if there are mitigating
circumstances for some. But clearly he does not attribute an
equal degree of malice in sin to everyone, any more than he

[1] Eph. 4: 17-19; cf. 1 Thess. 4: 5.
[2] According to a hypothesis of M. Goguel (pp. 155-56), this passage of
Romans does not refer to a general state in mankind, not even to contemporary paganism; its object is 'the origin of sin, not in the individual,
but in the race'. In the disobedience of Adam Paul would have seen
'an allegorical account of the idolatry of the first men'. The author himself admits the very conjectural nature of this interpretation, and it is
difficult to reconcile with the texts in which Paul showed that he took
the details of the creation and of the Fall very literally. And so, to cor-
roborate his thesis, M. Goguel quotes the allegory taken from the story
of Isaac and Ishmael. But it is one thing to attach a prophetic meaning
to a story understood historically, and another thing to interpret one and
the same story as referring to real past events, but on one occasion keeping to the material reality of the circumstances, and on another seeing
in them only a free symbolic representation of events. To admit such a
difference in attitude, we should have to show that Paul spoke far more
clearly than he did in Rom. 1.
[3] Wisdom 14: 11-21; 15: 4-13.

197

means to accuse everyone of homosexuality. He is not unaware of the influence of example and of false doctrines. He speaks of them more than once in his epistles, in passages which are in the first place directed at the faithful.[1] But it goes without saying that he considers that the pagans are even more exposed to this danger, since in 1 Cor. 15:33 he warns against corrupting company by quoting a verse of the pagan poet Menander.

This evil extends far beyond original sin and the responsibility of men is involved in it. The pagans know God's law (Rom. 1:32): they have the law written in their hearts (Rom. 2:15), so clearly that they are able to observe it and some of them are better than Jews who break the law (Rom. 2:27). Paul, with his clipped phrases, does not make it clear to what extent pagans can do good. He is anxious that the task of judging those who are outside should be left completely to God (1 Cor. 5:13). The sins that followed the first transgression were not always merely its inevitable consequence; in some cases they were the result of a real freedom to do good or evil. And yet at the same time each man feels the weight of the legacy of his first father and of the influence (by word and example) of the society in which he lives. There is an avalanche of sins,[2] in which Paul does not try to find out the determining part of each factor; he proclaims to all, Jew and Greek, the good news of salvation in Jesus Christ, the pardon of each and every sin.

Conclusion

From this study of Paul's thought we can see its depths and

[1] Seduction by false doctrines: Rom. 16: 18; Eph. 5: 6; Col. 2: 8; Titus 1: 10-11. Corrupting influence: 2 Tim. 3: 6, 13. Wicked example: Rom. 14: 13; 1 Cor. 8: 10, 13. Weakness of children: Eph. 4: 14.
[2] M. Meinertz, Vol. II, p. 30.

also its very unsystematic character. In different passages the apostle reveals various aspects of our condition, without indicating exactly how they are connected.[1]

In Rom. 1 : 19-32 attention is centred on the present guilt of men. The evil is a collective one, idolatry; but it comes from a free will that knows God and yet refuses to honour him. Rom. 5 : 12-21 states the universal influence of Adam's sin. Up to the time of Moses men did sin but without any knowledge of the divine law, so that there was no responsibility, at least on a universal scale. What leads to death is not personal malice but one sin, which spread from the first father. Rom. 7 : 7-24 describes the influence in each individual of a concupiscence that leads each to sin.

In Rom. 5 and 7 (unlike Rom. 1) Paul finds a certain excuse for sins that have actually been committed because of a universal racial influence and, for a certain time, absence of the law, or because of internal psychological constraint. In his eyes this is real sin, a real separation from God, entailing the objective consequence of death but involving no inward malice, no personal revolt against God, no deliberate transgression. The outward act reveals an already existing state.

While some passages describe the reign of sin and the redemption brought by Christ, others consider mankind as a son passing through a period of youthful dependence before arriving with Christ at the age when it can freely dispose of its inheritance. The texts suggesting that our bodily weaknesses and our inglorious condition are quite normal can easily be connected with this last view. Here Paul is taking up thoughts more fully developed in the Wisdom books, while elsewhere he surpasses

---

[1] J. Freundorfer, p. 216, underlines the fact that in Rom. 5 Paul's main object is not to teach what is the origin of sin, but to exalt the work of Christ.

his predecessors by teaching that the solidarity of the human race entails not only some suffering but a real contagion of sin.

Thus the epistles present the destiny of mankind under two aspects in turns: the aspect of sin spreading, increasing and dominating; and the aspect of a providential growth, reaching adult stature by stages. In this way they explain the teaching offered in a synthetic fashion by the parable of the weeds.

However we look at it, Christ is the source of good, either because he delivers us from sin or because he brings a development to its conclusion. He alone is the Saviour, according to the belief of the whole of the New Testament. Paul, in company with the other inspired authors, is a witness to this conviction of the Christian community. But he is the only one to compare Adam, the author of universal perdition, with the Saviour of all.

To remain faithful to Paul's thought, we need not present original sin either as the sole source of evil in mankind or as more powerful than the forces of salvation. Of course, in Paul's opinion, all men will not be saved. But the love of God, which acted by raising up Christ, the dispenser of justification and life, is more effective than the sin and death that came through Adam.

THE SPECIAL DOCTRINE OF ORIGINAL SIN

6

Original Sin and the Justice of God

THE doctrine of original sin frequently raises a difficult problem for some people : how can a just God allow each man to be the victim of a fault committed by a distant ancestor ? Now that we have tried to find the precise nature of original sin according to the Scriptures, there remains the question whether these same Scriptures allow us to solve, or at least lessen, this difficulty which seems so shocking to many. In fact the biblical authors did not dwell on the question. But, if they have no ready-made solution to offer us, nearly all of them did emphatically state the principle of God's just retribution and some described its application to problems similar to the one that has just been stated. Even in an exposition of biblical theology, careful to distinguish methodically between the exploration of Scripture and the systematic elaboration of the information thus gained, it is, therefore, possible to suggest some points that speculative theology will have to take into account.

If the faith of Israel had long been satisfied with the idea of a justice that it considered only approximate and applying to social groups, families or peoples rather than to individuals, nowhere did the inspired witnesses of this faith completely lose sight of the individual. And almost every book of the Bible contains, if not the actual words : 'God will requite man according to his works',[1] at least some indication of a firm belief in providential justice towards the individual, even at a time when the idea of collective retribution was predominant.[2]

The references that could be listed are inevitably a little vague in outline. One passes imperceptibly from statements concerning collective justice to statements concerning individual justice. For example, in certain cases, where the punishment falls on

---

[1] The formula: 'God will render to every man according to his works' appears with slight variations in the following texts: Jer. 17: 10; 32: 19; Psalm 62: 13; Prov. 24: 12; Job. 34: 11; Ecclus. 16: 12-14; 35: 24; Matt. 16: 27; Rom. 2: 6; 1 Cor. 3: 8; 1 Peter 1: 17; Apoc. 2: 23; 20: 12-13; 22: 12. In the following texts it is only a question of an individual or a definite category: 2 Sam. 3: 39; Jer. 25: 14; Psalm 18: 21; 28: 4; Lam. 3: 64; 2 Cor. 11: 15; 2 Tim. 4: 14; Apoc. 18: 6. The same idea appears again in a slightly different form in 1 Sam. 2: 30; 26: 23; Isaias 59: 18; Psalm 18: 26-27; Eccles. 12: 14; Ecclus. 11: 26 (G); John 5: 29; Rom. 14: 12; 2 Cor. 5: 10; 11: 15; Gal. 6: 5; Eph. 6: 8. And it underlies the countless assertions of divine justice.

[2] Abimelech pleads his good faith in order not to be punished by God for an unconscious guilt: Gen. 20: 4-7. Abraham intercedes on behalf of Sodom because of the just that it contained: Gen. 18: 25. The plague of hail spares the Egyptians who listened to Moses: Exod. 9: 19-21; Moses is spared in the threatened destruction of the people: Exod. 32: 10; Deut. 9: 14. The general punishment of the murmurers makes an exception of Caleb and Joshua: Num. 14: 20-24, 30-31. The law provides that only the culprit should be put to death: Deut. 24: 16. Rahab escapes the condemnation of Jericho: Joshua 6: 25. Abimelech perishes because of his wickedness: Judges 9: 56-57. Ruth is rewarded for her faithfulness. The sons of Heli are killed in the battle against the Philistines: 1 Sam. 4: 17. Saul loses the kingdom, which is given to another more worthy: 1 Sam. 15: 28. David realizes that he ought to be punished personally for his fault: 2 Sam. 24: 17. The young son of Jeroboam is the only one to receive a decent burial, for he is the only good one in the family: 1 Kings 14: 13. A foreigner, the widow of Sarepta, who had been kind to Elias, is preserved from the famine and obtains the return of her son to life: 1 Kings 17: 11-24. Josias, on account of his penitence on the occasion of the finding of the law, obtains the grace of dying before the national catastrophe: 2 Kings 22: 19-20. Joachim is to have neither burial nor successor on the throne, because of his hostility towards Jeremias: Jer. 36: 30. The false prophet Ananias is struck by an early death for preaching revolt against Yahweh: Jer. 28: 17.

the guilty and not on the whole people, there are still traces of collective retribution, since the immediate family is involved in the fate of its head: so it was with Core, Dathan and Abiron, or Achan.[1]

At the time of the exile two prophets stated explicitly what had up to then only been glimpsed more or less clearly, and asserted in the most formal manner the individual nature of divine sanctions. Jeremias and Ezechiel protest against the proverb that was passing from mouth to mouth among their contemporaries: 'The fathers have eaten sour grapes, and the children's teeth are set on edge.'[2] Both announce that in future everyone will bear the penalty for his own sins only. On the one hand, this categorical teaching brings to a head the conflict between the demands of justice and the fact of solidarity in sin between the generations but, on the other hand, it offers a complete solution, for it places the reward of each according to his merits in the future. Without denying the facts of experience it makes it clear that they are not Providence's last word.

It is instructive to study briefly the vicissitudes of the reflexion started by the two prophets on the theme of retributive justice. Although neither of them denied the actual truth expressed in the saying that they condemned,[3] certain minds have thought it possible to maintain that suffering was always the penalty for an earlier, personal sin. This stringent theory was introduced into the Bible only to be energetically rejected by the book of Job and by Ecclesiastes: the misfortunes that befall the

---

[1] Num. 16: 25-32; Joshua 7: 24. Even in the cases mentioned above, n. 2. a similar mixture of collective and individual retribution is to be noticed, David chooses to see his people decimated by the plague and only then realizes that he ought to be punished personally: 2 Sam. 24: 12-17. Joachim is punished with his family and his people: Jer. 36: 31.
[2] Jer. 31: 29; Ezech. 18: 2.
[3] Jer. 32: 18; Ezech. 21: 8.

innocent are a tragic reality, which cannot be set aside by any *a priori* argument.

Eventually the disproportion between the individual's fate and his deserts, which had long been a source of scandal to faithful souls, was seen as temporary. A psalmist, after describing his sadness and surprise, shares the thought that finally set his mind at rest : sudden ruin will bring the insolent triumph of the wicked to nought, and the faithful soul has above all the happiness, which is greater than anything else, of being always with his God (Psalm 73). It may be asked whether these profound verses refer to the future life or are confined to the joy given here below by the divine presence.[1] At all events they prepared the way for the doctrine of the book of Wisdom, which sets providential retribution in the next life.[2]

For this late book misfortunes that befall the just, early death or even violent death in persecution, are nothing in comparison with eternal life, which is destined for those who remain faithful, but only as a test to reveal those who are worthy of God (Wisdom 3 : 1-9). The anomaly of the success of the persecutors and the torment of their victims is of short duration : decease will come to re-establish order and open the way to a world where Providence's designs for man will be put into effect.

Clearly the author is considering an extreme case, but one that is valuable as an example. He wants to suggest his thought in a concrete fashion rather than proceed by the statement of abstract principles. For him, everyone (even the just and happy

[1]For a recent discussion on this point, see R. Martin-Achard, *De la Mort à la Résurrection d'après l'Ancien Testament*, (1956), pp. 127-33. Many points complementary to the subject treated briefly in this chapter are dealt with in a general way in this book. See especially pp. 165-70 on God's justice.
[2]Consult M. -J. Lagrange, 'Le livre de la Sagesse. Sa doctrine des fins dernières', in *RB.*, (1907), pp. 85-104; R. Schütz, *Les idées eschatologiques du livre de la Sagesse*, (1935).

man, dying in a ripe old age, although such a case is not mentioned) will in the end receive according to his works—not here below but after death which is a mere seeming for the just, who will enjoy the close company of God, but is the beginning of frightful torment for the wicked.[1]

After a long period of groping on the part of the sages, the latest of them sheds decisive light on the problem by placing in an indefinite future, beyond the present, earthly existence, the realization of individual retribution promised by the two prophets Jeremias and Ezechiel, contemporaries of the exile. The principle that God renders to each according to his works, which was part of Israel's faith from the beginning, is upheld but without the naïve applications it had previously known. The lessons of experience forced them to defer the manifestation of divine justice promised by the prophets beyond the realms of experience. Wisdom shows the way to harmonize two frames of mind that had hitherto remained in a state of unresolved tension : audacious hope and simultaneous acknowledgement of evil in the world.

However this book did not diagnose the whole extent of the evil from which mankind is suffering, for it did not explicitly envisage a universal original sin, a real separation from God, independent of the individual will. It provides only the setting in which a fact, only fully brought to light by Paul, can be fitted without detriment to the justice of Providence.

In a certain sense the Christian can be more pessimistic than the author of Job or Ecclesiastes. For, far from denying the facts revealed by the old sages, he knows that they have a

[1]Apart from the book's essential contribution, the doctrine of eternal life, the idea that divine justice takes account of the subjective conditions of each man may be found in passing: 'For the lowliest man may be pardoned in mercy, but mighty men will be mightily tested' (Wisdom 6: 6).

gravity that had been scarcely suspected up to then. In his view, everyone, as a consequence of a fault that he did not commit, undergoes not only something that affects his well-being but a real deterioration in his religious condition. The physical or mental sufferings, the moral errors or difficulties that face man, have a definite connection with a stain of sin which really contaminates us. The result of this is always, in part at least, a moral powerlessness and often anguish of conscience.

Such a doctrine provides a clear framework for a valid description and explanation of our wretched condition but it does not leave God's justice free from criticism. For, if the deliberate fault of the creature is presented as the root of evil, then the scandal of a poisoned heritage passing from one generation to another assumes even greater proportions, since it is not only a question of misfortune but of sin. The sour grapes eaten by the fathers are seen to be infinitely more harmful to the children then the contemporaries of Jeremias and Ezechiel ever imagined. The problem that the two prophets had to face has become more acute. It must be resolved along the lines of thought marked put by them and continued into a future life by the book of Wisdom, that is to say not by looking back for past causes but by looking forward in hope to a just judgement to come.

Of all the books in the Bible there is none that reveals more clearly all delicate nuances of divine justice than the book that announces the Good News of grace. In harmony with the teaching that was the great achievement of the book of Wisdom, Jesus teaches that persecution, with all its mortal dangers, is not to be feared. It can have only limited effects: it can kill the body but it cannot affect the soul. In the midst of all dangers the hairs of our heads are numbered.[1] What is beyond man's

[1] Matt. 10: 28-30; Luke 12: 4-7; cf. 21: 18.

powers of estimation does not escape the precise knowledge of God and will be the object of an accurate judgement. A divine retaliation will be carried out in due course and in due measure.[1] The Son of Man, the judge foretold by the prophet Daniel, will come in all his glory, rendering to each according to his works and taking no account of the skill that a man may have shown in preserving his life in difficult times or of apparent successes such as the conquest of an empire.[2]

God knows men's hearts and it may be, as in the case of the pharisees, that what men consider sublime is an abomination in God's eyes.[3] But on the last day the assessment of true values, which now is beyond human powers, will infallibly be carried out by the ministry of the angels.[4] Jesus teaches that real uncleanness comes from the violation of the commandments as a result of a personal choice of the heart, not from chance external contacts, which cannot be avoided.[5] What is more, he teaches that the transgressions themselves will be judged, not according to some abstract rule of morality but in view of the concrete opportunities offered to each in the gifts that have actually been received. The judgement pronounced on Sodom, that typical example of pagan corruption, will be more lenient than that which falls on the towns of Galilee, which rejected the news of salvation in the days of Jesus.[6] It was only because they lacked the miracles that were worked so freely in Corozain and Bethsaida that Tyre and Sidon were not converted like the Ninivites threatened by Jonah: thus gentile towns will obtain greater

[1] Matt. 10: 32-33; Luke 12: 8-9; Mark 8: 38; Luke 9: 26; cf. Matt. 7: 1; Mark 4: 24; Luke 6: 30.
[2] Matt. 16: 27; cf. 25: 31-46; Daniel 7: 13-14.
[3] Luke 16: 15; cf. Matt. 23: 28.
[4] This is the conclusion of the parable of the weeds: Matt. 13: 41.
[5] Matt. 15: 1-20; Mark 7: 1-23.
[6] Matt. 10: 15; 11: 24; Luke 10: 12.

indulgence on the day of judgement.[1] Then, perhaps, after long delays, 'that servant who knew his master's will, but did not make ready or act according to his will, shall receive a severe beating. But he who did not know, and did what deserved a beating, shall receive a light beating. Everyone to whom much is given, of him will much be required'.[2] That is why each man will be judged according to his words, to be justified or condemned according to his knowledge of God's law.[3]

On the day of the final reckoning those who have put the same effort into the development of a capital that was originally different for each individual will receive the same reward, according to the parable of the talents.[4] Those who originally received equal capital will receive reward in proportion to the effort put into its development, according to the parable of the pounds.[5] And laziness and lack of effort will be punished. Even where it seems to be a picture of undeserved generosity, careful scrutiny reveals a more exact justice than that of human payments and one that is able to take intentions into account. When evening has come the owner of the vineyard gives the same wages to all his workers. Those who did not find employment till late in the day, in spite of their good intentions, receive a silver piece, exactly the same as those who have worked since morning.[6]

All these various Gospel stories suggest and in the end impose the idea of a strict fairness, scrupulously exact but not petty, a justice that will take into account all the initial determination of our free activity by temperament, social environment and all

[1]Matt. 11: 21-22; Luke 10: 13-14.
[2]Luke 12: 47-48.
[3]Matt. 12: 37; cf. 25: 26-27; Luke 19: 22; John 5: 45-46; 15: 22-24.
[4]Matt. 25: 20-33.
[5]Luke 19: 16-19.
[6]Matt. 20: 1-15.

the varied circumstances that give or prevent access to the common economy of salvation.

This Gospel teaching finds an echo in St Paul. God is the just judge (2 Tim. 4 : 8), whose judgement is just towards the persecutors and their victims (2 Thess. 1 : 5-7). The judgement that is passed rightly falls on those who do evil (Rom. 2 : 2). With God there is no respect of persons, that is to say, he is not influenced by considerations of race[1] or class.[2] He will render to each according to his works. At first sight this statement suggests the idea of external works, within the range of human observation (Rom. 2 : 6-8), but it is soon to be made clearer. In fact, account must be taken of the different degrees of knowledge that everyone has of the law : 'All who have sinned without the law will also perish without the law, and all who have sinned under the law will be judged by the law' (Rom. 2 : 12). This knowledge possessed by the individual is an essential element of the divine judgement and Paul insists on the increased responsibility of anyone who claims to have the light : it can happen that a man condemns himself by approving (Rom. 14 : 22) or condemning others (Rom. 2 : 1). He was himself once a persecutor : but he acted in ignorance, and was able to obtain mercy (1 Tim. 1 : 13). Paul goes so far as to say : 'Sin is not counted where there is no law' (Rom. 5 : 13), a formula that rather simplifies matters and calls for some further precision. For, apart from the external promulgation of the law of Moses, there is the fact that God has secretly written his law in the hearts of pagans (Rom. 2 : 14-15). The existence of this internal law, which is open to a good deal of obscurity in its subjective certainty, as well as in its translation into deeds, makes judgement here and now impossible : so it is reserved for the future

[1] Rom. 2: 11; Gal. 2: 6.
[2] Eph. 6: 9; Col. 3: 25.

(Rom. 12 : 19). The Lord will one day reveal secret intentions, which for the moment are still hidden in the hearts of every man.[1] For the present the Christian cannot claim to judge those who are outside, Jews or pagans (1 Cor. 5 : 13), for what the law says is said to those who are under the law (Rom. 3 : 19) and its demands cannot simply be applied to those who have no knowledge of it.

Together with this teaching about the judgement according to works, there is something that at first has a very different sound. As so often happens in the Bible, Paul is expressing various truths one after the other, without directly showing how they fit together. So there are divine actions that are determined by prevenient grace and not by the desire to do justice to everyone.

Amongst the people of Israel in Paul's time, some recognized in Jesus the Saviour announced by the prophets, as in the time of Elias seven thousand men had remained faithful to the true God : 'So too at the present time there is a remnant chosen by grace. But if it is by grace, it is no longer on the basis of works; otherwise grace would no longer be grace' (Rom. 11 : 5-6). And what is true of the Israelites is equally true of the pagans, amongst whom a certain number were called to salvation in Christ : 'For by grace you have been saved through faith; and this is not your own doing, it is the gift of God—not because of works, lest any man should boast.'[2]

When he exalts the grace of God in this way, because it acts independently of any consideration of works, the apostle is not speaking of the judgement that will decide the fate of each on the last day but of the call to a privileged state : the possession of the Christian faith. The fact that some receive this gift and

[1] 1 Cor. 4: 4-5; Rom. 2: 16.
[2] Eph. 2: 8-9; cf. Gal. 2: 16; Rom. 3: 28; Titus 3:5; 2 Tim. 1: 9.

others do not is not due to the greater or less perfection of the works that have gone before. Divine favour alone, which owes nothing to anybody, makes the decision. This fact is perfectly compatible with a further judgement according to the use that is made of the gifts received. And this is precisely what Paul means when he goes on to teach that the faithful are 'created in Christ Jesus for good works, which God prepared beforehand, that we should walk in them' (Eph. 2 : 10).

It is in this light that we must understand the election and the hardening of which Rom. 9 speaks. Among the descendants of Abraham, in the course of successive generations, the grace of God again made its choices. The alliance was not bound automatically to membership of a certain family. God chose between Isaac and Ismael, between Jacob and Esau. He shows mercy to whom he chooses and he hardens whom he will, as can be seen from what Scripture says about Moses and Pharaoh; and he finds his glory in his adversaries as well as in his servants. Nothing can oppose his will. God is as free with regard to men as the potter who makes vessel destined for different purposes from the same clay; and the handiwork cannot ask the maker the reasons for his decisions (Rom. 9:20-21). This was a classical metaphor in Israel, used to describe the creation of man by God[1] and above all the sovereign freedom of God with regard to his creatures.[2] It is noticeable, however, that Jeremias chose to bring out something other than an independence that had no need to justify itself to anyone, when he developed this comparison. For him the pliable clay, before it is baked, represents the action of God, always capable of modification in accordance

[1] Gen. 2: 7; Isaias 64: 7; Job 10: 9; 33: 6.
[2] Isaias 29: 16; 45: 9. Paul takes the terms of the first text according to the Septuagint literally and draws inspiration from the second. Cf. also Ecclus. 33: 13; Wisdom 15: 7 (which does not apply to the work of God); 2 Tim. 2: 20.

with human actions: the divine 'repentance' corresponds to conversion, and conversely the unfaithfulness of a people brings the cancelling of the blessings that had been given in the first place.[1] There is indeed a decision of God that sometimes precedes the decision of man, but this does not suppress the operation of a just final retribution.

No doubt, when Paul speaks of Moses and Pharaoh, he has not the same idea in his mind as Jeremias when he was reflecting on the work of the potter. For the moment, his attention is fixed on the place given to each in the visble economy of salvation. It is the all-powerful will of the Lord that decides this, but that does not prejudge the eternal fate reserved for everyone on the basis of his conduct.[2] Paul clearly taught that there was a judgement to come that would be based on the free use made by men of the gifts that they had received. In this way he could have no difficulty in distinguishing between a situation that was favourable or unfavourable in the official regime of revelation and the worth of every person in God's eyes.[3] Earlier he did in fact contrast the man who was outwardly a

---

[1] Jer. 18: 1-10; cf. 26: 13, 19; Zac. 1: 3; Mal. 3: 7.

[2] M. -J. Lagrange writes: 'He (Paul) is speaking of the call by God to a privileged position in the order of salvation. . . . What is said of the action of an individual in history must not be understood of his moral destiny in eternity', *Saint Paul, Epître aux Romains*, (1916, 1931), pp. 246-47. In the same way a protestant exegete, E. Gaugler, writes: 'It is only a question of the role of the ruler in the history of salvation, it is not a question of this man's personal fate at the judgement', *Der Römerbrief*, II, (1952), p. 53; quoted by O. Michel, *Der Brief an die Römer*, (1955), p. 209, n. 3.

[3] This is disputed by a recent commentator, O. Michel: 'A distinction between the historic role that God assigns to man and the eternal judgement that is passed on him is difficult to maintain', *Der Brief an die Römer*, p. 209. Unfortunately there is nothing to support this denial. And the distinction in question is to be found in the words of Jesus about Sodom, Tyre or Sidon (Matt. 10: 15; 11: 21-24; Luke 10: 13-15), or in the parable about the workers employed at the eleventh hour (Matt. 20: 1-16), not to mention St Paul (1 Cor. 5: 12).

Jew, circumcised according to the flesh, and the man who was a Jew at heart, whose praise comes not from men but from God (Rom. 2 :29). He even considered expressly the paradox of a persecutor of the Chosen People, such as Pharaoh, acting in good faith. He was once a blasphemer himself and persecuted the first disciples, and he found mercy because of his ignorance : an example of God's patience towards the believers (1 Tim. 1 :13-16). Thus the call of grace and the judgement according to works are not mutually exclusive, because they do not refer to the same stages of salvation. Sometimes we can even see how the call of grace does not indeed anticipate the definitive judgement but is roughly in keeping with certain laws of justice, and in this there is a promise for the future. In spite of his sinful past Paul was received in grace, excused as he was by his ignorance. And Cornelius, the Roman centurion, obtained the grace of hearing the Christian Gospel by his prayers and almsgiving (Acts 10 :4, 31, 35).

Now that we have seen the scriptural evidence for the delicacy and accuracy of divine justice and its universal application, we should do well to consider some other ideas as well. In this way new points of view on the problem of providential justice will emerge which a systematic exposition of original sin will have to take into account. The biblical writers, confronted with the unutterable mystery of God, delight in an abundance of expressions that are deficient in themselves, and they are not content to use one that could be considered exhaustive. It would, therefore, be imprudent to seize on a principle, even one drawn from a great number of texts, without careful examination to see whether there is not a complementary principle which would compel us to tone down the application of the first. Alongside the very approximate justice that reveals itself in this present life, alongside the perfect justice that is promised in the future life, Scripture speaks of God's intention to test and instruct men.

More than any other book of the Bible, Genesis was anxious to show how the consequences of an ancestor's conduct make themselves felt in his race, after him.[1] There is a certain justice in this, which must not be overlooked even if its collective nature prevents it from being fully satisfying. The theology of original sin runs smoothly along this line of thought, which sees the present determined by the past. However in the book of Genesis, so constantly prone to show suffering as the penalty for sin, we find a most striking example of an entirely different idea : the ordeal of Abraham (Gen. 22). The frightful situation in which the patriarch finds himself, commanded to sacrifice his dearly loved son, is not connected with the expiation of any earlier fault : it is a test to which God puts his faithful servant before confirming the promises already made to him.

On occasion, this idea of a test appears again in the Bible.[2] It underlies the story of Job, although the word itself is not mentioned. It offers a different religious explanation of suffering from the more ordinary one, that used to call it the punishment of a fault, the universal validity of which the book of Job sets out to contest. Sometimes this idea of a test is the object of wider development. Thus a meditation in Deut. 8 on the vicissitudes of the wandering in the desert after the departure from Egypt sees in all the privations suffered by Israel the effect of a fatherly solicitude : Yahweh intended to test his people, to see whether or not they would keep his commandments, and at the same time to instruct them as a father instructs his son.

[1] The various peoples or tribes are normally traced back to an ancestor from whom they received both their name and their own character.
[2] Exod. 15: 25; 16: 4; 20: 20; Deut. 13: 4; 33: 8; 2 Chron. 32: 31; Psalm 17: 3; 26: 2; 66: 10; Tob. 12: 14; Ecclus. 2: 1-6; 4: 17; Wisdom 3: 5-6.

The scarcity imposed by circumstances taught a lesson, which they could not have learned in any other way, obliging them to do without certain satisfactions, which they had hitherto taken for granted, in order that they might receive a new and better satisfaction, thus increasing their confidence in a Providence rich in all its ways.[1]

This suffering, which is a trial and at the same time a lesson, can be the result of sin : in that case it is a punishment in addition. The three ideas are associated in the prologue of the book of Judges : the continued existence of the former populations of Canaan among the newly established Israelites was the punishment of their negligence in not expelling them, a providential occasion for testing the faithfulness of the people, and finally a help in training the younger generations in the art of war (Judges 2 : 20 to 3 : 6).

The fact that the various ideas come together in this particular case must not be taken as a statement of a general principle, in the sense that all suffering that serves to test or educate derives in every case from sin. Such a principle is not valid in the case of the individual considered in isolation and has been rejected in the most categorical fashion by the book of Job and Ecclesiastes. Experience shows that everyone may have to suffer without deserving it, as a punishment for his faults.

Even if one considers large groups, or mankind as a whole, such a strict generalization cannot be maintained. Certainly, by and large, a group considered over a certain period of time more regularly meets the fate that it deserves than does an individual :

[1]The metaphor of the crucible in which metals are purified conveys the idea of a trial and at the same time the idea of education, sometimes that of punishment as well: Isaias 48 : 10; Jer. 6 : 27-30; 9 : 6; Ezech. 22 : 17; Mal. 3 : 3; Zac. 13 : 9; Psalm 66 : 10; Prov. 17 : 3; Wisdom 3 : 6; 1 Peter 1 : 7. The idea of a painful education is found again in Prov. 3 : 11-12; Psalm 119 : 71; Ecclus. 6 : 18-26.

in the long run chance events cancel one another out. However, even on this level of global consideration, there are exceptions : for example, Psalm 44 denies that the current national distress is the effect of any infidelity on the part of the people.

Thus the Bible appeals to ideas other than the punishment of sin to explain suffering, and does not always link these with the idea of punitive justice. Because of our condition as creatures, we are subject to a trial, in which our freedom may lead to failure but in which difficulties can become the occasion for progress. Any theology of original sin or rather original justice should take this as a warning to be cautious. To describe the state that went before the Fall, Genesis was content with some very discreet suggestions whose sobriety becomes even more apparent when compared with the profusion of detail given by the apocryphal writings of about that time.[1] It is difficult to go farther than the inspired book and make a mental reconstruction of the state of original innocence by abstracting from the limitations and sufferings of our present condition, as if these could only be the consequence of an original fault. For the Bible gives no authority for such a principle.

If we must now summarize the conclusions to be drawn from the examination that we have followed, we can say that Scripture shows us divine justice exercised on two different levels. First of all in the present life, a certain approximate justice is at work, and its reality is all the more noticeable if a group of some importance is considered over a fairly long period of time. From this, the existence of original sin is to be deduced : a state of separation from God, existing in a whole race and resulting from the act of separation freely committed in Adam's

[1]On this point details may be found in F. R. Tennant, *The Sources of the Doctrine of the Fall and Original Sin*, (1903), chaps. 6-10, or in J. Bonsirven, *Le judaïsme palestinien au temps de Jésus-Christ*, (1935), Vol. II, pp. 12-18.

sin. This halting justice is not, however, the only principle by which we can explain the facts of the human condition : alongside it must be set the divine plan to test and educate his creatures. After this present life merit will be rewarded, no longer in a rough and irregular fashion but with perfect delicacy and accuracy. No inspired author has explicitly applied this second principle to original sin.

7
Original Sin in the Light of Modern Science and Biblical Studies

In the preceding chapters we have discussed the teaching on original sin as it is contained in the various books of the Bible and have tried to give an idea of the exact contribution of each book. The question remains how this dogma of Christian faith is to be understood, on the one hand in the light of all the information that has emerged during our exegetical enquiry and on the other in the light of what we learn from a scientific knowledge of the world and of man which is so very different from that possessed by the inspired authors.[1] Moreover, since biblical times there have been numerous theological speculations: the Fathers of the Church, theologians and Christian thinkers have all tried systematically to work out the doctrinal

[1] This concluding chapter was already written when I came across P. Smulders, *La vision de Teilhard de Chardin, Essai de réflexion théologique,* (1964) (translated and adapted from the third Dutch edition, 1963). This work is not simply an objective account of Teilhard's thought; it goes deeply into some of the questions that this thought posed for Christian theology. There are two appendices on 'Evolution and Original Sin' and 'Monogenism' (pp. 173-209). I have not rewritten the chapter or the notes, but I do want to point out that there are many points of agreement between P. Smulders and myself.

218

elements contained in or suggested by Scripture or philosophy. Local and general councils have made statements on this subject and have settled some of the main points. Since not everything that has emerged from all this activity is of the same decisive value, it may be useful to consider in particular those points which do have a more direct connection with the testimony of Scripture, and not to insist on certain constructions that do not imitate the reserve and lack of arbitrary statements to be found in the biblical texts. A certain moderation is suggested by the doctrine of the Wisdom books, which regard as normal the initial imperfection of a creature destined to undergo a test.

I. Mankind Separated From God Before the Advent of Christianity

During these last years the attention of the exegetes has[1] been focused more and more on the biblical idea of 'the sin of the world' (John 1:29). Perhaps this shift of interest owes something to the reflections on collective guilt started by contemporary historical circumstances.[2] However that may be, there are numerous indications scattered throughout Scripture. At the beginning of Genesis we find ancient traditions on the simultaneous development of technical culture and violence

[1]For example, L. Ligier, *Péché d'Adam et péché du monde;* vol. 1: *L'Ancien Testament,* (1960): vol. 2: *Le Nouveau Testament,* (1961). I reviewed this work in *RSPT,* 45 (1961), pp. 74-6 and 47 (1963), pp. 72-4. For an account more systematic than exegetical cf. also P. Schoonenberg, 'Erbsünde und "Sünde der Welt"' in *Orientierung* 26 (1962) pp. 65-9 and 'Zonde der Wereld en erfzonde' (with a summary in German) in *Bijdragen,* XXIV, (1963), pp. 349-89.
[2]For example K. Jaspers, *Die Schuldfrage. Ein Beitrag zur deutschen Frage,* (1946).

(Gen. 4:22-24) and the division of mankind into different languages (Gen. 11 : 1-9). Although the prophets' message, with its denunciations of their infidelity and its promises of pardon, was directed primarily at Israel, there are some oracles devoted to the pagan nations, who are guilty too (Isaias 13-21; Jer. 46-51; Ezech. 25-32; Amos 1-2). The Gospel reminds us of the uninterrupted succession of sins of infidelity on the part of Israel, culminating in the generation that rejected its Messias, Jesus, and thus set the seal on the work of its forefathers (Matt. 23 : 32). In the speech that was to lead to his condemnation St Stephen took up the same reproaches (Acts 7 :2-53). And St Paul speaks of the pagan nations as steeped in sin : 'they are darkened in their understanding, alienated from the life of God because of the ignorance that is in them, due to their hardness of heart they have become callous and have given themselves up to licentiousness, greedy to practise every kind of uncleanness' (Eph. 4 : 17-19; cf. 1 Thess. 4 :5; Eph. 2 : 1-2; Titus 3 :3-5). For St Peter, Christian salvation consists in escaping 'the defilements of the world through the knowledge of our Lord and Saviour Jesus Christ' (2 Peter 2 :20). While for St John all that is in the world is sinful lust and does not come from the Father (1 John 2 : 16).

Two books[1] in particular use the story of the Fall and also give an uncompromising description of the moral corruption of the pagan : we might even be inclined to think the picture painted by Wisdom or the Epistle to the Romans exaggerated as a result of excessive generalization. A religious error, idolatry, was at the root of this depraved conduct. Men made no effort to get to know God properly, they even reduced him to the status of a creature and fashioned false gods for them-

[1] Wisdom 13-15; Romans 1:18-32. For their references to the story of the Fall cf. Wisdom 10:1; Romans 5.12-19.

selves and so eventually became worthy of death. The book of Wisdom noted the corrupting influence exercised by idols, 'traps for the souls of men and a snare to the feet of the foolish' (14:11; cf. 14:21; 15:5), whereas Paul, intent on showing the culpability of paganism, did not even note that one man's fault can be another's excuse. In such surroundings, given over as they are to error and sin, a child will obviously not find the stimulus he needs for his moral and religious formation. Because of what he sees and hears around him, he cannot help being steeped in false ideas and perverse habits. Paul's silence on this point is not a denial, for we find quite clear statements in other places (1 Cor. 15:33; Eph. 4:14).

We need not draw up an exhaustive list of these details here : what we have noted briefly will suffice to show the place occupied in Scripture by the idea of the collective dimensions of sin and of its universal extent, what can be called in short 'the sin of the world', to use a biblical expression.

And so before Christ, mankind was plunged collectively into sin : pagan and Jew alike belonged to a more or less corrupt environment and suffered, at least involuntarily, a separation from God that showed itself in religious error and ignorance, moral perversion—in short in conditions most likely to render impossible a trusting approach to God as a father. This is what the story of the Garden of Eden expresses by the sinful couple's reaction of flight from Jahweh.

II. WAS THERE A SINGLE OR A MULTIPLE SIN AT THE BEGINNING?

This universal captivity in sin is not only the result of the fact that all men without exception sin personally, but also the result of a law of spiritual and social heritage at work along-side the laws of physical heredity. Sin is passed on from one generation to another, either in a certain family, in a certain people or in the whole of mankind. This disposes the believer to proceed from determined historical faults to the very origins of the human race, to look for a series of successive faults, one conditioning the other from the beginning to the end, and hence to make a mental reconstruction of the first sin.[1] This is not solely responsible for all the ills that beset mankind, but it was the first to break a harmonious balance that could never again be perfectly restored.

The reader who, instead of concentrating exclusively on two texts (the Eden narrative and St Paul's commentary on it), is alive to this contemporary corruption so frequently described in the Bible together with its proximate causes, is in a position to ask a question :

Does the narrative of the fault of the first couple describe the clearly defined failure of two individuals, who alone are the ancestors of all men, or does it give a general representation of the law of spiritual heritage dominating the life of mankind? Parables like that of the wicked rich man or of the pharisee and the publican give us a living and concrete description of a religious and moral way of life that numerous individuals can realize, independently of each other, in very different circumstances. But there is more than that here : the essential aim of the Genesis narrator is to show that the free conduct of the ancestor foreshadows and conditions the situa-

[1] The conviction that the first sin did not become known through historical tradition or immediate revelation, but as the result of a mental reconstruction, is expressed by H. Renckens, *Urgeschichte und Heilsgeschichte*, (1959), p. 40, (translated from the Dutch, *Isräels visie op het verleden*, (1957); and by K. Rahner, in the article on 'Atiologie,' in *Lexikon für Th. u. K.*, I, (1957), col. 1011-1012; and by many others.

tion of his descendants. The passing on of a state of separation from God and the various misfortunes that are its consequences forms the basic teaching of this passage. In consequence all are sinners, as St Paul was to say : sinners, i.e., not necessarily responsible because of any personal act of guilt, but separated from God, incapable of behaving as his sons and prone to act against his will.

All have need of redemption, for all are sinners by reason of the corrupting influences passed on from generation to generation. But do these ascending lines of filiation in evil, which accompany natural filiation and embrace the whole human race like a fan, converge at the beginning in one, absolutely unique point? Must we affirm the existence of a first couple as Genesis at first sight seems to say? Or may we think of a more complex network of sin and contagion? Are we faced here with a diagrammatic representation, true in the way of such representations, but not as a photograph is true with the truth of an individual document?

In Genesis the characteristics and the destiny of different peoples or tribes are traced back to the action of one ancestor giving to each his name and his psychological characteristics. There is some artificial simplification here, but to speak of error would be to fail to understand that truth can be expressed in many and varied ways. The biblical authors were very conscious of the connection between the successive links of a line. In their eyes the divine choice was conditioned by membership of a particular race. And conversely the faults of an individual were visited on his children and their children to the third and fourth generation (Exod. 20 : 5; 34 : 7; Deut. 5 : 9; Num. 14 : 18; Jer. 32 : 18). So they were able to portray in one single ancestor and the sentence pronounced on his descendants the common effect of multiple sins, the consequence of disturbances which go on diminishing. It is then possible that the whole of mankind with the constant factors of its condition, was consciously represented in the story of Adam, whose name means 'man'.

If this interpretation is admitted, original sin is not a unique catastrophe at the birth of our species; it is the continually perpetuated perversion of mankind, in which new sins are conditioned more or less by the preceding sins and carry on the existing disorder. Instead of a disturbance that would die away in three or four generations, there is a generalized and anonymous corruption, with everyone its victim and many its authors, but in such a way that more often than not it is impossible to pinpoint any individual responsibility. In the story of the Tower of Babel (Gen. 11 : 1-9) one of these collective faults is shown bringing in its train dire consequences, which remain for later generations. It is easy to see that this passage involves a great deal of generalization and simplification, when it reduces to one localized event a number of facts leading to the divergence of language and opposition between peoples. The question is whether it is unfaithful to the intention of the inspired author, or whether the teaching of St Paul is gravely compromised, if we admit an analogous literary genre in Chapter 3 of the same book.

St Augustine was struck by the Bible texts that told of ancestors being punished in their posterity and he put forward a theory that theologians have sometimes considered strange, but that could still be very stimulating.[1] In his eyes original

[1]On this Augustinian theory cf. A.-M. Dubarle, 'La pluralité des péchés héréditaires dans la tradition augustinienne', in *Rev. Et. Aug.*, II, (1957), pp. 113-36. This theory found a certain echo among the theologians of the Middle Ages and at the Council of Trent. At the end of the article the discussion that this theory provoked at that time is studied.

sin is modified in each generation by the merits or demerits of
individuals; parents increase or lessen for their children the
burden of penalty and sin, which is passed on by the act of
generation. Compared with the catastrophic corruption
brought on by the fault of our first father these additions or
subtractions remain relatively unimportant and original sin is
not gradually obliterated in a long line of just men. Only the
grace of Christ can succeed in remitting it entirely. These ideas,
when compared with the questions being asked by modern literary criticism, can help in forming the concept of a universal
state of original sin, but one that proceeds from multiple
sources. This leaves room for a certain individual variability,
although the main common features are present everywhere.

What we suffer from is not only the fault of a distant
ancestor but as much and above all far closer sins, which in
their turn were provoked by earlier sins. We could speak today
of a chain reaction and such an idea seems to us to fit in with
what we see elsewhere of mankind's condition. Each of us, because he is born into a world and a race contaminated by sin,
is born a sinner. 'That which is born of the flesh is flesh' (John
3 : 6). He cannot enter the kingdom of God without first being
cleansed.

Many modern exegetes refuse to see in the story of the Fall
the story of an individual event. In their eyes it is only a kind
of parable, illustrating the universal fact of sin in mankind.
From the point of view of literary criticism such an interpretation is far from unfounded. But what it ignores or overlooks,
what catholic dogma proclaims with insistence and teaches us
not to add to the text but to recognize in it, is the fact that sin
like all other elements of man's destiny is not a strictly individual matter. Its consequences weigh heavy on the posterity of
the culprits. In the case of man and his wife it is the whole of

mankind that is now in the grip of fear at God's approach, banished far from the garden of happiness, condemned to death and the penalty of work by the sweat of the brow. Underlying the text is the idea of a heritage of sin.

Between the interpretation of many modern exegetes, who see in Chapter 3 of Genesis only the stylized outline of individual sin, and the early and usual interpretation, which sees in it the account of a particular sin at the beginning which had consequences for the whole of mankind, there is room for an intermediate position, admitting the schematic and universal nature of the narrative but not missing the main point, a sin handed on by inheritance : what the text describes is the effect of a countless multitude of individual sins.

Perhaps a faithful catholic is not today in a position to provide unanswerable arguments in support of this interpretation. Perhaps the positive science of human origins, which at the moment is unable to affirm the existence of a single couple, the ancestors of all men, will one day succeed in finally rejecting this or in incontrovertibly proving it. Perhaps the theologians will agree to accept the idea offered them by biblical exegesis : the idea of a symbolic and schematic account, intending to describe not a strictly individual event but a universal condition passed on by inheritance. Perhaps on the other hand they will succeed in showing that strict unity of physical origin is so necessarily bound up with the universality of original sin that the first cannot be denied without the second being abandoned. It is not always easy to discover at the outset the remote consequences of a new idea, nor is it easy to form a complete picture of all the internal connections of revealed truths and so estimate the repercussions of a denial that may at first seem unobjectionable.

For the moment it will be enough, now that the problem has

been set out, to note that the Council of Trent in its dogmatic decree on original sin (1546), while clearly assuming the existence of an individual Adam, does not directly set out to affirm the strict unity of original sin : it takes it for granted. When it does speak of it, it is in an interpolated relative clause in a canon whose main object is to define the remedy for original sin, namely the reconciliation won by the blood of Christ. And even the mention of the unique origin of sin spread among all men is only a remark leading up to the statement that this sin is nevertheless multiplied in each person. By this statement the Council ruled out the opinion of Albert Pighius, and the revised version of the text omitted any reference to the ideas of St Augustine mentioned above, which had met with support and opposition in the course of the debates before the final vote.[1]

Nearer to our own time the encyclical *Humani Generis* (1950) set out to uphold the authentic idea of original sin as the Council of Trent had defined it (Denz 3891). Then, on the subject of the scientific hypothesis of polygenism, it stated (Denz 3897) : 'Christians cannot admit a theory that claims . . . that the word "Adam" means some group of our primor-

[1]On this point cf. the article already mentioned: A. -M. Dubarle, 'La pluralité des péchés héréditaires dans la tradition augustinienne'. The draught of the conciliar canons contained a brief reference to *original* sin, which was intended to rule out the Augustinian view. After various objections a rephrasing of the sentence turned it towards an entirely different object. Although unique in its origin the sin of *Adam* is multiplied in each by its presence in each man ('origine unum est . . . omnibus inest unicuique proprium'; cf. Denz. 790 or 1513). This was intended to rule out a view of A. Pighius (cf. H. Jedin, *A History of the Council of Trent*, II, (1961), p. 145) and avoided any pronouncement on the multiple original sins that St Augustine's view might have allowed one to envisage. The assertion of the unity of Adam's sin was taken for granted by the Fathers of the Council and was only a preparation for the statement that this sin is multiplied in the descendants. So there is nothing in this canon that can indirectly affect a modern polygenist theory, admitting sins in each independent line.

dial ancestors, granted that it does not appear how such a view can be reconciled with what the revealed sources of truth and the acts of the Church's magisterium lay down on the subject of original sin, which is the result of a sin really committed by one individual, Adam, and which is passed on to all men by generation and so is in each of us and belongs to each of us.' Obviously a loyal catholic cannot for a moment entertain any hypothesis that clearly contradicts his faith: it is also normal for him to dislike toying with a hypothesis, so long as it remains doubtful whether it can be reconciled with his faith. That is why the pontifical document, which combines a practical directive and the grounds for it in one and the same complex clause (which too many translations have made into two independent and categorical statements), does not consider the hypothesis of polygenism as freely acceptable, in contradistinction to the open attitude adopted with regard to evolution.

More than once it has been pointed out that there is a difference between declaring a reconciliation impossible and stating that we cannot see how it can be reconciled.[1] In the second case it is possible to envisage a later modification of the intellectual situation. This is not, therefore, excluded by the encyclical, which in any case is not an irrevocable document. In fact studies in exegesis and conciliar history lead us to ask whether the intention of the author of Genesis, of St Paul and of the Fathers of the Council of Trent was really directed at the strict unity of origin of the human race and not rather at the universality of sin.

[1]C. Muller, 'L'encyclique Humani Generis' in *Synthèses*, V, (1950-51), pp. 296-312, cf. p. 304. L. Boros, 'Evolutionismus und Anthropologie' in *Wort und Wahrheit*, XIII, (1960), pp. 15-24, cf. p. 23. P. Chauchard, *La science détruit-elle la religion?* (Je sais- je crois series), 1960, p. 78. Also M.B., *Orientierung*, 24 (1960), pp. 145-47; P. Schoonenberg, *Bijdragen* XXIV (1963), pp. 349-89, cf. p. 374; A. Bec, *Scholastik* 26, (1951), pp. 52-59.

Can original sin and the sin of the world be equated? This question is being asked at the moment by catholic theologians.[1] It is not at all clear that the answer must be a categorical negative. But it is understandable that some should hesitate before questioning concepts that have long been held by the Church, although they have never been directly sanctioned by the magisterium of the ecumenical councils or papal definitions.[2]

The question may be left open. But what should not create any difficulties is the recognition that in the perspective of Scripture original sin is continued, relayed and conveyed to us by the sin of the world. It is well, then, to complete and balance an oversimplified view of things by the inexhaustible riches of biblical ideas. It has recently been remarked that the

---

[1] P. Schoonenberg, 'Erbsünde und "Sünde der Welt" ', in *Orientierung*, XXVI, (1962), pp. 65-69: 'Zonde van de Wereld en erfzonde', (with a German summary) in *Bijdragen* XXIV, (1963), pp. 349-89, cf. pp. 375 ff. A little less clearly in R. Leys, 'Teilhard dangereux?' in *Bijdragen* XXIV, (1963), pp. 1-20, cf. pp. 17-18.

[2] Against this one can quote the following lines of a philosopher, who, while professing to be ready to accept any possible future decision, makes use of the initiative of thought for the moment: 'if the council definitions, particularly those of the Council of Trent, referring to Adam, are given a *sensus plenior* (a collective sense with Adam representing the whole human race), the meaning of the conciliar definitions is not in the least modified, but their scope is better understood . . . The Fathers of the Council of Trent, like the majority of thinkers of their time and following St Augustine, interpreted *adam* as a proper name, indicating a particular individual. But progress in the reading of the Hebrew text (which St Augustine did not read) has shown that the Genesis narrative did not take *adam* in an individual sense, but in the specific sense . . . And so, until the Church makes a formal definition, we think that we can use the freedom of a Christian thinker, who puts forward suggestions that the Church in her wisdom can accept or reject'. C. Tresmontant, *La Doctrine morale des prophètes*, (1958), p. 159, n. 1. It may be useful to remember that any definition of the Church on a subject that exegesis at the moment believes would be better left open would not be made because of any new revelation, over and above what was entrusted to the apostles, but because of a better judgement, made necessary by new circumstances, of the implications of already revealed truths and of their agreement or disagreement with recent theories.

usual presentation of Christian doctrine in catechesis and theology 'passes directly from original sin to the Incarnation'[1] as if there were nothing between these two which was a positive preparation for salvation or which made its need still more acute by new sins. But St Paul tells us: 'the free gift following many trespasses brings justification' (Rom. 5:16).

III. THE ORIGINAL STATE OF MAN

Modern theories of evolution have already been mentioned in the discussion on the unity or plurality of the source of original sin. We can now consider them more directly, not in order to expose or discuss them in themselves, but to consider them in their bearing on the idea of original sin.

The evidence of modern science leads us to think of mankind as issuing from an animal stock. Gradually the human organism, as we see it today, was formed by multiple modifications, which we can observe or reconstruct thanks to the discoveries of fossil remains. Parallel to this the human psyche came from an animal psyche, which does not imply stupidity or brutishness: we should rather think of the industrious spirit, provident and co-operative, that can be shown by an animal society. Human industry, recognized as such by the manufacture of tools on a large scale, however primitive they may be, is associated with skeletons that seem to us a far cry from our ideal of plastic beauty.

Our Christian faith assures us that at a given moment a qualitative threshold was passed. God created man in his own image, as a spiritual being, using and dominating from then

[1] P. Grelot, *Sens chrétien de l'Ancien Testament: Esquisse d'un traité dogmatique*, (1962), p. v. In this work there are some remarks about the historical development of collective sin: pp. 107, 116, 356.

on the corporal and psychic organism that was the result of animal evolution. Arguments from analogy show us that this threshold is not necessarily perceptible to external observation. If, and this experiment has been made, the reactions of a human baby and those of a young monkey are simultaneously followed and compared, it is not possible to say at what moment truly human intelligence begins to appear. But it is certain that in three or four years the differentiation is complete. In the same way, if *per impossibile* we had sufficient palaeontological documentation at our disposal to follow closely over the course of time the transformations in body and technical ability of a group of hominids, we admit that we should still be unable to pinpoint the generation in which human nature appeared. For our positive sciences hominisation is a fact that extends over a period of time, but this does not contradict the religious or philosophical idea that maintains that a creature either is or is not a man, whatever may be the actual appearances of human spirituality perceptible to external observation.

These extremely modest beginnings suggested by the modern theory of evolution form a strange contrast with the descriptions in classical theological treatises, brought to life for us in the great Christian works of art: an Adam clothed in splendour, endowed with perfect physical beauty and wide knowledge, and of such moral integrity that he not only dominates his passions but has the same control of will over them as over the movements of his muscles, an Adam blessed with sanctifying grace and preserved from suffering and death. We are told that all this is the effect of a privilege of grace, which could be lost without nature being affected or mutilated thereby. If it is admitted that this nature was the result of a slow process of evolution and not instantaneous creation, this privilege determines a new state that can really be nothing but a 'marvellous parenthesis',[1] since the Fall caused by sin soon intervenes. The laws of evolution, suspended or surpassed for a moment, come into play again, and we cannot hope to be able to look back and discover definite traces of these brief moments when an emerging humanity was crowned with grace.

Such a reconciliation between the modern theory of evolution and the classical representation of the original state of man is not absurd, considered in itself. But there is still the danger that it will not entirely remove the uneasiness felt by many people who are accustomed to the disciplines of science and who see the happiness of paradise as a poetic legend, in which we can, of course, as in many legends, pick out a more or less profound moral truth but need not recognize a real happening.

This is the point at which we may well ask ourselves what our Christian faith teaches us in its most authentic documents. In the first place we can say this. The Council of Trent passed over a doctrinal draft in which Adam's exceptional gifts were described in the classical way,[2] and simply promulgated a

---

[1]This expression comes from M. Labourdette, *Le péché originel et les origines de l'homme*, (1953), p. 178. However the author already introduces some restrictions into the pictures of the original perfection drawn by classical theology, particularly as regards the extent of their knowledge.
[2]*Concilium Tridentinum edidit societas Goerresiana*, vol. XII, pp. 566-69: Decreti de peccato originali minuta (ineunte mense iunio 1546) . . . '. . . "Fecit Deus hominem rectum et inexterminabilem" (Eccles. 7:29; Sap. 2:23). Et hoc secundum corpus et secundum animam et secundum mentem ac spiritum. Secundum enim corpus fecit eum non subjectum corruptioni et morti, non laboribus aut doloribus subditum et infirmitatibus, sed sanum, integrum . . . Secundum animam vero ita bene compositum reddidit ac temperatum rectitudine et justitia, ut omnino corpus animae subiceretur et pars inferior animae, ubi passiones gignuntur, superiori parti, in qua ratio viget, sicut ordo ipse bene institutae naturae poscebat, miro modo consentiret, minime contumax, superior autem pars id est ratio et ipsa mens, Deo creatori suo, ut par erat, obedienter obtemperaret. Quare cum nudi essent, "non erubescebant" (Gen. 2:25), nulla scilicet existente erubescentiae causa, cum nihil in eis contra decorem et rationem pugnaret. Denique secundum mentem . . .' (p. 567, 1.10-21).

canon stating that by his sin the first man lost 'the holiness and righteousness in which he had been constituted'.[1] These words correspond to those defining man's role on earth in the book of Wisdom (9:2-3). They do not imply that this holiness and righteousness were the equal of what the theologians call sanctifying grace, making men 'partakers of the divine nature' (2 Peter 1:4). In the following session, which was devoted to justification, the Council went on to teach that authentic Christian righteousness replaces the original righteousness lost by Adam, without making clear whether it surpasses it or not.[2]

The Genesis narrative shows us man in a divine garden, a sort of luxurious oasis (cf. Gen. 2:19), giving names to the animals, thus exercising over them his powers of intellect and will, but there is no need to see all this as a sign of any exceptional infused knowledge. He recognizes the value of the gift made to him in the person of the woman: he is not a child. The first couple are naked and feel no embarrassment, for the physical climate is clement and there is not yet any dissimulation between individuals, nor any of those artificial social distinctions symbolized by clothing. Peace also reigns between God and man.

The author of this passage wanted not so much to give a

---

[1]'Sanctitatem et iustitiam in qua *constitutus* fuerat' (Denz. 788 or 1511). This formula was definitively sanctioned and replaced one in an earlier draft: 'sanctitatem et iustitiam in qua *creatus* fuerat', which was inspired by Eph. 4:24: 'novum hominem qui . . . creatus est in iustitia et sanctitate veritatis'. The similarity of words, which was quite deliberate, might suggest an equality between the condition of the first man and the sanctifying grace given to the Christian. The formula that was actually adopted by the council reproduced, but apparently without realizing it, the words of Wisdom 9:2-3: 'constituisti hominem . . . in aequitate et iustitia', where 'sanctitate' would be a better translation of the Greek '*hosioteti*' than the 'aequitate' of the Vulgate.
[2]Session VI, Decree on justification, ch.7; Denz. 800 or 1531.

detailed description of, as to suggest, a state in which the harsh facts of the human condition that we experience did not make themselves felt (death, mutual distrust, slavery, the difficulty of work, the anxieties of motherhood, the hostility of surrounding nature and the moral struggles that men now experience). He had no intention of describing any magic state, supposing other physical or psychological laws than those now in force. Clearly he had no idea of evolution and the ideal picture that he drew was a retouched picture of the life of the small Palestinian peasant seeing in his home and the fruits of the earth the marks of divine favour (cf. Psalm 128).

Then sin appeared to disturb this happy harmony and to spoil the excellence of the Creator's work. And the essential point in the Garden of Eden story, as also in St Paul's teaching, is that this perversion has disastrous consequences for the sinner and also for his posterity. Man hides from God and this foreshadows the future reaction of even the most favoured persons; individuals experience embarrassment before one another. Man must work hard to live; woman must put up with subjection to her husband and the pains of childbirth; all must die; and finally all must struggle against the serpent. But while the narrator described the main features of the state of fallen humanity so precisely, he only sketched, and then with great restraint, the better conditions that went before. The Wisdom authors laid particular emphasis on all that is normal in the limitations and difficulties of a creature whose freedom is being tested.

In the mental reconstruction that we may be inclined to make of the state preceding the Fall, we should be warned by these examples against increasing the divergence between this state and our present condition and imagining exemption from the laws governing life or the physical world. This can be applied even to death, the wages of sin according to St Paul (Romans 6 : 23), who brings together in this passage many Old Testament texts, beginning with Gen. 2 : 17 and 3 : 22. On this point we should remember what a wealth of meaning the Bible has put into this word 'death'. At the beginning of its semantic development there was certainly the idea of corporal decease; but around this basic meaning crystallized the idea of misfortune, shame and separation from God. Death is a return to the earth and from this point of view it is normal for man, who was taken from the earth; but, considered in the light of all the secondary meanings attached to the word, it is also the downfall of the sinner. In this sense it did not exist before sin: 'God did not make death' (Wisdom 1 : 13).

To be faithful to the statements of Genesis and St Paul we do not need to postulate a corporal existence immune from decease. The inspired authors saw a consequence of sin in these tragic experiences surrounding decease (physical sufferings, family separations and a feeling of hopeless failure). They did not speculate explicitly on what a state of innocence would have been like or on the possible dissociation between physical decease and death as the sum of human ills.[1]

The magisterium of the Church has made no irrevocable pronouncement on this point. One provincial Council, that of Carthage in 418, did directly condemn the denial of Adam's corporal immortality.[2] But this canon was not specifically

---

[1]We do not attribute any real theological authority to these lines of C. Péguy, but they are quite apposite.

    Ce qui depuis ce jour est devenu la mort
    N'était qu'un naturel et tranquille départ.
    Le bonheur écrasait l'homme de toute part.
    Le jour de s'en aller était comme un beau port. *Ève*, st. 26.

[2]'Whoever says that Adam, the first man, was made mortal, so that, whether he sinned or not, he was going to die in his body, that is that he was going to leave his body, not through the merit of sin but by the necessity of nature, let him be anathema' Denz. 101 or 222.

approved by Pope Sosimus in the letter that he addressed to the whole Church on the subject of grace and original sin.[1] The ecumenical Council of Trent did not take up this canon of Carthage, while it did reproduce almost the exact text of another canon of the same council. A draft condemnation was left in the archives, and it was worded in this way : 'if anyone says that Adam was bound to die in any way, even if he had not sinned, let him be anathema'.[2]

So without contradicting any irrevocable doctrinal authority, scriptural or ecclesiastical, we can, in conformity with the suggestions of the evolution theory, admit that mankind emerged from the animal world. Leaving aside the existence of a spiritual soul, the transition may have been very gradual. In the case of the soul, which either does or does not exist, there can have been no gradual transition, although all its rich potential would not have been immediately manifest to external observation. Man began gradually to diverge from the

---

[1] The letter (Tractoria or Tractatoria) of Sosimus on the council of Carthage has been lost. Only a few extracts have been preserved by St Augustine (cf. *PL*, 20, 693-95), who would certainly have reproduced with care any passage concerning the immortality of the first man. On this and related points cf. P. M. de Contenson in *RSPT*, XXXIX, (1955), p. 58, n. 40, in a review of the work of M. Labourdette, *Le péché originel*.

[2] 'Qui ergo dixerit Adam omnino moriturum etiam si non peccasset, anathema sit'. This draft, which was not discussed, can be found in *Concilium Tridentinum . . .*, vol. XII, p. 567, 1.47. The Council of Trent did take up a canon of the provincial Council of Orange (529), but with a modification that has made it lose its indubitable bearing on the present question. The Council of Orange declared that Adam had handed on to his posterity bodily death, which is the penalty of sin, and sin, which is the death of the soul (Denz. 175 or 372). The Council of Trent states that Adam passed on to his posterity death and bodily sufferings and sin, which is the death of the soul (Denz. 789 or 1512). After this rearrangement it is no longer clear that the text is speaking of bodily death to the exclusion of 'death' in the very full biblical sense of the word, all the more so as the definitive text left out a clause of the draft, which spoke of sin 'to which is due both the death of the body and of the soul as a penalty' (*Conc. Trid.*, vol. V, p. 196).

animals in his way of life, while sin began to form that heritage of perversion that was handed on at the same time as the heritage of technical culture.

Such a theory, attempting to do justice to the evidence of our modern knowledge of human origins as well as to the biblical data taken as a whole and not just the two solitary texts of Genesis 3 and Romans 5, does not compromise the gravity of original sin. Instead of concentrating on the loss of wonderful and gratuitous gifts, whose disappearance does not really injure our nature in itself, this theory fixes its attention on quite concrete troubles that we find in our actual experience and that the Genesis narrative represented in a stylized way : a poisoning of our trusting relationship with God and various sufferings. The doctrine of original sin consists in stating that not everything that worries us can be explained by the still incomplete development of man's spiritual powers or by the failures of an evolutive system that would leave room for mistakes or a process of trial and error on man's own level as well as on the level of the formation of the species. In the present state of humanity there is a disorder (not just something missing) on the religious as well as the human level, and this is the result of deliberate sin. Individuals are embroiled in this disorder whether they like it or not : and it is of small importance whether the point of departure was close to the animal state, as modern evolution theory thinks, or raised far above it, as was thought for a long time by theologians who did not have the information that we possess today. The essential point is that the present state of mankind, with the baneful influence that it exercises on newcomers to existence, is the result of deliberate faults and that even the initial religious state of young children is vitiated by it.

IV. Generation, the Means of Passing On Original Sin

On three occasions the Council of Trent expressed the view that original sin is transmitted by propagation (Denz. 790), that it is contracted by generation (Denz. 791) and that men propagated by Adam's seed are born unjust, for by this propagation they contract their own unrighteousness, when they are conceived (Denz. 795).

This doctrine echoes the thought of the Fathers and theologians.[1] In general there cannot be any doubt as to its meaning. But it should be noted that it is never put forward in the strictly defining part of a canon, but in an interpolated relative clause (Denz. 790), or in an explanation put after the anathema (Denz. 791), or in a chapter of doctrinal exposition and then in a comparison meant to throw light on the main point of the teaching, namely justification. Moreover there is no very clear-cut precision; in the first case it is hardly more than a formula put in as a parallel to the negative formula *'non imitatione'*. So it is permissible to think that this is not a dogmatic definition strictly demanding our faith, but that a certain latitude for theological interpretation remains possible.[2]

[1] Cf., for example, St Thomas, *ST.*, Ia, IIae, q. 81, a. 4 and 5. This doctrine of the Council of Trent was meant to rule out the Pelagian idea, according to which original sin became diffused 'imitatione, non propagatione' (cf. St Augustine, *De peccatorum merito et remissione*, I, ix, 9; *PL*, 44, 114). According to Pelagius every man is born with free will; but Adam's example more or less drags every man into sin, which justifies the words of St Paul in Romans 5. St Augustine reacted very energetically against this explanation of Pelagius. The Council of Carthage, which the Council of Trent reproduced almost word for word on this point, ruled out this doctrine by speaking of young children who have not yet been able to commit any (personal) sin but who still have need of purification (Denz. 102 or 791, 223 or 1514).

[2] These conciliar texts were intended to rule out certain mistaken ideas, and this intention must be kept in sight. A transmission of original sin consisting solely in a conscious and deliberate imitation of Adam's sin (according to the teaching of Pelagius) cannot be held. But 'physical generation' is not the only possible alternative and it is on this point

It may seem strange to the modern mind that a spiritual disorder like sin could be passed on by way of physical generation. Recent research in genetics tells us that an organic peculiarity, whether defective or not, is transmitted by heredity : for example the colour of the eyes, the shape of the body, or the absence of a finger joint. But a defect in the spiritual order and a defect produced during the life of the first generator does not seem the sort of thing that could be contracted by virtue of the laws of heredity. We know that each generation must learn things for itself. And when we remember that it is desirable to seek understanding of the mysteries of the faith from analogy with the objects of our natural knowledge,[1] we are, to say the least, disturbed at the thought of a spiritual disorder like original sin being transmitted by generation.

But perhaps in this matter we are the victims of the extreme precision of our scientific terms. Sacred Scripture sometimes gives a very wide meaning to the term sonship. The Wisdom books refer to the disciple as the 'son' of his master: the convert pagans become sons of Abraham (Gal. 3:7, 29; Rom. 4:10; cf. Matt. 3:9): and sinners are the sons of the devil (Matt. 13:39; John 8:44; Acts 13:10; 1 John 3:10). So an influence in the moral order that is not generation in the precise sense of the geneticists can be called filiation. Even Christ's words to Nicodemus: 'that which is born of the flesh is flesh' (John 3:6), should not be taken too literally, since they are followed by a parallel proposition: 'that which is

that there can be a certain freedom of interpretation. This is admitted by J. de Fraine, *La Bible et l'origine de l'homme*, (1961), pp. 109-11; and also by K. Rahner, 'Theologisches zum Monogenismus' In *Zeits. für kath. Theol.*, LXXVI, (1954), pp. 14-15 (reprinted in *Schriften zur Theologie*, vol. I, (1954), pp. 269-71. Eng. trans. *Theological Investigations*, vol. I).

---

[1] It is one of the procedures indicated by the Vatican Council I, by which reason may gain a fruitful understanding of mysteries: Session III, the Constitution of the catholic Faith, ch. 4., Denz. 1796 or 3016.

born of the Spirit is spirit', where it is not a question of physical generation.

Genesis does not make physical generation responsible for all the influence, when it traces the destiny and character of every people and tribe back to the person of an ancestor. Spiritual factors such as curses and blessings and paternal education are mentioned too (Gen. 18 : 19). It is clearly a social tradition that the author has in mind and not any innate instinct when he speaks of the taboo on a certain type of food observed by Jacob's sons in memory of a dramatic episode in their father's life (Gen. 32 : 32).

Without too much artificiality the tribes or peoples could be considered as nothing more than enlarged families, because that corresponded in general with the social conditions of the patriarchal period. In the same way the character of a definite people could be bound up with the destiny of its ancestor and the general condition of mankind with the deliberate sin of Man or Adam, without any particular efforts being made to arrive at an accurate knowledge of the physiological causes and the social and psychological causes. At a time when the family was practically the only centre of education, the son was much more the work of the father than in our modern society, where the child is subjected to all the various influences of school, street, youth movements, radio, television, etc. A global view of the facts of heredity corresponds very well with the Genesis narrative, which encourages us to distinguish various influences in the heritage passing from one generation to another.

At this point it is worth while calling to mind what modern research in psychoanalysis has made us understand more deeply. There can be no comparison between the influences brought to bear on a child at an early age, when it is still lacking internal structure, and those brought to bear on an adult, who is already in possession of his autonomy, his reflex consciousness and his moral principles. A young baby has absolute need of affective contacts if it is to awaken to a human life : corporal sustenance is not enough to activate the spiritual faculties. A psychological incubation must take place after generation and gestation. During this period of childhood the human being is extremely open to injuries that may be inflicted on it by defective behaviour on the part of those about it. But it does not necessarily react by strict imitation; for example it may respond to harshness not by harshness but by weakness and fear. Now among these influences that an individual undergoes there are some (possibly continuing till the advent of maturity) that form part of the internal makeup of the person and others that merely provide encouragement, superficial attraction or information.

If we pay attention to these facts, which we need not describe in further detail here, we may come to envisage psychological factors alongside physical heredity, which already passes on certain blemishes or disorders, in order to explain the universal propagation of a state of sin in all men. It is inevitable that there should be some injurious and deforming contacts among the multitude of human relationships in which a young child becomes involved and which he needs absolutely for his formation, just as he needs food to build up his body. Between generation in the strict sense of the word and the bad example received from an adult there is an incalculable mass of social and psychological influences brought to bear on a subject in the process of formation, providing him of necessity with the instruments of his psychic life (language for example). It is fair to say of the interior result of all this physical heredity and spiritual heritage that it exists in each person *'propagatione non imitatione*', to repeat the formula of the Council of Trent on the subject of original sin.

Thus in each person there are dispositions more or less seriously disordered from the moral point of view as a result of organic or psychological dispositions. There is a more or less complete ignorance of God, because the environment in which the child is brought up is more or less contaminated by sin and is thus unable to exercise on the child the incorrupt and healthy influence that would be desirable in principle.[1] We have only to think of the example that Scripture gives us in the picture of an idolatrous and corrupt pagan society (Wisdom 13-15; Rom. 1 : 18-32). There are deviations from which nobody can escape entirely.

In the notion of descent Genesis includes all the influences brought to bear on the member of a race, but at the same time it sometimes suggests that they are not all of the same nature. Many of the Fathers of the Church, particularly from the time of St Augustine, understood this descent in the narrow sense of physical generation and considered this as the cause of the transmission of original sin.[2] And they stressed the point (which is debatable, though not in their eyes) that this generation was realized in an act that involved more or less grave

[1]Analogous ideas are developed at length by P. Schoonenberg, 'De erfzonde als situatie', in *Bijdragen*, XXII, (1961), pp. 1-30, as well as in the articles mentioned above, p. 219, n. 2. He describes original sin as the situation that results for a young child from his presence in an environment in which he is encouraged to do evil or in which the encouragement to do good is more or less completely lacking.

[2]However, before St Augustine various Christian writers explained the necessity of baptism by the need of a remedy against future temptations. This opens the way to a more flexible view of the contagion of original sin spread over time and not concentrated in the single moment of generation. On these writers (though not expressly on the consequence suggested here) cf. J. C. Didier, 'Le pédobaptisme au IVe siècle. Nouveaux documents', in *Mélanges de Sc. R.*, VI, (1949), pp. 233-46. 'Un cas typique de développement du dogme', ibid., IX, (1952), pp.

moral disorder. Thus in each link of the chain an actual disorder conditioned the propagation of the hereditary disorder into the next generation. This idea was close enough to the biblical idea, although unfortunately associated with the act of sexual union, which they considered to be inevitably sinful, and this was a frame of mind scarcely in conformity with the mind of the Bible.[1]

The theologians of the Middle Ages defined original sin as the loss of a gratuitous gift, granted by God to mankind in the person of its first father, Adam. This gift was lost at the beginning and quite naturally the privation was perpetuated in mankind on the occasion of generation. The analogy was borrowed from the hereditary privileges of the nobility, which were granted by the sovereign and could be lost as the result of some misdemeanour. This institution seemed quite natural in a feudal society, but we can see its conventional and arbitrary nature better and so we find ourselves paying more attention to the indications in the Bible of a view of the transmission of a heritage that is less exclusively bound up with physical generation.

'That which is born of the flesh is flesh' (John 3 : 6). Every man is a son of man : this radical dependence on his origin is an essential characteristic of his condition. For better or worse a new individual shares the history of those who have passed

191-214. Origen, in a commentary on Romans 5-14: 'death reigned from Adam to Moses', declares that children receive the contagion of sin not only through generation but also through education. He distinguishes the age at which the child is still under the complete influence of the parents and the age at which he begins to exercise his freedom; he takes the example of idolatry (*PG*, 14, 1018 BC and 1024 AB).

---

[1] That is why the virgin conception of Jesus was of such prime importance in their eyes. For St Augustine or St Leo this was the necessary condition if the contagion of original sin was not to affect Christ. Nowadays these views have been abandoned.

through life before him. Because he comes from a race and an environment contaminated by sin, he is himself tainted by this contagion, which enters his being through all the avenues of intrapersonal influence, before he is able to offer the least resistance. He is flesh and therefore he has earthly thoughts and desires; he is flesh and therefore he is incapable of approaching the living God without dying (Deut. 5 : 26). He has to be purified in the water of regeneration, to be renewed by the Holy Ghost, in order to be able to enter the kingdom of God (John 3 : 3-6).

The main purpose of this study has been to make contact with the inexhaustible wealth of Scripture. Following that, we have tried to check this exegetical enquiry against the most essential and authoritative teaching of the Christian faith, as the Council of Trent formulated it, while acknowledging the questions raised by the findings of modern science and without insisting on safeguarding theological constructions that are not the object of faith at all costs. Now we can take one last comprehensive look. We see original sin now as a truly tragic and actual situation : no longer merely the loss of wonderful gifts at a great remove from our day and condition, but the moral and religious perversion in which every man finds himself inevitably plunged by reason of his birth into a perverted environment : ignorance of God, or idolatry and a more or less profound corruption.

Mankind is oppressed by a countless mass of sins : it is impossible accurately to pin point the individual responsibility for this. In each generation the harmfulness of this distant downfall is reactivated by new sins. And the pressure of the social environment forces some of this corruption into the empty souls of children, just as physical heredity transmits blemishes or some lack of balance. Nobody can claim to have escaped this condition : everyone needs a Saviour.

The grace of Christianity now appears not only as a free gift, giving something better than what went before, but also as the pardon of a condemned prisoner, the salvation of something that was lost. 'Save yourselves from this crooked generation' (Acts 2 :40). 'You know that you were ransomed from the futile ways inherited from your fathers, not with perishable things such as silver or gold, but with the precious blood of Christ, like that of a lamb without blemish or spot' (1 Peter 1 : 18-19).